AND THE COW JUMPED OVER THE MOON

By Pam Schiller and Thomas Moore

Other books by the authors

Thomas Moore

Do You Know the Muffin Man? by Pam Schiller and Thomas Moore

Humpty Dumpty Dumpty by Thomas Moore

Where Is Thumbkin? by Pam Schiller and Thomas Moore

Pam Schiller

The Bilingual Book of Rhymes, Songs, Stories, and Fingerplays by Pam Schiller, Rafael Lara-Alecio, and Beverly Irby

The Complete Book of Activities, Games, Stories, Props, Recipes, and Dances by Pam Schiller and Jackie Silberg

The Complete Book of Rhymes, Songs, Poems, Fingerplays, and Chants by Pam Schiller and Jackie Silberg

The Complete Daily Curriculum for Early Childhood: Over 1200 Easy Activities to Support Multiple Intelligences and Learning Styles by Pam Schiller and Pat Phipps

The Complete Resource Book for Infants by Pam Schiller

The Complete Resource Book for Toddlers and Twos by Pam Schiller

The Complete Resource Book: An Early Childhood Curriculum With Over 2000 Activities and Ideas by Pam Schiller and Kay Hastings

Count on Math: Activities for Small Hands and Lively Minds by Pam Schiller and Lynne Peterson

Creating Readers by Pam Schiller

Do You Know the Muffin Man? by Pam Schiller and Thomas Moore

Earth and Me by Mike Artell and Pam Schiller

The Instant Curriculum, Revised: Over 750 Developmentally Appropriate Learning Activities for Busy Teachers of Young Children by Pam Schiller and Joan Rossano

Parties Kids Love: Great New Party Ideas for Birthdays, Holidays, or Just For Fun by Mike Artell and Pam Schiller

The Practical Guide to Quality Child Care by Pam Schiller and Patricia Carter Dyke

Practices in the Early Childhood Classroom by Pam Schiller

Rainy Day Recess by Pam Schiller and Mike Artell

Sensitive Situations by Pam Schiller

Start Smart: Building Brain Power in the Early Years by Pam Schiller

Under Construction: Beginning Math by Pam Schiller and Lynne Peterson

The Values Book: Teaching 16 Basic Values to Young Children by Pam Schiller and Tamera Bryant

Where Is Thumbkin? by Pam Schiller and Thomas Moore

Children's Books

A Chance for Esperanza by Pam Schiller and Alma Flor Ada

Humpty Dumpty by Pam Schiller and Thomas Moore

Roll-On, Roll-On by Pam Schiller

Sara Sidney: The Most Beautiful Iguana in the Whole World by Pam Schiller and Tamara Bryant

Sing a Song of Opposites by Pam Schiller

The Itsy Bitsy Spider by Pam Schiller

The Zebra on the Zyder Zee by Pam Schiller

Books in Press

Starting With Stories: Engaging Multiple Intelligences Through Children's Books by Pam Schiller and Pat Phipps

Series of 8 CD/book sets by Pam Schiller

- *Bountiful Earth*
- *Bugs, Bugs, Bugs*
- *Critters and Company*
- *Fabulous Food*
- *Honk, Honk, Rattle, Rattle*
- *Me, My Family , and Friends*
- *School Days*
- *Wild, Wild West*

For Toddlers and Twos

And the Cow Jumped Over the Moon!

Over 650 Activities to Teach Toddlers Using Familiar Rhymes and Songs

Pam Schiller
and
Thomas Moore

gryphon house, inc.
Lewisville, NC

Copyright

Published by Gryphon House, Inc.
PO Box 10, Lewisville, NC 27023
800.638.0928; 877.638.7576 (fax)

Visit us on the web at www.ghbooks.com

Illustrations: Deborah Wright

Reprinted December 2015

Library of Congress Cataloging-in-Publication

Schiller, Pamela Byrne.
And the cow jumped over the moon / by Pam Schiller and Thomas Moore.
p. cm.
Includes index.
ISBN 978-0-87659-296-0
1. Music--Instruction and study--Juvenile. 2. Early childhood education.
3. Education, preschool. 4. Children's songs. I. Moore, Thomas, 1950-II. Title.
MT920.S35 2006
372.87'049--dc22

2005031539

Bulk purchase

Gryphon House books are available for special premiums and sales promotions as well as for fund-raising use. Special editions or book excerpts also can be created to specification. For details, contact the Director of Marketing at Gryphon House.

Disclaimer

Gryphon House, Inc. and the authors cannot be held responsible for damage, mishap, or injury incurred during the use of or because of activities in this book.

Be sure to use non-toxic materials at all times when working with toddlers. Some of the activities in this book use materials that may pose a choking hazard to young toddlers. Always use caution when working with toddlers.

Appropriate and reasonable caution and adult supervision of children involved in activities and corresponding to the age and capability of each child involved, is recommended at all times. Do not leave children unattended at any time. Observe safety and caution at all times.

Table of Contents

And the Cow Jumped Over the Moon

Music is an integral part of a quality early childhood curriculum. It plays a role in setting the tone of the classroom, developing skills and concepts, helping children make transitions, and building a sense of community. Of course, if you ask the children, they will tell you that singing is part of their daily activities because it's just plain fun.

Talking With Toddlers

Toddlers are in the most fertile time of their lives for picking up the elements of language. They are learning to understand and produce sounds, fine-tuning the art of taking turns when talking, and understanding grammatical nuances. Singing is a great springboard into language acquisition by toddlers, as are reading and speaking.

Always talk to children at their eye level. Often, this means getting down on your knees or sitting on the floor beside them as they play. Eye contact lets children know that they are your partners in communication. It also adds importance to your words and their words. It says, "I am interested in what you have to say," or on the flip side, "What I have to say is important."

Singing, like talking and reading, is more effective at children's eye level. Eye contact not only supports the value in the activity but also ensures that children are able to see the shape of your mouth as you sing the lyrics.

Toddlers acquire language skills as they are exposed to singing, reading, and speaking, but the journey is individual—each child moves at his or her own pace. There are, however, strategies to use along the way to support each child's journey. Below are tips for helping children as they progress from being a non-speaker to becoming a more advanced speaker. Notice that there are no ages assigned to these strategies. Some children will be great communicators before they are two, and others may not be skilled at communicating until they are closer to three—the speed of acquisition does not signal that one child is more advanced than another.

Tips for Talking With Non-Speakers

- Talk to non-speaking toddlers freely all day in a clear and expressive tone. Even when they do not seem to understand what you are saying, they are listening.
- Read children's faces and actions. Express in words what a toddler shows in gestures and facial expressions.

- Make sure children watch your face when you speak to them. They can understand a lot by your expression and even more by following your eyes. We tend to look at things we are talking about and toddlers learn to follow our gaze. If necessary, use your hands to direct their eyes.
- Use a normal tone of voice and facial expression with toddlers and twos. Refrain from using "baby talk" and a high-pitch level of voice that is commonly used with infants. Save exaggerated facial expressions and character voices for story time. Children are sponges during the toddler years—we want their communication skills to be natural.
- Vocabulary is an important part of what you are teaching children, but don't forget that equally important are the small sounds that make up language. Poems, rhymes, and rhythms help children hear those little sounds and, at the same time, encourage them to experience joy in the sounds of language.
- One-way conversations are not easy. If at a loss for something to talk about, tell the child about something you did last night.
- Read! Sing! Talk! Communication skills are learned by experience. The sounds of language vary in the three formats used to deliver it—reading, singing, and speaking. The more experience children have with language in each of these forms, the better they become at discriminating the various sounds of language and the better command they have of vocabulary.

Tips for Beginning Speakers

- Most toddlers understand more words than they can say and more complex grammar than they can produce. When speaking to toddlers, try to match their understanding of words rather than their ability to produce them. If a child calls water "wa-wa," don't imitate him. Respond with the correct pronunciation of "water." Sing or make up simple songs that use the vocabulary most familiar to children, such as "If You're Happy and You Know It." You can change the words to any song to make the vocabulary more familiar!
- During routines such as feeding and diaper changing, or while playing with toddlers, provide vocabulary for the things around you. If something is nearby and you know a song or rhyme about it, sing or say the rhyme.
- Be consistent in the words you use when toddlers are beginning to speak. If you call a container they are putting blocks into a "container" today, don't change the word to "bucket" tomorrow. As toddlers gain control of their vocabulary, around the age of two or so, help them expand it by using the many different words that can identify the same object.
- Toddlers are often difficult to understand, but it is important to try and understand what they are saying. Ask them to show you what they are saying by using gestures. Ask other adults or children for help in understanding. Pretending to understand is easier, but you will miss the value of the message. Children always need to know that their words are important, but at the beginning stages of speech, it is even more crucial.
- Provide time for toddlers to respond. They are not able to process information as quickly as adults or even older children, and they are new

at expressing themselves. If you remain patient and allow them plenty of time to respond, you will be surprised at how quickly they improve their speed and accuracy when responding. Waiting also signals that you respect their thoughts and ideas.

- Read stories and sing songs that stretch children's vocabularies. This is a delicate balance and will not be the same for every child. Don't read a book or sing a song that is too advanced. A good rule of thumb is to make certain that at least half of the vocabulary is familiar to the child.

Tips for More Advanced Speakers

- By age two, most children are beginning to put words together. The words they use to form these early sentences tend to be the names of objects (car, toy) and people (me, Mommy), and verbs (have, want) or words they use like verbs ("allgone"). For example, "Car go" or "Me doit."
- Toddlers often speak in fragmented sentences with limited use of proper syntax. For example, they may say, "Me do it" or "Gone, gone." Expand their sentence structure by repeating the correct sentence back. For example, "Me do it" becomes "You did it," and "Gone, gone" becomes "The milk is gone." As a toddler's language becomes more complex, help her expand it even more fully. "I do it" becomes "I can put my shoes on," and "Milk gone" becomes "I drank all of my milk."
- Keep sentences short and simple, and use an active voice when speaking. For example, "The boy ate the ice cream" instead of "The ice cream was eaten by the boy."

Model courtesy, respect, and good listening skills. Apologize if you have to divert your attention, and make sure you come back to the speaker when you are able. Say, "Excuse me" when leaving a conversation, wait your turn to speak, and provide others their turn to speak. Children learn more from watching us than from instruction.

Brain Research and Opportunities for Building a Foundation for Literacy

In recent years, with a strong national focus on early brain development, we have begun to examine and define the valuable roles that singing songs and reciting chants and rhymes play in laying the foundation for reading readiness. We know, for example, that singing songs and reciting chants and rhymes help build vocabulary and develop sound discrimination. The size of a child's vocabulary (oral language) and his or her skill in being able to discriminate sounds (phonological sensitivity) are strong predictors of how easily a child will learn to read when exposed to formal instruction. But oral language and phonological awareness are not the only skills that are developed when children are exposed to songs, chants, and rhymes. Songs, chants, and rhymes also help develop listening and thinking skills (comprehension). With conscious effort, we can use singing to build a foundation for literacy.

Following is a chart that shows the windows of opportunity for wiring vocabulary, sound discrimination, and thinking skills (comprehension). You will notice that toddlers and twos are at the optimal age for the wiring of each of these skills. How often children are read to, sung to, and spoken to will have a direct correlation to how strongly each of these skills is wired. Experience wires the brain and repetition of experience strengthens the wiring.

Window for:	Wiring Window	Greatest Enhancement Opportunity
Language	4—24 months	8 months—6 years
Early Sounds	4—8 months	
Vocabulary Development	0—24 months	2—7 years
Emotional Intelligence	0—48 months	4—8 years
Trust	0—14 months	
Impulse Control	16—48 months	
Social Development	0—48 months	4—12 years
Thinking Skills	0—48 months	4 years—puberty
Cause and Effect	0—16 months	
Problem Solving	16—48 months	
Motor Development	0—24 months	2—5 years
Vision	0—24 months	2—2 years
Reading Skills	0—24 months	2—7 years
Early Sounds	4—8 months	8 months—10 years
Vocabulary	0—24 months	2—5 years

Developing Children's Desire to Read

In order for children to become avid readers they must have mastery of the skills (mechanics), but they must also have the desire to read (disposition). Disposition grows from positive experiences. Singing songs and reciting chants and rhymes provide a natural ways to develop skills and ensure that children acquire the disposition to read.

And the Cow Jumped Over the Moon is a collection of traditional songs, chants, and rhymes with suggestions for ways they can be used to support the development of vocabulary, sound discrimination, and comprehension. Just singing the songs and reciting the chants and rhymes with children is a great first step, but if we really want to capitalize on the full range of benefits inherent in using songs, chants, and rhymes as a springboard to literacy, we need to intentionally use them as real learning opportunities. The Language Enrichment and Extension Activities that accompany the songs, chants, and rhymes in this book provide opportunities for enhancing the development of listening and oral language development skills, as well as opportunities for building comprehension skills and sound sensitivity (phonological awareness).

Cross-Generational Links

Children should be introduced to songs, chants, and rhymes that span time. This includes selections that are traditional—so traditional that their grandparents, even great-grandparents, will recognize them (songs such as "Twinkle, Twinkle, Little Star" and "Yankee Doodle" and poems and rhymes of poets such as Robert Frost and Langston Hughes). Children also need to experience songs, chants, and rhymes that are modern traditional such as "Itsy Bitsy Spider," "Miss Mary Mack," and "Peanut Butter." These are selections, words, tunes, or both that will be familiar to their parents. Finally, children need to have their own songs, chants, and rhymes—new selections that will someday be the classics of their generation. These might include "Sign Along with Me," "Once There Were Three Brown Bears," and "Humpty Dumpty Dumpty."

Songs, chants, and rhymes that span several generations help maintain threads of unity as a society, as a culture, and as a perspective on history. They tie us to tradition while respecting our evolution into the future. Songs, chants, and rhymes are markers for each generation—a way to say, "This is who we were." Some fond memories might include singing with your families—at church, around the piano at family gatherings, in the car, while you worked, maybe even singing to your new baby brother. Nothing is more fun and satisfying than singing together. Do you remember the first time you came home from school singing a song and your mother or father said, "Hey, I know that song!"

To provide this link for children, they need exposure to many songs, chants, and rhymes. The wider the breadth of that exposure, the greater the ability one has to see the threads that link us to one another. *And the Cow Jumped Over the Moon* embraces the concept of cross-generational music and rhymes and, although we hope children will have some at home, we want to widen the exposure of both familiar and new songs, chants, and rhymes in the classroom.

Regional Links

Songs, chants, and rhymes are also diverse when viewed from a geographical perspective. Not everyone in this country knows every song in this book. There are a few exceptions, but for the most part songs, chants, and rhymes are regional and sometimes even local. However, the wider the exposure the more likely children are to grow into adults who can stand around a piano and sing their old favorite songs with any group of people from any age group and from any geographic location. Again, the goal is to connect people to each other.

What Does Brain Research Say About Singing?

Singing lightens our mood and generally triggers us to feel happy. When we feel happy, our body releases endorphins into our system that help boost our memory. Singing also requires that we take in additional oxygen, which increases our alertness. Singing builds a sense of community and bonds us to one another. It is a universal language and is by its nature inclusive. Singing is a great activity for enhancing brain functions.

Using This Book

There are more than 250 songs, chants, and rhymes in *And the Cow Jumped Over the Moon.* The follow-up activities for each selection focus on using the song, chant, or rhyme to enhance the development of literacy skills. Literacy skills for toddlers include oral language development, auditory discrimination and auditory memory (later referred to as phonological awareness), and comprehension. Each selection also includes suggestions for story time, outdoor play or music and movement, and extension activities. Because questions are a great way to stimulate both thinking (**comprehension**) and speaking (**oral language**), we have included suggested questions to ask children in many of the activities. Stimulating discussions are a great way to build oral language and comprehension skills. This is an often overlooked opportunity for building literacy skills. The book also provides reflection questions to use at the end of each day. (All questions appear in italics.) Research suggests that this is one of the best ways to help children process what they have learned.

The appendix includes a list of suggested American Sign Language signs to use as teaching opportunities with songs, chants, and rhymes. The appendix also includes a thematic reference chart and a list of suggested resources that will support your musical and literacy journey.

And the Cow Jumped Over the Moon can be used to support your theme or domain-based lessons or can be used as stand-alone lessons/activities. There is a theme chart (appendix page 236) that provides a map for how songs, chants, and rhymes might fit in with specific themes or concepts. This allows you to use the selections as a support to the themes you are teaching. If you want to use the songs, chants, and rhymes as support to specific aspects of literacy, you can use the index. For example, if you are looking for activities to support the development of listening skills, simply look under "listening" in the index to find those songs, chants, and rhymes with specific suggestions for listening. You can do the same for other areas, including oral language, sound discrimination, and comprehension.

Themes or Developmental Domains?

The term "toddler" spans a large chronological range and, consequently, creates a large developmental gap. Children between the ages of 18 and 24 months are not ready for traditional early childhood themes. We need to prepare activities for them that fit into the framework of developmental domains. Two-year-olds are generally ready to understand the concept of themes and learning centers, but it will still take time for the concepts to be internalized. You will notice that we provide both a developmental domain and a learning center reference for all extension activities. Generally, we consider children less than 24 months as younger toddlers and children beyond 24 months as older toddlers. The use of domains and centers and of older and younger references will help you stay focused on the individual needs of each child.

The songs, chants, and rhymes in this book make great transition activities. Print your favorites on index cards and keep them in your pocket. Take one out during transitions and watch it work its magic.

Keep the Joy

Please be careful not to over-teach lessons. Choose only one or two of the follow-up activities each time you use the selection. Do not lose the song, chant, or rhyme in the drill and practice of skills. Over-teaching lessons will turn children off, and the joy of the song, chant, or rhyme may be lost to them forever.

Don't forget your own joy. Singing comes from within all of us and there is truly no such thing as a person who cannot sing. Singing is your internal voice of celebration and although you may not be a Pavarotti, Garth Brooks, Patti LaBelle, or Barbara Striesand, you have a voice that is uniquely yours. If you say you can't sing, you will model that thinking for children. If you don't sing, you send the same subtle message. No one should deny his or her joyful expression. We want all children to find their internal voice of joy, and you are their guide. "Children... seem to have a clearer understanding of what constitutes a good voice. The children I know hear every voice for what it has to offer: Beauty. Power. A way for human beings to connect. The opening of a soul." [Moore, T. (2002, July). If you teach children, you can sing. **Young Children**, page 84-85.]

When You Don't Know the Tune

There may be traditional songs in this book that are unfamiliar to you. Familiarity with songs is determined by life experiences, geographic location, cultural background, family traditions, and an array of circumstances that may never be identified. What is so wonderful is that the great diversity of traditional songs created by these differences provides opportunities for us to continue to add new songs to our personal collections throughout our lives.

If you come to a song you don't know, look it up on one of the websites provided in the appendix (page 245). Most sites provide an opportunity to actually hear the lyrics. (Throughout this book, references to CDs on which songs can be heard are provided whenever possible.) If there is a song you can't find, say it as a chant or rhyme. The inherent value of the rhyme and rhythm will still provide a rich language experience for the children.

Learn While the Children Learn

One of the best things this book offers is the opportunity inherent within the songs, chants, and rhymes to help children enhance the development of early literacy skills. It will also help you better articulate the value of singing and reciting chants and rhymes. With accountability knocking at the door of the early childhood classroom, it is critical to speak to the educational and learning value of these activities. This is a new era for all of us. The best way to grow with our profession is by experiencing firsthand the kinds of activities that can best guide the literacy journey for young children. There is no teacher like experience.

We know that you and the children in your classroom will enjoy the activities in *And the Cow Jumped Over the Moon.* Singing and reciting chants and rhymes are just plain fun for all of us. You can't help but fall in love with language when you experience it with rhythm, cadence, rhyme, and melody. Keep a song in your heart and a poem in your pocket—they are great tools for developing a foundation for literacy. And remember, you are also creating joyful memories, which in turn creates a joyful disposition toward literacy.

The Alphabet Song

The Alphabet Song (Tune: Twinkle, Twinkle, Little Star)
A — B — C — D — E — F—G,
H — I — J — K — L — M — N — O — P,
Q — R — S — T — U — V,
W — X — Y and Z.
Now I've said my ABC's
Next time won't you sing with me?

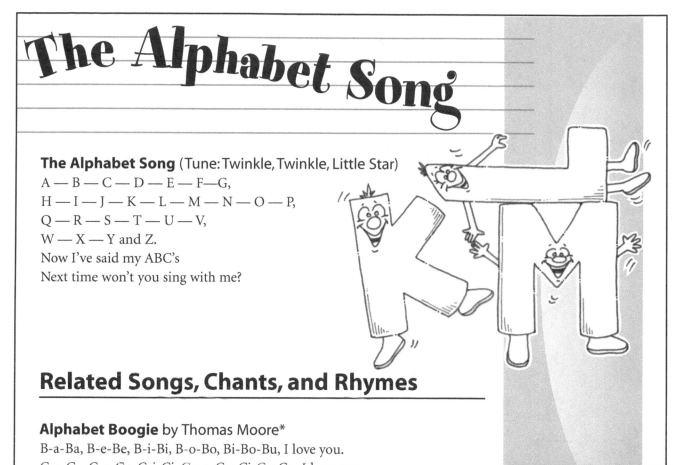

Related Songs, Chants, and Rhymes

Alphabet Boogie by Thomas Moore*
B-a-Ba, B-e-Be, B-i-Bi, B-o-Bo, Bi-Bo-Bu, I love you.
C-a-Ca, C-e-Ce, C-i-Ci, Co-o-Co, Ci-Co-Cu, I love you.

**I Am Special* CD, Thomas Moore Enterprises

The Alphabet Chant by Pam Schiller
A, B, C, and D,
Say these letters with me.
E, F, G, and H,
It's easy—don't you see?
I, J, K, and L,
Keep going, you're doing well.
M, N, O, and P,
Hmm, I like these letters so.
Q, R, S, and T,
It's almost time to take a rest.
U, V, W and X and Y, (*say these letters slowly*)
Almost time to say goodbye.
Z,
That's it—no more ABCs.

Nursery Rhyme Rap by Jean Feldman
(Tune: Ninety-Nine Bottles of Pop on the Wall)
Jack and Jill went up the hill
To get a pail of water.

SEE ALSO

"Counting Rhyme," page 142
"One, Two, Buckle My Shoe," page 142

Jack fell down and broke his crown
And Jill came tumbling after.
Oh, A B C D E F G...H I J K L...M N O P...Q R S... TUVWXYZ!
Humpty Dumpty sat on a wall
Humpty Dumpty had a great fall.
All the king's horses and all the king's men,
Couldn't put Humpty together again.
Oh, A B C D E F G...H I J K L...M N O P...Q R S...TUVWXYZ!
Little Miss Muffet sat on her tuffet
Eating her curds and whey.
Along came a spider and sat down beside her
And frightened Miss Muffet away.
Oh, A B C D E F G...H I J K L...M N O P...Q R S...TUVWXYZ!
Hey, diddle diddle, the cat and the fiddle,
The cow jumped over the moon.
The little dog laughed to see such a sight,
And the dish ran away with the spoon.
Oh, A B C D E F G...H I J K L...M N O P...Q R S...TUVWXYZ!
Little Boy Blue, come blow your horn,
The sheep's in the meadow, the cow's in the corn.
Where is the boy who looks after the sheep?
He's under the haystack fast asleep.
Oh, A B C D E F G...H I J K L...M N O P...Q R S...TUVWXYZ!
Hickory, dickory, dock,
The mouse ran up the clock.
The clock struck one, the mouse ran down,
Hickory, dickory, dock.
Oh, A B C D E F G...H I J K L...M N O P...Q R S...TUVWXYZ!

STORY TIME SUGGESTIONS

Chicka Chicka Boom Boom by Bill Martin, Jr. and John Archambault
Eating the Alphabet by Lois Elhert

Follow-Up Questions

- *What are ABC's?*
- *Which letter is the first letter of the alphabet? Which letter is last?*

Language Enrichment

- Print each child's name on a strip of paper. Point out each letter. Ask the children to point to the first letter in their names.
- Read a short story to the children. Point out the letters in the title of the book. Remind the children that these letters are in "The Alphabet Song."
- Show the children how to make the first letter of their names using finger spelling (see appendix page 244). If the first letter of their name is one of the more complicated finger spellings, teach them how to make the letter *A*. For children who show an interest in finger spelling, teach them how to make the letters *B* and *C*.

Extension Activities

Cognitive Development/Language

Magnetic Letters

Provide magnetic letters and a cookie tray. Sit with the children as they play with the letters. Help older children use the letters to spell their names. *Can you find the first letter of your name? Which letter is the first one mentioned in the song?* Younger children will enjoy exploring the magnetic attraction of the letters.

Cognitive and Social-Emotional Development/Blocks

Alphabet Blocks

Make Paper Bag Alphabet Blocks. Print each letter of the alphabet on small lunch bags, one letter per bag. Stuff crumpled newspaper into each bag until it is three-quarters full. Fold the top of the bag over and tape it down with masking tape or duct tape. Encourage the children to build with the blocks. Talk with them as they build. *Can you find the block with the letter that your name starts with? Can you name any of the letters on the blocks?* Show younger children the blocks that have the first letter of their names. This activity is for awareness only. Don't expect the children to recognize or identify the letters. Some will; most won't.

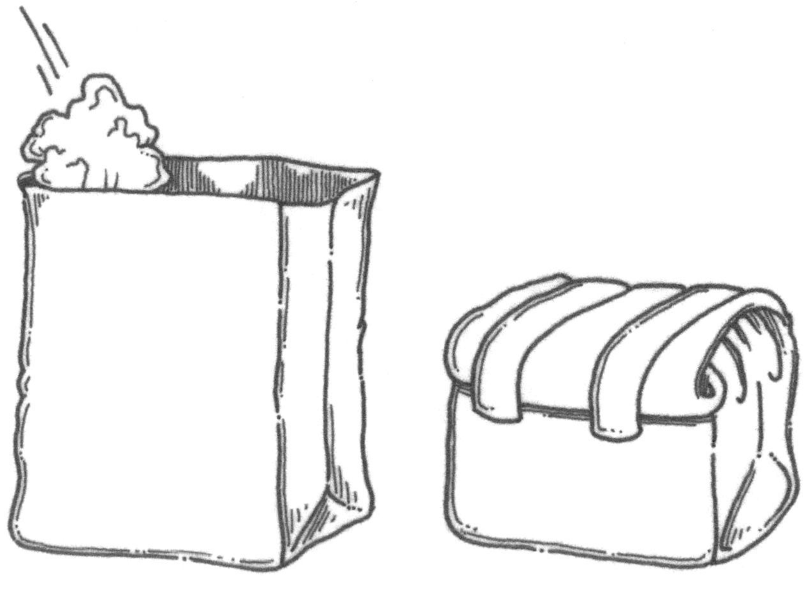

Physical and Cognitive Development/Gross Motor

Alphabet Saucers

Print alphabet letters on 6" paper plates. Create a *tossing* "line" by placing a strip of masking tape on the floor. Encourage the children to toss the plates into a box or basket. Identify the letters on the plates as the children toss them. Make sure each child tosses a plate with the first letter of his name on it. This activity is for awareness only. Don't expect the children to recognize or identify the letters.

Physical Development/Fine Motor

Playdough Letters

Show the children how to shape letters out of playdough. Demonstrate rolling the dough into balls and pinching the dough to make a design or break it apart. Working with the dough is more important than making letters. It strengthens all three hand muscles that will be needed for writing. Older children will enjoy watching you shape the first letters of their names.

Outdoor Play or Music and Movement

- Play Alphabet Jump. Print alphabet letters on paper plates. Spell each child's name on the floor using the letter plates. Encourage the children to "jump" the letters of their names. Call out each letter as they jump on it.
- Encourage the children to sing along with songs on *A to Z, the Animals and Me* CD, (Kimbo), "Nursery Rhyme Rap" (*Dr. Jean and Friends* CD, Jean Feldman), or "Alphabet Forward and Backwards" (*Keep on Singing and Dancing* CD, Jean Feldman).
- Chant along with the "Alphabet Boogie" (*I Am Special*, Thomas Moore).

REFLECTIONS ON THE DAY

- *What letters can you name?* (The order doesn't matter.)
- *What letter does your name begin with?*

Annie Mae

Annie Mae (Tune: Traditional)
Annie Mae, where are you going?
Up the stairs to take a bath.
Annie Mae with legs like toothpicks
And a neck like a giraffe.
Annie Mae stepped in the bathtub.
Annie Mae pulled out the plug.
Oh, my goodness!
Oh, my soul!
There goes Annie Mae down that hole.
Annie Mae? Annie Mae?
Gurgle, gurgle, glug.

Related Songs, Chants, and Rhymes

After My Bath
After my bath I try, try, try
To rub with a towel till I'm dry, dry, dry.
Hands to dry, and fingers and toes,
And two wet legs and a shiny nose.
Just think how much less time it'd take
If I were a dog and could shake, shake, shake!

Evan's Bath Song by Richele Bartkowiak (Tune: Rockabye, Baby)
Splishin' and a splashin'
In the bathtub.
When we take a bath
We clean and we scrub.
With a washcloth
And a little shampoo,
And when it's all over
We smell good as new.

Splishin' and a splashin'
That's what we do.
Don't forget Ducky.
He likes it, too.
Watchin' the bubbles
Dance in the tub.
Oh, how we love bath time
Rub-a-dub-dub!

SEE ALSO

"Dirty Old Bill," page 38
"Michael Finnegan," page 38
"Slippery Soap," page 39
"This Is the Way We Wash Our Face," page 197
"This Is the Way We Wash Our Hands," page 196
"Tiny Tim," page 215

Rub-a-Dub-Dub
Rub-a-dub-dub
Three men in a tub
And who do you think they be?
The butcher, the baker, and the candlestick maker
Turn them out, knaves all three.

Follow-Up Questions

- *Have you ever worried about going down the drain when the water drains out of the tub? Do you think you could fit in the drain hole?*
- *Where do you think Annie Mae went?*
- *What is your favorite part of bath time? Why?*

Language Enrichment

- Discuss the vocabulary that relates to the bathtub, such as *faucet, drain, tub, shower,* and *plug.*
- Discuss the vocabulary that relates to bath time, such as *bath mat, towel, soap,* and *shampoo.*
- Ask the children what they think the words of the song that describe Annie Mae's legs as toothpicks means. *What do you think her legs look like? What does her neck look like?*
- Teach children the American Sign Language sign for *bath* and *water* (see appendix page 239).

STORY TIME SUGGESTIONS

Bath Time by Eileen Spinelli
Caillou Bath Time by Joceline Sanschagrin
Elmo's Tub-Time Rhyme by Kara McMahon

Extension Activities

Cognitive Development/Art

Craft Stick Collage
Give the children a sheet of drawing paper, craft sticks, and glue or paste. Encourage them to use the craft sticks to make a collage. Draw a stick figure for the children and invite them to use the craft sticks to make the legs. Talk with the children about the craft sticks. *Are the craft sticks skinny?* Show the children the skinny side of a craft stick and the wide side of a craft stick. *Which is skinnier? If Annie Mae's legs were fat, what might we use to describe them?*

Cognitive Development/Discovery

Will It Fit?

Cut a 4" diameter hole in the bottom of a copy paper box (or a similar-size box). Turn the box over. Give the children balls of several different sizes, such as tennis balls, ping-pong balls, and bouncing balls. Encourage the children to see which ball will fit through the hole. Have them predict the outcome prior to testing. Discuss size. *Which balls are large? Which balls are small?* Give younger children only balls that will fit into the hole. They will enjoy putting the balls in the hole.

Physical Development/Fine Motor

Soapy Hands

Provide a shallow tub of water, a towel, and several different-sized bars of soap. Let the children explore the different sizes of soap. Show them how to turn the soap over in their hands to lather up. *Which soap size is easier to use? Have you ever seen the soap go down the drain?*

Social-Emotional Development/Dramatic Play

Bathe the Baby

Provide a shallow tub of water, plastic or rubber dolls, soap, and towels. Encourage the children to bathe the babies. Talk with them as they work. *Did you wash the baby's toes? Did you shampoo baby's hair? How does baby like the water?*

Outdoor Play or Music and Movement

- Cut out an arch on two sides of four or five medium-size boxes. Arrange the boxes side by side on the floor to create a tunnel. Encourage the children to crawl through the tunnel. If the children are not frightened by the thought, you can pretend that the tunnel is Annie Mae's drain. Flashlights will add to the fun.
- Sing along with "Annie Mae" (*Me, My Family and Friends* CD, Schiller Educational Resources, LLC) or "Anne Mae" (*Laugh 'n Learn Silly Songs* CD, Kimbo).

REFLECTIONS ON THE DAY

- *Have you ever lost a toy down the drain? Did you get it back? How?*
- *Which balls fit inside the hole in the box? Which ones didn't fit?*

The Ants Go Marching

The Ants Go Marching (Tune: Traditional)
The ants go marching one by one,
Hurrah, hurrah.
The ants go marching one by one,
Hurrah, hurrah.
The ants go marching one by one,
The little one stops to suck his thumb.
And they all go marching down
To the ground,
To get out
Of the rain.
BOOM! BOOM! BOOM! BOOM!

...two...tie her shoe...
...three...climb a tree...
...four...shut the door...
...five...take a dive...

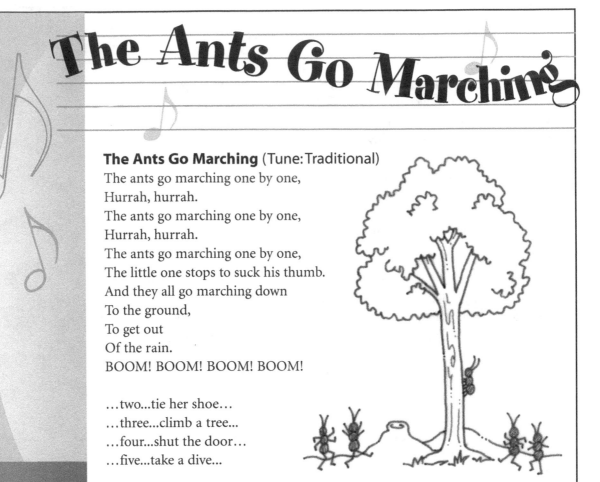

SEE ALSO

"The Grand Old Duke of York," page 61
"My Busy Garden," page 80

Related Songs/Chants/Rhymes

Little Ants by Pam Schiller (Tune: This Old Man)
Little ants marching by,
In a line that's mighty long,
With a hip, hop, happy, hi
Won't you join my song?
Little ants are marching on.

Little ants hopping high,
In a line that's mighty long,
With a hip, hop, happy, hi
Won't you join my song?
Little ants are hopping on.

Little ants dancing by,
In a line that's mighty long,
With a hip, hop, happy, hi
Won't you join my song?
Little ants are dancing on.

Little ants spinning by,
In a line that's mighty long,
With a hip, hop, happy, hi
Won't you join my song?
Little ants are spinning on.

Little ants sneaking by,
In a line that's mighty long,
With a hip, hop, happy, hi
Won't you join my song?
Little ants are sneaking on.

Little ants waving bye,
In a line that's mighty long,
With a hip, hop, happy, hi
Won't you join my song?
Little ants are waving bye.

Little Ant's Hill by Pam Schiller (Tune: Dixie)
Oh, I stuck my foot
On a little ant's hill,
And the little ant said,
"You better be still,
Take it off! Take it off!
Take it off! Remove it!"

Oh, I didn't take it off,
And the little ant said,
"If you don't take it off
You'll wish you had.
Take it off! Take it off!"
Ouch! I removed it!

Follow-Up Questions

- *Have you ever been bitten by an ant? Where?*
- *Have you ever seen ants traveling in a line? Where?*

Language Enrichment

- Discuss the words in the song that may be new vocabulary, such as *marching, climb, shut, dive*, and *hurrah.*
- Talk with the children about the words *hurray* and *hurrah. When do we use the word hurray? Can you think of something you celebrate by saying hurrah or hurray?*

STORY TIME SUGGESTIONS

Hey, Little Ant by Phillip M. Hoose
The Little Red Ant and the Great Big Crumb by Shirley Climo

- Sing "Little Ants" (see page 22) with the children. Discuss the verbs that describe the ants' actions in each verse. Ask a child to demonstrate each action.
- Teach the children the American Sign Language sign for *ant* (see appendix page 239).

Extension Activities

Cognitive Development/Discovery

Ant Pictures

Collect pictures of ants. Place the photos in plastic sleeves and into a binder to make a book. Encourage children to look at the photos. Talk with them as they look at the ants. *What are the ants doing? How many ants are in the picture? How many legs do the ants have? Are ants small or large?* Younger children will enjoy looking at the photos. Ask them simple questions. *What is the bug in the picture called?*

Cognitive Development/Games

Ant Puzzles

Make ant puzzles by cutting out three 4" diameter circles from brown construction paper. Draw a face on one of the circles. Cut out two antennae and six legs from black construction paper. Laminate the pieces, if possible. Work with children individually to put the ant together. Talk about the body parts of an ant as you help the children construct the ant.

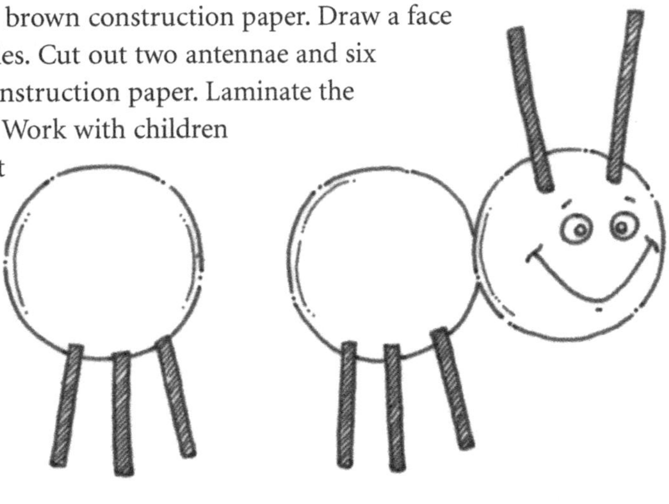

Physical and Cognitive Development/Art

Ant Prints

Provide fingerpaint and paper. Show the children how to make three connected fingerprints to create an ant. Add six legs and two antennae to each ant. Talk with the children about the body parts of the ant. *How many legs do ants have?*

Physical and Social-Emotional Development/ Gross Motor

Don't Step on the Ants!

Make several fingerprint ants on a piece of paper and draw circles around them. Cut them out and lay them in a path on the floor. Use masking tape to outline the pathway. Challenge children to walk through the path without stepping on the "ants." As the children become more skilled at stepping around the ants, add more ants to make the path more difficult.

Outdoor Play or Music and Movement

- Play marching music and teach the children how to march. March with big steps and march with small steps. Encourage the children to put their hands on the ground and try marching with four "legs." Show the children how to march one by one and two by two. Hold younger children while you march around the room. They will feel the rhythm.
- Teach older children a movement pattern that includes marching, such as march, march, march, turn; march, march, march, turn. Another pattern is march, march, jump; march, march, jump; and so on.
- Sing along with "The Ants Go Marching" (*Bugs! Bugs! Bugs!* CD, Schiller Educational Resources, LLC), "The Ants Go Marching" (*Where Is Thumbkin?* CD, Kimbo), or "The Ants Go Marching" (*Get Funky* CD, The Learning Station).

REFLECTIONS ON THE DAY

- *Does an ant have more legs or fewer legs than you do?*
- *Tell me something you know about ants.*

Are You Sleeping?

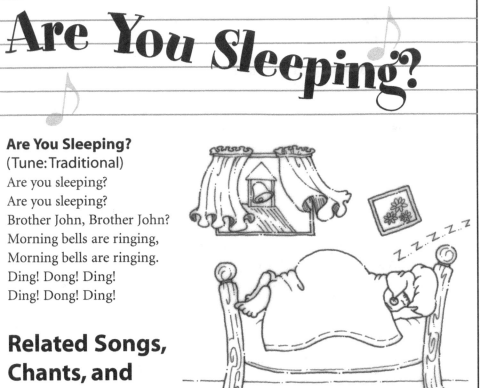

Are You Sleeping?
(Tune: Traditional)
Are you sleeping?
Are you sleeping?
Brother John, Brother John?
Morning bells are ringing,
Morning bells are ringing.
Ding! Dong! Ding!
Ding! Dong! Ding!

Related Songs, Chants, and Rhymes

Dream Fairy (Tune: Traditional)
A little fairy comes at night,
Her eyes are blue, her hair is brown,
With silver spots upon her wings,
And from the moon she flutters down.

She has a little silver wand,
And when a good child goes to bed,
She waves her hand from right to left,
And makes a circle round its head.

And then it dreams of pleasant things,
Of fountains filled with fairy fish,
And trees that bear delicious fruit,
And bow their branches at a wish.

Frère Jacques (Tune: Traditional)
Frère Jacques,
Frère Jacques,
Dormez vous?
Dormez vous?
Sonnez les matines,
Sonnez les matines,
Din, din, don!
Din, din, don!

SEE ALSO

"Giant Stomp," page 51
"Hickory, Dickory, Dock," page 70
"Little Boy Blue," page 95
"Rock-a-Bye, Baby," page 165
"Six in the Bed," page 179
"Wynken, Blynken and Nod," page 193

Wee Willie Winkie (Tune: Traditional)
Wee Willie Winkie
Runs through the town,
Upstairs and downstairs
In his nightgown.
Rapping at the windows,
Crying through the lock,
Are the children all in bed?
For it's now eight o'clock.

Follow-Up Questions

- *Sing the song, substituting some of the children's names in place of Brother John. Does changing the name change the song?*
- *Who wakes you up in the morning? How does he or she wake you up?*

Language Enrichment

- Show the children several different alarm clocks. Ask them what they know about alarm clocks. Identify the parts of the clock (hands, face, numerals, and so on).
- Discuss the line "morning bells are ringing." If children seem able to understand, explain that these are probably church bells that are sometimes rung to welcome the new day. Tell them that in their homes, the morning bell might be an alarm clock.
- Invite the children to sing the song saying the sound *da* instead of words. (**Note:** Using a syllable sound like *da* or a letter sound like /d/ instead of words helps focus on one of the discrete sounds of language. For some toddlers, this is easier than saying the words. When children enter school and formal reading instruction begins, they will need to be able to hear both the discrete source of syllables and individual letters. Early experiences with these sounds wire them in the brain so they will be familiar to children later.)
- Teach the children the American Sign Language sign for *goodnight* (see appendix page 239).

Extension Activities

Cognitive Development/Discovery

Bells, Bells, Bells

Give the children a variety of bells, such as a timer, rhythm band bells, jingle bells, and an alarm clock to explore. Talk with them about the bells. *Which bells are used in which situations? Which bell makes the loudest sound? Which bell makes the softest sound?* **Safety Note:** Watch carefully to make sure that children do not put bells in their mouths.

STORY TIME SUGGESTIONS

Goodnight Moon by Margaret Wise Brown
Hey! Wake Up! by Sandra Boynton
Pajama Time! by Sandra Boynton

Physical Development/Fine Motor

Bell Ringer Comparisons

Cut 2" holes in the lids of potato chip cans. Give the children large jingle bells and have them drop some bells inside. Encourage them to shake their cans to see whose can makes the loudest sound. Talk with the children about why some cans make louder sounds than others. Challenge older children to arrange the cans by sound—from loudest to softest.

Physical Development/Gross Motor

Ring That Bell!

Place a service bell in the middle of the floor. Make a throw line by placing a strip of masking tape on the floor. Give the children a beanbag and encourage them to toss the bag to hit the bell. Talk with the children about the sound the bell makes when it is hit. *Does it sound like a ding? Dong? Ping?*

Social Development/Dramatic Play

Bedtime

Provide props for bedtime (pillows, blankets, stuffed animals, and story books) and let the children play. Encourage their conversations. *Do you like to sleep with a pillow? Do you like a big pillow or a small pillow? Do you sleep with a stuffed animal?*

REFLECTIONS ON THE DAY

- *Which bell sounds did you like best today? Would you want to wake up to bells that sound like those bells?*
- *Would you rather wake up to a bell ringing or to someone rubbing your back and calling your name?*

Outdoor Play or Music and Movement

- Set an alarm clock so that it will ring in five minutes. Hide the clock and challenge the children to find it before it rings by listening for the ticking sound.
- Sing with "Are You Sleeping?" (*Me, My Family and Friends* CD, Schiller Educational Resources, LLC) or "Are You Sleeping?" (*Here Is Thumbkin,* Kimbo Educational).

Baby Bumblebee

Baby Bumblebee adapted by Richele Bartkowiak
(Tune: Baby Bumblebee)
I caught myself a baby bumblebee.
Won't my mommy be so proud of me?
I caught myself a baby bumblebee
Ouch! He stung me!

I'm talking to my baby bumblebee.
Won't my mommy be so proud of me?
I'm talking to my baby bumblebee.
"Oh," he said, "I'm sorry."

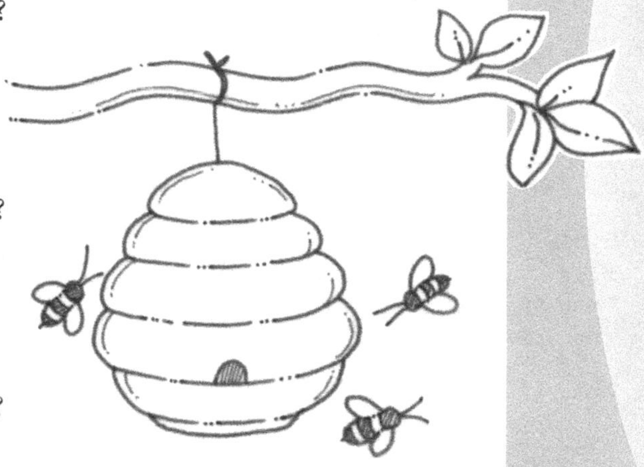

I'm letting go my baby bumblebee.
Won't my mommy be so proud of me?
I'm letting go my baby bumblebee,
Look, he's happy to be free!

Related Songs, Chants, and Rhymes

The Bee and the Pup (Tune: Traditional)
There was a bee-i-ee-i-ee
Sat on a wall-i-all-i-all
And he went buzz-i-uzz-i-uzz
And that was all-i-all-i-all.

There was a pup-i-up-i-up
Sat on a bee-i-ee-i-ee
Someone went ki-yi-yi-yi-yi
And that was he-i-ee-i-ee.

Buzzy, Buzzy Baby Bee
Buzzy, buzzy baby bee,
Won't you say your name to me? *(point to a child)*
Madison.
Good morning, Madison!
I'm so glad you're here with me.

SEE ALSO

"My Busy Garden," page 80

Here Is the Beehive

Here is the beehive.
Where are the bees? (*hold up fist*)
Hidden away where nobody sees. (*move other hand around fist*)
Watch and you'll see them come out of the hive, (*bend head close to fist*)
One, two, three, four, five. (*hold fingers up one at a time*)
Bzzzzzzzz… all fly away! (*wave fingers*)

Little Bee's Hive by Pam Schiller (Tune: Dixie)

Oh, I stuck my hand
In a little bee's hive,
And the little bee said,
"Goodness, alive!
Take it out! Take it out!
Take it out! Remove it!"

Oh, I didn't take it out,
And the little bee said,
"If you don't take it out
You'll wish you had.
Take it out! Take it out!"
Ouch! I removed it!

STORY TIME SUGGESTIONS

Buzz-Buzz, Busy Bees by Dawn Bentley
The Honey Makers by Gail Gibbons

Follow-Up Questions

- *Have you ever seen a bee? Where did you see one? What was it doing?*
- *How do bees move?*
- *Have you ever been stung by a bee?*

Language Enrichment

- Discuss the vocabulary in the song, including *bumblebee, stung, and proud.*
- Ask the children what they think the little girl/boy said to the bumblebee. If the children don't know, tell them that the child told the bee to please not sting him/her again.
- Talk to the children about the ending of the song. *Why do you think the child let the bee go?*
- Teach the children the American Sign Language sign for *bee* (see appendix page 239).

Extension Activities

Cognitive Development/Discovery

Bee Pictures

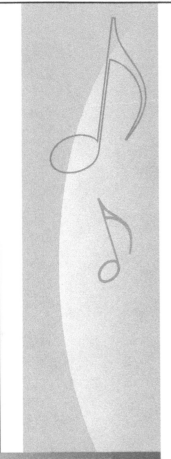

Collect photographs of bees, place them inside plastic sleeves, and put them into a three-ring binder to create a book about bees. Encourage the children to look through the book. Talk with them about the pictures. *How many wings does a bumblebee have? Where are its antennae?*

Cognitive Development/Science

Flower Garden

Provide potting soil, paper cups, and marigold seeds. Encourage the children to plant the seeds and then watch their plants grow and bloom into flowers. Discuss the process of planting the seeds. *What is the dirt called? What shape is the seed? What will the plant need to grow?*

Social and Cognitive Development/ Dramatic Play

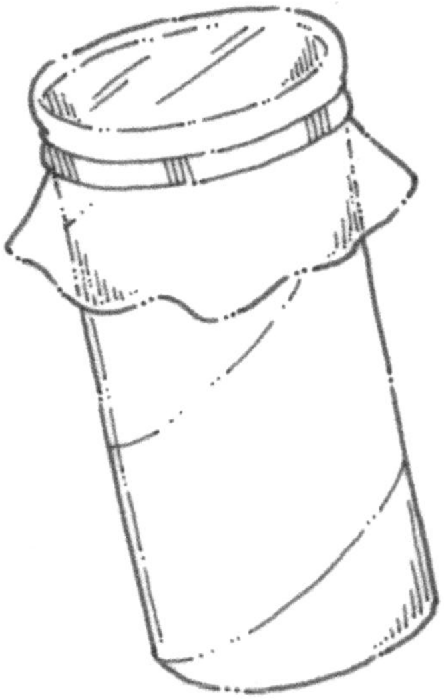

Kazoos

Make kazoos by placing a circle of wax paper over one end of an empty toilet paper tube and securing it with a rubber band. Give each child a kazoo and show them how to use the kazoos to make buzzing sounds. Talk with the children about the sounds they can make with their kazoos. *Are the sounds similar to bees buzzing?*

Social Development/Snack

Toast and Honey

Serve toast and honey for snack. If possible, find honey that has a honey comb inside the jar so children can see what a honey comb looks like. Discuss honey and its origin with the children. Keep it simple.

Safety Warning: Check for any food allergies.

Outdoor Play or Music and Movement

- Play classical music and encourage the children to fly like bumblebees around the room. Provide strips of yellow cellophane for wings.
- Sing along with "Baby Bumblebee" (*Bug, Bugs, Bugs* CD, Schiller Educational Resources, LLC) or "Baby Bumblebee" (*Here Is Thumbkin* CD, Kimbo).

REFLECTIONS ON THE DAY

- *What did you learn about bees today?*
- *Bees fly. What other bugs fly?*

Bubbles in the Air

Bubbles in the Air by Pam Schiller
(Tune: If You're Happy and You Know It)
Bubbles in the air, in the air.
Bubbles in the air, in the air.
Bubbles in the air…bubbles everywhere.
Bubbles in the air, in the air.

Bubbles in my hair, in my hair.
Bubbles in my hair, in my hair.
Bubbles in my hair…I don't even care.
Bubbles in my hair, in my hair.

Bubbles in the air, in the air.
Bubbles in the air, in the air.
Bubbles in the air…pop them if you dare.
Bubbles in the air, in the air.

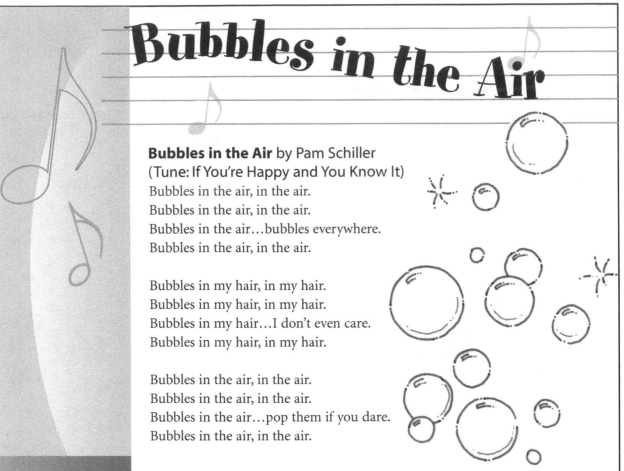

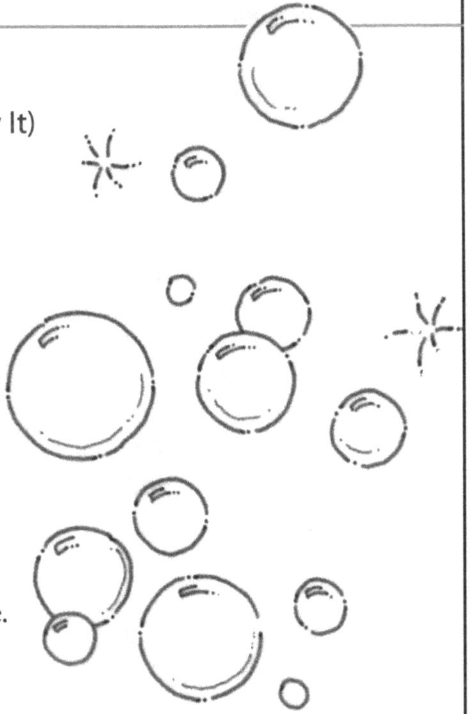

SEE ALSO

"Evan's Bath Song," page 19
"Tiny Tim," page 215

Related Songs, Chants, and Rhymes

B-B-B-Bubbles by Pam Schiller (Tune: K-K-K-Katie)
B-b-b-bubbles, beautiful bubbles.
We love you more and more and more and more and more.
B-b-b-bubbles, beautiful bubbles.
You're the b-b-b-bubbles we adore.

Let's All Watch the Bubbles
Let's all watch the bubbles, the bubbles, the bubbles
Let's all watch the bubbles go way up high.
There are big ones and tiny ones
And fat ones and shiny ones,
Let's all watch the bubbles go way up high.

Pop the Bubbles (Tune: Little Red Wagon)
Let's pop, pop, pop those bubbles.
Pop, pop, pop those bubbles.
Pop, pop, pop those bubbles.
Now everybody stop! Pop, pop!

Follow-Up Questions

- *Have you ever had a bubble land on your head? What happened?*
- *What do bubbles feel like when you pop them? What does the liquid feel like on your hands?*

Language Enrichment

- Ask children questions about bubbles. *How do you make a bubble solution? Can you make bubbles move where you want them to go? How?*
- Invite the children to discuss their experiences with bubbles.
- Make bubble soap with the children. Mix 1 teaspoon glycerin, ½ cup liquid detergent, ½ cup water in a container. For best results, let the mixture sit overnight before blowing bubbles. Discuss the ingredients and the amount used.
- Teach children the American Sign Language sign for *bubbles* (see appendix page 239).

Extension Activities

Cognitive Development/Art

Bubble Art

Provide a cake pan or a tub with just enough non-toxic tempera paint to cover the bottom. Cut large-size bubble wrap into small squares. Give each child a square of bubble wrap and a sheet of drawing paper. Encourage the children to dip the square of bubble wrap into the tempera paint and press it on their drawing paper to make designs. Talk with the children about their designs. *What shape do the bubbles make?*

Physical and Cognitive Development/Outdoor

Bubble Prints

Mix non-toxic tempera paint with bubble solution. Encourage the children to blow bubbles over a large sheet of butcher paper. When the bubbles land on the paper and pop, they will leave a colored circle print. Talk with the children about the print the bubbles make when they pop. *What shapes are on your paper?*

STORY TIME SUGGESTIONS

Bubbles, Bubbles by Kathi Appelt

Pop! A Book about Bubbles by Kimberly Brubaker Bradley

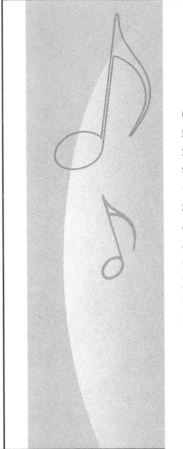

Physical Development/Fine Motor

Bubbles From My Hand

Provide a small tub of water and liquid soap (bubble bath soap works well). Demonstrate how to form a loose fist, dip the hand (fist) in the water, rub soap over the circle made by the thumb and the index finger, and then gently blow. A bubble will appear from the underside of the fist. Talk with children as they blow bubbles. *That was a large bubble.*

Safety Note: Make sure children do not put soap on their lips. Tell them to keep their hands at least a few inches from their mouths when blowing bubbles.

Physical Development/Gross Motor

Bubble Pop

Give the children large-size bubble wrap and let them try popping the bubbles by stomping on them. *What sounds do the bubbles make when they pop? How is the sound different from the sound bubbles make when you blow them?*

REFLECTIONS ON THE DAY

- *How did you make bubbles with your hands?*
- *What did you learn about bubbles today?*

Outdoor Play or Music and Movement

- Blow bubbles and challenge the children to keep the bubbles in the air by chasing them and using their breath to keep them up. Show them how to use a sheet of paper or a paper plate to fan the air to lift the bubbles up.
- Sing along with "Bubbles in the Air" (*School Days* CD, Schiller Educational Resources, LLC).

Cap, Mittens, Coat, and Boots

Cap, Mittens, Coat, and Boots by Pam Schiller
(Tune: Head, Shoulders, Knees, and Toes)
Cap, mittens, coat, and boots,
Coat and boots.
Cap, mittens, coat, and boots,
Coat and boots.
And pants and belt, and shirt and tie
Go together wet or dry,
Wet or dry!

Related Songs, Chants, and Rhymes

Cap, Mittens, Boots, and Scarf by Pam Schiller
(Tune: Head, Shoulders, Knees, and Toes)
Cap, mittens, boots, and scarf,
Boots and scarf.
Cap, mittens, boots, and scarf,
Boots and scarf.
And shoes and socks and coat and sun
Keep me warm for winter fun,
Winter fun!

Stop, Drop, and Roll (version 1) by Pam Schiller
(Tune: Hot Cross Buns)
Stop, drop, and roll.
Stop, drop, and roll.
If ever your clothes catch on fire,
Stop, drop, and roll.

Remember this rule,
This golden safety rule.
If ever your clothes catch on fire,
Stop, drop, and roll.

SEE ALSO

"One, Two, Buckle My Shoe," page 142
"There Was an Old Woman," page 193

Stop, Drop, and Roll (version 2) by Pam Schiller
(Tune: Hot Cross Buns)
Stop, stop, stop—don't run,
Stop and drop and roll.
If ever your clothes catch on fire,
Stop and drop and roll.

Stop, stop, stop—and drop,
Roll and roll and roll.
If ever your clothes catch on fire,
Stop, drop, and roll and roll.

Which Things Go Together? by Pam Schiller
(Tune: Sweetly Sings the Donkey)
Which things go together?
My foot and its shoe.
Which things go together?
Earrings, one and two.
Matching, matching, matching
So much fun to do!

Which things go together?
Rain and rubber boots.
Which things go together?
Ties and dress-up suits.
Matching, matching, matching
So much fun to do!

STORY TIME SUGGESTION

Caps, Hats, Socks and Mittens by Louise Borden

Follow-Up Questions

- *What kind of clothes do you wear to school?*
- *What kind of clothes do you wear when it rains?*

Language Enrichment

- Discuss seasons and the clothes you need for each season. *What do you wear when the weather is warm? What do you wear when it is cold outside?*
- Make up a new song using the same tune but with different clothing items (shorts, sandals, shirt, and hat or jeans, sweater, belt, and shoes). Sing the new version of the song and discuss the items that are mentioned in the new lyrics.
- Sing "Head, Shoulders, Knees, and Toes" and then sing "Caps, Mittens, Coat and Boots." *Is the tune of the songs the same?*
- Talk about hats. *What is the difference between a cap and a hat? What kind of hats have you seen people wear? When do you wear hats?*

Extension Activities

Cognitive Development/Language

Sock Sort

Collect socks in solid colors and prints. Place them in a basket and invite the children to match and fold them. Discuss the prints on the socks and the many ways that people fold them. Discuss other clothing items that come in pairs (shoes, mittens).

Cognitive Development/Math

Shoe Match

Provide several pairs of shoes all mixed together. Encourage the children to match the shoes one-to-one. Use the correct terminology (*one-to-one* and *pairs*). Discuss the different ways shoes fasten—Velcro, laces, snaps, and so on.

Cognitive and Physical Development/Art

Sponge Painting

Cut sponges into mitten and hat shapes. Provide non-toxic paint and paper and encourage the children to make mitten and hat prints. Ask questions. *What kind of hat are you making? Do you wear this kind of hat in the winter or the summer?* Younger children will enjoy exploring the paint and sponges.

Social-Emotional Development/Dramatic Play

Dress Up

Provide a variety of clothing items. Be sure to include both male and female clothing and lots of accessories, such as hats, purses, ties, and jewelry. Provide a mirror so the children can see how they look when they put on their outfits. Talk about the different articles of clothing. Help them name and describe the items as they select their attire. Discuss fasteners.

Outdoor Play or Music and Movement

- Play Pass the Hat. Collect enough hats for every child to have one. Ask the children to sit in a circle. Play music and have the children pass their hats from head to head. When the music stops, each child keeps the hat on her head. Start the music again and invite the children to stand and dance.
- Use masking tape to make a line on the floor. Have the children place a hat on their heads and then walk the line.
- Sing along with "Cap, Mittens, Coat and Boots" (*Me, My Family and Friends* CD, Schiller Educational Resources, LLC) or "Stop, Drop and Roll" (*School Days* CD, Schiller Educational Resources, LLC).

REFLECTIONS ON THE DAY

- *Can you name some clothing items that come in pairs?*
- *Do you wear hats? What kind do you like to wear?*

Dirty Old Bill

Dirty Old Bill
(Tune: Turkey in the Straw)
I know a man named Dirty Old Bill
He lives in a house on Garbage Hill.
And he never took a bath and he
never will.
Phew-wee! Dirty Old Bill!

Related Songs, Chants, and Rhymes

I Wish I Were
(Tune: If You're Happy and You Know It)
Oh, I wish I were a little bar of soap (bar of soap),
Oh, I wish I were a little bar of soap (bar of soap),
I'd go slidee, slidee, slidee,
Over everybody's body.
Oh, I wish I were a little bar of soap (bar of soap).

Michael Finnegan (Tune: Traditional)
There was an old man named Michael Finnegan.
He had whiskers on his chinnegan.
They fell out and then grew in again.
Poor old Michael Finnegan,
Begin again.

There was an old man named Michael Finnegan.
He went fishing with a pin again.
Caught a fish and dropped it in again.
Poor old Michael Finnegan,
Begin again.

There was an old man named Michael Finnegan.
He grew fat and then grew thin again.
Then he died and had to begin again.
Poor old Michael Finnegan,
Begin again.

SEE ALSO

"Annie Mae," page 19
"Rub-a-Dub-Dub," page 20
"This Is the Way We Wash Our Face," page 197
"This Is the Way We Wash Our Hands," page 196
"Tiny Tim," page 215

Slippery Soap by Pam Schiller
Slippery, slippery, slippery soap
Sliding and slipping through my hands.
Slippery, slippery, slippery soap
Slipping and sliding from my hands.
Slippery, slippery, slippery soap
Where are you hiding, slippery soap?
Silly, slippery, sliding, hiding soap.

Follow-Up Questions

- *Do you like taking a bath? Why do you think Bill doesn't want to take a bath?*
- *Who helps you take your bath? Which part of your bath do you enjoy most?*
- *Why do you think that Bill lives on Garbage Hill?*

Language Enrichment

- Ask the children to help you sequence the steps in taking a bath (turn on the water, take off clothes, put soap on washcloth, and so on).
- Encourage the children to name all the things they need when they take a bath.
- Talk with the children about the use of the term *phew-wee.* This is every child's favorite part of the song. Toddlers will probably remember hearing this term used to describe their diapers. *What does it mean? What other ways do we say something doesn't smell good?* (stinky, smelly). *Do you think it hurts Bill's feeling when people say "phew-wee?"*
- Teach the children the American Sign Language sign for *bath* (see appendix page 239).

STORY TIME SUGGESTIONS

Elmo Wants a Bath by Joe Mathieu
Harry the Dirty Dog by Gene Zion
Mrs. Wishy-Washy by Joy Cowley

Extension Activities

Cognitive Development/Blocks

Bill's House
Crumple paper to make a "garbage hill." Make a house for Bill from a small box. Invite the children to try to place the house on the garbage hill. *Is it hard to get the house to stay on the hill? What would make it easier?* Provide a towel to cover the garbage hill. *Will the house stay now?* Younger children will enjoy watching boxes slide and roll off the hill.

Cognitive and Social Development/Listening

Dirty Old Bill

Tape record yourself singing the song or, if possible, tape a parent or school staff member singing it. Place it in the listening center for the children to enjoy and sing along with.

Physical Development/Fine Motor

Nice Smells

Provide a shallow tub of water and several different scents of bar soap. Encourage the children to explore the different soap aromas. *Which fragrance smells the best?* Provide hand lotions to use after their hands are all clean. *Which fragrance do you like best?* **Safety Note:** Supervise closely so that toddlers do not get soap in their eyes and/or mouths.

Social Development/Dramatic Play

Wash-Up Time

Provide a tub of water, some rags, soap, and rubber animals to wash. Talk with the children as they give the animals a bath. *Which animal are you washing? Does he have fur or hair? Do you need some shampoo?*

REFLECTIONS ON THE DAY

- *Were you able to get Bill's house to stay on top of the garbage hill? How did you do it?*
- *Why do people think that Bill smells? What do people say when they smell Bill?*

Outdoor Play or Music and Movement

- Hide a bag of potpourri in the classroom and see if the children can use their noses to find it. **Safety Note:** Make sure the bag is sealed tightly so potpourri cannot be removed.
- Sing along with "Dirty Old Bill" (*Me, My Family and Friends* CD, Schiller Educational Resources, LLC), "Michael Finnegan" (*Where Is Thumbkin?* CD, Kimbo Educational), or "I Wish I Were" (*Laugh 'N Learn Silly Songs* CD, Kimbo Educational).

Do You Know the Muffin Man?

Do You Know the Muffin Man? (Tune: Traditional)
Oh, do you know the muffin man,
The muffin man, the muffin man?
Oh, do you know the muffin man
Who lives on Drury Lane?

Oh, yes, I know the muffin man,
The muffin man, the muffin man.
Oh, yes, I know the muffin man
Who lives on Drury Lane.

Related Songs, Chants, and Rhymes

Hot Cross Buns (Tune: Traditional)
Hot cross buns,
One-a-penny buns;
One a penny,
Two a penny,
Hot cross buns.

Fresh, sweet buns,
Come and buy my buns;
One a penny,
Two a penny,
Fresh, sweet buns.

Nice, light buns,
Buy my currant buns;
Come and try them,
Then you'll buy them,
Nice, light buns.

I Like Jelly on My Toast
(Tune: She'll Be Comin' 'Round the Mountain)
I like jelly on my toast, yes, I do (yes, I do!),
I like bacon with my eggs, 'cause that's good too (good too!),
I like jelly on my toast and bacon with my eggs,
I like jelly and toast and bacon and eggs. Don't you?

SEE ALSO

"Chew, Chew, Chew Your Food," page 152
"Drink, Drink, Drink Your Milk," page 152
"Peanut Butter and Jelly," page 151
"Peas Porridge Hot," page 101

I like cookies with my milk, yes, I do (yes, I do!),
I like ice cream with my cake, 'cause that's good too (good too!),
I like cookies with milk and ice cream with my cake,
I like cookies and milk and ice cream and cake. Don't you?

Polly Put the Kettle On (Tune: Traditional)
Polly, put the kettle on,
Polly, put the kettle on,
Polly, put the kettle on,
We'll all have tea.

Sukey, take it off again,
Sukey, take it off again,
Sukey, take it off again,
They've all gone away.

Blow the fire and make the toast,
Put the muffins on to roast,
Blow the fire and make the toast,
We'll all have tea.

Shortnin' Bread
Put on the skillet, slip on the lid.
Mama's gonna make a little short'nin' bread.
That ain't all she's gonna do.
Mama's gonna make a little coffee, too.

Chorus:
Mama's little baby loves shortnin', shortnin',
Mama's little baby loves shortnin' bread.
Mama's little baby loves shortnin', shortnin',
Mama's little baby loves shortnin' bread.

Three little children, lyin' in bed,
They were sick—covers over their heads.
Sent for the doctor, and the doctor said,
"Give those children some shortnin' bread."

(Chorus)

When those children sick in bed,
Heard that talk about shortnin' bread.
Popped up well to dance and sing,
'Cause short'nin' bread's their favorite thing.

(Chorus)

STORY TIME SUGGESTIONS

Bread, Bread, Bread by Ann Morris
Bread Is for Eating by David Gershator
The Tortilla Factory by Gary Paulsen

Follow-Up Questions

- *Do you prefer muffins or bread? Why?*
- *What does the muffin man do? Do you think he sells other types of bread or just muffins?*
- *Where does the muffin man live?*

Language Enrichment

- Talk with the children about muffins. *Do you like muffins? Which flavor of muffin do you like best? How are muffins like cupcakes?*
- Show the children a real muffin or a photograph of a muffin. Ask them to describe what they like to eat with or on their muffins.
- Invite older toddlers to name as many different types of muffins as they can. Make a list of the muffin types on a sheet of chart paper.
- Ask the children how they think adding jelly beans to muffins would make the muffins taste. *What other foods could we add to muffins? Would raisins make the muffins taste better or not?*

Extension Activities

Cognitive Development/Art

Muffin Assortments

Cut round circles from light brown construction paper to represent muffins. Give the children small blue, brown, and yellow circles to glue on the muffins to make blueberry muffins, chocolate chip muffins, and banana muffins. Talk with them about the type of muffin they choose to make.

Cognitive Development/Math

Muffin Tin Fill

Cut red, yellow, orange, blue, green, and purple felt circles to fit inside the crates of a muffin tin. Provide colored beads and encourage the children to sort the beads by matching each bead to the color in the bottom of the crates. To make this activity more challenging, give the children a large scoop to use to move the beads from the bucket to the correct crate in the muffin tin. Discuss the use of muffin tins when they are used for cooking.

Physical Development/Fine Motor

Making Muffins

Provide playdough and baking props, such as a rolling pin, muffin tins, cookie cutters, and so on. Encourage the children to make *cookies* and *muffins*. Talk with them as they work. *What kind of a muffin or cookie are you making? How do you make muffins?* Younger children will simply enjoy exploring the playdough. Talk with them about the texture of the dough and show them how to pinch it, pat it, and roll it.

Physical and Social Development/Gross Motor

Muffin Toss

Give the children pretend muffins (rolled socks) to toss into a basket. Make a throw line by placing a piece of masking tape on the floor 2' away from the basket. As children become proficient, move the basket further from the throw line. Let younger children place socks in the basket. Talk with them about how many "muffins" will fit in the basket before the basket is too full to hold any more.

REFLECTIONS ON THE DAY

- *Which kind of muffin did you like best?*
- *How did you make muffins?*

Outdoor Play or Music and Movement

- Create a path to the muffin man's *house* using masking tape. For more fun, make the path "zig" and "zag." Encourage the children to crawl along the path to find the muffin man. Make sure there are "muffins" at the end of the path (muffin shapes cut from poster board and pretend plastic/wood muffins). Create a *house* for the muffin man by decorating a cardboard box.
- Sing along with "Oh, Do You Know the Muffin Man?" (*Fabulous Foods* CD, Schiller Educational Resources, LLC), "Oh, Do You Know the Muffin Man?" (*Baby Faces* CD, (Kimbo Educational), or "Muffin Man (*Greg and Steve: We All Live Together Vol. 3,* Youngheart).

Do Your Ears Hang Low?

Do Your Ears Hang Low? (Tune: Turkey in the Straw)
Do your ears hang low? (*point to your ears*)
Do they wobble to and fro? (*move your hands side to side*)
Can you tie them in a knot? (*make a tying motion*)
Can you tie them in a bow? (*pretend to tie a bow*)
Can you throw them over your shoulder, (*toss clasped hands over shoulder*)
Like a Continental soldier? (*salute*)
Do your ears hang low? (*point to your ears*)

Related Songs, Chants, and Rhymes

Are You Listening? (Tune: Are You Sleeping?)
Are you listening?
Are you listening?
Boys and girls, girls and boys?
Come and join our circle,
Come and join our circle,
Sit right down.
Sit right down.

Here Are My Ears
(suit actions to words)
Here are my ears,
Here is my nose,
Here are my fingers,
Here are my toes.

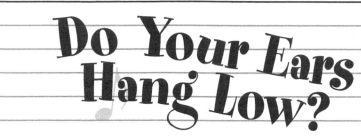

Here are my eyes,
Both open wide,
Here is my mouth
With white teeth inside.

Here is my tongue
That helps me speak,
Here is my chin,
And here are my cheeks.

Here are my hands
That help me play,
Here are my feet,
For walking today.

SEE ALSO

"Humpty Dumpty's New Ears," page 73
"Where, Oh, Where Has My Little Dog Gone?," page 231

Stop, Look, and Listen

Stop, look, and listen
Before you cross the street.
First use your eyes and ears,
Then use your feet.

This Is the Way We Wash Our Ears

(Tune: Here We Go 'Round the Mulberry Bush)

This is the way we wash our ears,
Wash our ears, wash our ears.
We scrub behind, we scrub inside
Every time we take a bath.

Follow-Up Questions

- *What do the words, "Do your ears hang low mean?" Is the song talking about an animal? Can a child's ears hang low?*
- *Where are your ears? How many ears do you have?*

Language Enrichment

- Ask the children if they can think of animals that have ears that hang low.
- Discuss the vocabulary in the song, including *wobble, Continental soldier, knot,* and *bow.*
- Teach the children the American Sign Language sign for *ear* (see appendix page 239).

STORY TIME SUGGESTIONS

Do Your Ears Hang Low? by Caroline Jayne Church

Toes, Ears, and Nose by Marion Dane Bauer

Extension Activities

Cognitive Development/Art

Bow Collage

Collect discarded gift wrap bows. Provide paper, glue or paste, and bows. Encourage the children to make a collage with the bows. Make the connection between the line in the song that asks, "Can you tie them in a knot, can you tie them in a bow?" Ask the children if they can tie their ears in a bow. Show them how a bow is different from a knot.

Cognitive Development/Discovery

Ear "Stuff"

Give the children clip-on earrings, ear phones, and ear muffs to explore. Be sure to provide a mirror. Talk with them about the things that go on and over ears. *Why do we need ear muffs? Who wears earrings?*

Cognitive Development/Listening

A Story on Tape

Make a tape of a simple and familiar story. Encourage them to listen to the tape. Talk with them about using their ears and earphones to hear the story. For added fun, have family members record the story. *Does anyone recognize the voice of a family member?*

Cognitive and Social-Emotional Development/Science

Ears Up Close

Encourage the children to use a magnifying glass to look at your ears and at the ears of their friends. Talk about the parts of the ear. *Where are the earlobes? Where is the top of your ear?*

Outdoor Play or Music and Movement

- Play some marching music and encourage the children to march like soldiers. Show them several types of soldier marches.
- Sing along with "Do Your Ears Hang Low?" (*Where Is Thumbkin?* CD, Kimbo Educational) or "Do Your Ears Hang Low?" (*Me, My Family, and Friends* CD, Schiller Educational Resources, LLC).

REFLECTIONS ON THE DAY

- *What did you learn about ears today?*
- *What things do we use our ears for?*

For He's a Jolly Good Fellow

For He's a Jolly Good Fellow (Tune: Traditional)
For he's a jolly good fellow,
For he's a jolly good fellow,
For he's a jolly good fellow,
Which nobody can deny.
Which nobody can deny.
Which nobody can deny.
For he's a jolly good fellow,
For he's a jolly good fellow,
For he's a jolly good fellow,
Which nobody can deny.

We won't go home until morning,
We won't go home until morning,
We won't go home until morning,
Till daylight doth appear.
Till daylight doth appear,
Till daylight doth appear,
We won't go home until morning,
We won't go home until morning,
We won't go home until morning,
Till daylight doth appear.

Sing again, changing the pronoun "he" to "she."

SEE ALSO

"Make New Friends," page 126
"The More We Get Together," page 126
"Morning Greeting," page 59
"Will You Be My Friend Today?," page 126

Related Songs, Chants, and Rhymes

Hello, Good Friend (Tune: Are You Sleeping?)
Hello, good friend,
Hello, good friend.
How are you?
How are you?
Say your name to us, friend,
Say your name to us, friend.
And we will clap for you.
We'll clap for you.

Punchinello (Tune: Traditional)

Directions: *Choose one child to be Punchinello. The children stand in a circle around "Punchinello." Punchinello does an action, such as touching his toes, hopping, or twisting in the first verse. The other children copy his action in the second verse. The child in the center selects a child to take his place during the third verse.*

What can you do,
Punchinello, funny fellow?
What can you do,
Punchinello, funny you?

We can do it, too,
Punchinello, funny fellow,
We can do it, too,
Punchinello, funny you!

You choose one of us,
Punchinello, funny fellow,
You choose one of us,
Punchinello, funny you!

This Is Quinn by Pam Schiller
(Tune: Here We Go 'Round the Mulberry Bush)

Here is our friend
His name is Quinn,
His name is Quinn,
His name is Quinn.

Here is our friend.
We're glad he's here.
Say "hello" to Quinn.

Use names (and characteristics) for the children in your classroom. For example: "Her name is Kate, her hair is brown...".

Follow-Up Questions

- *What is a "jolly good fellow?"*
- *Would this be a good song to sing on someone's birthday? Why?*

Language Enrichment

- Discuss new vocabulary with the children, such as *jolly, fellow,* and *deny.*
- Sing the song, changing *jolly good fellow* to *fantastic fellow.* Try other words with three syllables. Treat each new word as new vocabulary and discuss it with the children.
- This is a song of celebration. Explain that people sing it when a friend does something worth celebrating, such as learning to walk or learning to balance on one foot. *What have you learned to do recently that we can celebrate by singing this song to you?*
- Teach the children the American Sign Language sign for *friend* (see appendix page 239).

STORY TIME SUGGESTIONS

The Baby Dances by Katherine Henderson
Good Dog, Carl by Alexandra Day
Look What I Can Do by Jose Aruego

Extension Activities

Cognitive Development/Library

Things to Celebrate

Gather books that show children doing milestone activities, such as hopping, skipping, jumping, and dancing. Look through the books with the children and encourage them to identify the activities that might make them feel like celebrating. They may need your help as they get started. Talk about the activities and why they are worthy of celebration. Remind the children of their own successes. Sing "For He's/She's a Jolly Good Fellow" to the children in the books.

Physical Development/Art

Confetti Collage

Provide paste or glue and small pieces of construction paper (confetti). Invite the children to smear the paste on their paper and then drop pieces of confetti on top to create a celebration design. Talk with them about their designs. *What color is the confetti? What makes the confetti stick to the paper? How is confetti used?*

Physical Development/Gross Motor

I Can Do It!

Use a strip of masking tape to make a start line. Encourage the children to jump as far as they can from the line. Mark their landing spots with strips of masking tape with their names on them. Ask each child to jump again with a goal of jumping beyond their first jump. Celebrate successes and encourage children to continue until successful. Use celebration vocabulary (*Yeah! Hurray! Way to go! Good job! You did it!*), as children meet their goals.

Social-Emotional Development/Music

Celebration Music

Provide rhythm instruments (or party noise makers) and encourage the children to play some celebration music. Help them think of reasons to celebrate with their music (*it is almost lunch time* or *time to go outdoors*).

Outdoor Play or Music and Movement

- Play the circle game "Punchinello" (see page 49) with the children.
- Sing along with "For He's a Jolly Good Fellow" (*100 Songs for Kids, Vol. 1* CD, Time/Life Music) or "Punchinello" (*Wee Sing and Play* CD; Price, Stern and Sloan).

REFLECTIONS ON THE DAY

- *Do your mommy and daddy do things that we can celebrate by singing "For He's a Jolly Good Fellow?"*
- *What does the word* jolly *mean?*

Giant Stomp

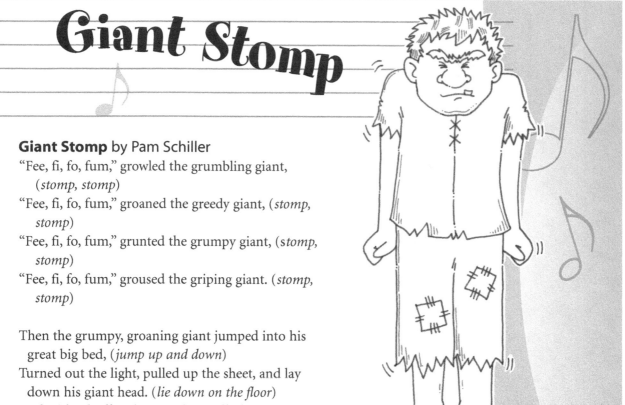

Giant Stomp by Pam Schiller
"Fee, fi, fo, fum," growled the grumbling giant, (*stomp, stomp*)
"Fee, fi, fo, fum," groaned the greedy giant, (*stomp, stomp*)
"Fee, fi, fo, fum," grunted the grumpy giant, (*stomp, stomp*)
"Fee, fi, fo, fum," groused the griping giant. (*stomp, stomp*)

Then the grumpy, groaning giant jumped into his great big bed, (*jump up and down*)
Turned out the light, pulled up the sheet, and lay down his giant head. (*lie down on the floor*)
And with a huff and a great big puff silently went to sleep. (*huff, puff and close eyes*)

Related Songs, Chants, and Rhymes

Five Huge Dinosaurs by Pam Schiller
Five huge dinosaurs dancing a jig, (*hold up five fingers and dance them*)
They rumble and grumble and stumble
Because they are so big. (*spread hands apart*)

Five huge dinosaurs floating on a barge, (*hold up five fingers make a boat with hands*)
They jiggle and wiggle and jiggle
Because they are so large. (*spread hands apart*)

Five huge dinosaurs singing a song, (*hold up five fingers and put hands beside mouth*)
They bellow and holler and ramble
Because they sing it wrong. (*shake head no*)

Five huge dinosaurs taking a bow, (*hold up five fingers and bow*)
They bobble and hobble and tumble
Because they don't know how. (*hold hands out to side*)

SEE ALSO

"Are You Sleeping?," page 26
"Lazy Mary," page 96
"Rock-a-Bye, Baby," page 165
"Six in the Bed," page 179
"Wee Willie Winkie," page 27

Five huge dinosaurs making me laugh, (*hold up five fingers and then hold tummy*)
They stumble when they dance. (*dance fingers on arm*)
They jiggle when they float. (*make boat with hands*)
They ramble when they sing. (*place hands beside mouth*)
They tumble when they bow. (*bow*)
But they can make me laugh! (*hold tummy, shake head yes*)

So Big!
How big is baby? (*hands out to side and shrug shoulders*)
So big! (*show size with hands—stretch out wide or hold up high*)

Who's That Traipsing on My Bridge?
Trip trap, trip trap
Who is traipsing on my bridge?
Get off, get off
Whoever you are.
I don't like anyone on my bridge!

Follow-Up Questions

- *Why was the giant so grumpy?*
- *How do you feel when you are sleepy?*
- *Discuss real and make-believe. What things are make-believe?*

STORY TIME SUGGESTIONS

Big and Little by Steve Jenkins
Big and Little by Margaret Miller

Language Enrichment

- Ask the children, *Who can show me how a giant might growl? Groan? Grunt?* If the children can't make these sounds, demonstrate them and have the children echo your sound.
- Discuss words that may be new vocabulary for the children, including *grumbling, greedy, grumpy*, and *gripe.*
- Ask the children why the giant didn't have someone to tuck him into bed. *Would he be less grumpy if someone read him a bedtime story?*

Extension Activities

Cognitive Development/Language

Grumpy Faces
Provide a mirror and encourage the children to make grumpy faces. Talk with them about things that make them grumpy. *What can you do to feel better when you are feeling grumpy? How can you tell when someone is feeling grumpy?* For younger children, you make a grumpy face. See if you can make them laugh.

Cognitive Development/Math

Giant and Small Sort

Collect a box of items that come in giant and small sizes (books, pencils, blocks, bags). Encourage the children to sort the items by size. Talk with them about things that they consider to be "giant" in size. For younger children, be sure the small items are really small and the big items are really big.

Physical Development/Gross Motor

Giant Stomps

Place several strips of large-size bubble wrap on the floor and encourage the children to stomp like giants on the bubbles in an effort to pop them. *How is a giant stomp different from a baby stomp?*

Social-Emotional Development/Dramatic Play

Goodnight, Giant

Have an adult lie on a piece of butcher paper and use a pencil to trace around the outline of his or her body. Cut out the large figure to represent a giant. Use a beach towel for a bed. Encourage the children to sing songs and read stories to the "giant." Ask the children to think of other things they can do to help the giant go to sleep. Point out that giants are only make-believe.

Outdoor Play or Music and Movement

- Show the children how to take giant steps and how to take baby steps. Encourage them to walk across the room taking giant steps and then return taking baby steps.
- Play some "heavy" music and encourage the children to move like giants. Use descriptive words to describe their movements, such as *slouch, heavy, gigantic,* and so on.

REFLECTIONS ON THE DAY

- *How are giants different from children?*
- *Are giants real or make-believe?*

Going on a Bear Hunt

Going on a Bear Hunt
We're going on a bear hunt.
Want to come?
Well, come on then.
Let's go! (*walk in place*)
Look! There's a river. (*children echo this line and the next three*)
Can't go over it,
Can't go under it,
Can't go around it,
We'll have to go through it. (*pretend to walk into the river, through the water, and onto other bank, then resume walking in place*)

Look! There's a tree. (*children echo this line and the next three*)
Can't go under it,
Can't go through it,
We'll have to go over it. (*pretend to climb up and over tree, then resume walking in place*)

Look! There's a wheat field. (*children echo this line and the next three*)
Can't go over it,
Can't go under it.
Can't go around it.
We'll have to go through it. (*pretend to walk through field, making swishing sounds with hands against thighs, then resume walking in place*)

Add verses to make the story as long as you want.

Look! There's a cave. (*children echo this line and the next six*)
Want to go inside?
Ooh, it's dark in here. (*look around, squinting*)
I see two eyes.
Wonder what it is. (*reach hands to touch*)
It's soft and furry.
It's big.
It's a bear! Let's run! (*retrace steps: run in place through wheat field, climb over the tree, run in place, cross river, run in place, then stop*)
Home safe. Whew!

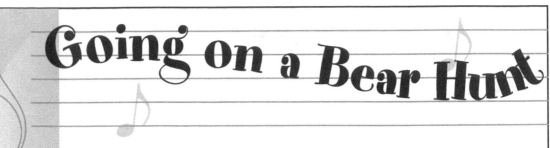

SEE ALSO

"Teddy Bear, Teddy Bear," page 188
"There Once Were Three Brown Bears," page 190
"Three Bears Rap," page 191

Related Songs, Chants, and Rhymes

The Bear Went Over the Mountain
(Tune: For He's a Jolly Good Fellow)
The bear went over the mountain,
The bear went over the mountain,
The bear went over the mountain
To see what he could see.

To see what he could see,
To see what he could see.
The bear went over the mountain
To see what he could see.

I Met a Bear (Tune: Sippin' Cider Through a Straw)
Teacher: The other day
Children echo: The other day
Teacher: I met a bear
Children echo: I met a bear
Teacher: A great big bear, oh, way out there.
Children echo: A great big bear, oh, way out there.
Everyone: The other day, I met a bear.
A great big bear, oh, way out there.

(*Continue with children echoing the teacher and everyone singing the repeat of the verse.*)

He looked at me.
I looked at him.
He sized me up.
I sized him up.
(*repeat verse together*)

He said to me,
"Why don't you run?
I think its time.
(*repeat verse together*)

I said to him,
"That's a good idea."
Now legs get going,
Get me out of here.
(*repeat verse together*)

And so I ran,
Away from there
But right behind me,
Was that bear.
(*repeat verse together*)

In front of me,
There was a tree,
A great big tree,
Oh glory be!
(*repeat verse together*)

The lowest branch
Was ten feet up
So I thought I'd jump,
And trust my luck.
(*repeat verse together*)

And so I jumped,
Into the air,
But I missed that branch,
Away up there.
(*repeat verse together*)

Now don't you fret,
And don't you frown,
I caught that branch,
On the way back down!
(*repeat verse together*)

This is the end.
There is no more.
Unless I see,
That bear once more.
(*repeat verse together*)

Follow-Up Questions

- *What was in the cave?*
- *Why did we run all the way back home?*

Language Enrichment

- Discuss positional vocabulary words, including *around*, *over*, and *through*. Ask a volunteer to demonstrate each direction using a carpet square as the item in relationship to the various actions. For example, hold the toddler's hand as he jumps *over* the carpet square. Put several carpet squares in two side-by-side stacks (about 1' apart) so that the volunteer can walk "through" the carpet squares.
- Talk about bears. If photos are available, use them to stimulate conversation. *How big are bears? What colors are bears? What do they eat? How do they move?*
- Teach children the American Sign Language sign for *bear* (see appendix page 239).

STORY TIME SUGGESTION

We're Going on a Bear Hunt by Helen Oxenbury

Extension Activities

Cognitive Development/Discovery

What's in the Box?

Make a Feely Box by cutting a 3" diameter hole in one end of a shoebox. Place an item inside the box when the children are not looking. Let the children stick their hands through the hole and use their fingers to examine the item inside. Ask them to describe what they feel. *What does the item feel like? Is it soft? Is it smooth? Do you know what this item is?* Change the item often.

Cognitive and Social-Emotional Development/Games

Bear Hunt

Hide a stuffed bear and encourage the children to find it. Provide flashlights for the children to use for their search. Stand close by and provide clues, if necessary.

Physical Development/Gross Motor

Over, Under, Around

Lay a large piece of butcher paper on the floor. Cut out an arch from a box to make a small cave. Cut out an irregular circle from blue butcher paper or construction paper to create a lake. Make a tree by adding green strips of paper to one end of an empty paper towel tube. Place the items on the paper. Draw a path that goes around each item and into the cave. Encourage the children to roll a toy car over the path. Talk with them about their course of travel.

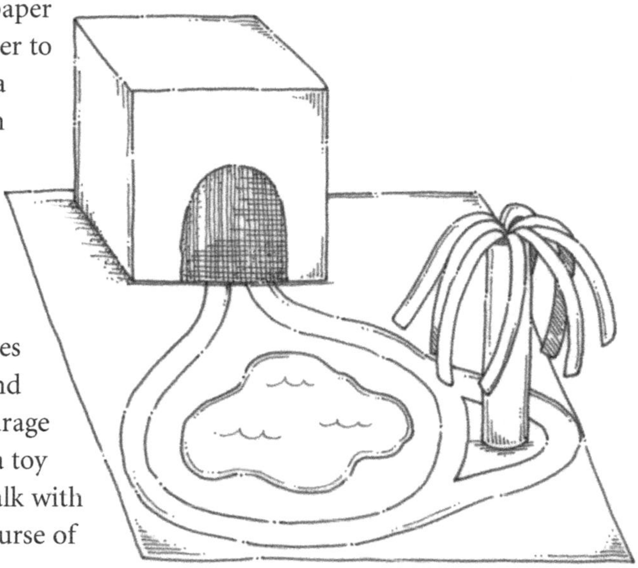

Social-Emotional Development/Dramatic Play

Cave Exploration

Cover a table with a sheet to make a tent (cave). Place a stuffed bear or several stuffed bears inside. Talk with the children about why a bear might be found in a cave. Explain that some bears sleep through the entire winter time (hibernation).

Outdoor Play or Music and Movement

- Take the children outdoors to search for any item you choose. Examples include a tricycle, ball, bird, bug, and so on. As they look for the item, use the positional vocabulary that is used in "Going on a Bear Hunt."
- Chant along with "Goin' on a Bear Hunt" (*Kids in Action* CD, Greg and Steve Productions).
- Sing along with "I Met a Bear" (*Laugh 'N Learn Silly Songs* CD, Kimbo Educational), "The Bear Went Over the Mountain" (*Favorite Songs for Kids* CD, or *Six White Ducks* CD, Kimbo Educational).

REFLECTIONS ON THE DAY

- *What things did we see on our "bear hunt?"*
- *Do you think the bear was scared when he saw people in his cave?*

Good Morning to You

Good Morning to You adapted by Richele Bartkowiak
(Tune: Traditional)
Good morning to you!
Good morning to you!
We're all in our places
With bright, shining faces.
Oh, this is the way to start a great day!

Good noontime to you!
Good noontime to you!
We're all in our places
With food on our faces.
Oh, this is the way to have a great day!

Good evening to you!
Good evening to you!
Stars and moon in their places
They go through their paces.
Oh, this is the way to end a good day!

SEE ALSO

"For He's a Jolly Good Fellow," page 48
"Make New Friends," page 126
"The More We Get Together," page 126
"Will You Be My Friend Today?," page 126

Related Songs, Chants, and Rhymes

Good Morning
(Tune: If You're Happy and You Know It)
Good Morning, (*child's first name and last name*).
How are you?
Good Morning, (*child's first name and last name*).
How are you?
How are you on this special day?
We're glad you came to play.
Good Morning, (*child's first name and last name*).
How are you?

Good Morning to You
(another version)
Good morning, good morning, good morning to you.
Good morning, good morning, good morning to you.
Our day is beginning, there's so much to do.
So, good morning, good morning, good morning to you.

Morning Greeting

Austin, Austin, howdy-do,
Hello, good day, how are you?

Follow-Up Questions

- *Who says good morning to you each day? Who do you say good morning to each day?*
- *Who says good night to you each evening?*

Language Enrichment

- If available, show the children pictures of things that happen in the morning and things that happen at night. Use the pictures to stimulate discussion.
- Sing "Good Morning" (see previous page) with the children. Encourage the children to practice answering the question, "*How are you?*" Sing the song in Spanish ("*Buenos Días*").
- Teach the children the American Sign Language signs for *good morning* and *goodnight* (see appendix page 239).

Extension Activities

Cognitive Development/Language

Smiling Faces

Sit in front of a mirror with the children. Make a funny face, a smiling face, and a frowning face. Talk about things that make you smile and things that make you frown. Encourage the children to think of things that make them smile.

Cognitive and Emotional Development/Art

Fingerpaint Happy Faces

Place non-toxic fingerpaint directly on the top of a table. Encourage the children to explore the paint. Draw happy faces in the paint. Ask children questions about things that make them happy. *Are you happy to see mommy or daddy (or other person) when he or she comes to pick you up? Are you happy when you get to play with a favorite toy?* Draw a sad face and ask questions about things that might make a child sad.

Social Development/Dramatic Play

Daily Routines

Encourage the children to pretend to get up in the morning and go to bed at night. Talk with them about their routines. *What do you do the first thing in the morning? What do you do before going to bed?*

STORY TIME SUGGESTIONS

Good Morning, Good Night by Michael Grejniec

Good Morning, Good Night Billy and Abigail by Don Hoffman

Social Development/Music

Me Puppets

Make a Me Puppet for each child. Make an enlarged copy of each child's photograph. Cut out the face of the child from each photo. Laminate each one and glue to a tongue depressor. Give each child her own Me Puppet. Put on some happy music and encourage the children to make their puppets dance. Talk with them about their happy faces. Ask the puppet, *How are you today?*

Outdoor Play or Music and Movement

- Play Good Morning, Good Night. Have the children walk around smiling and clapping while you recite the "Good Morning" chant (see page 58) using a variety of tones and voice inflections. After five or six greetings, suddenly say, *good night.* This signals the children to lie on the floor and pretend to be asleep. Sing or hum a lullaby ("Rock-a-Bye Baby"). At the end of the song, start the "Good Morning" chant again. When you say, *good morning,* this is the signal for children to get up and walk around again. Continue the game for as long as the children show an interest in playing.
- Sing along with "Good Morning" (*Songs for the Whole Day* CD, Thomas Moore Enterprises) or "Good Morning to You" (*School Days* CD, Schiller Educational Resources, LLC).

REFLECTIONS ON THE DAY

- *What do you say when someone asks, "How are you?"*
- *Who can show me how we say, "Good morning with our hands?"*

The Grand Old Duke of York

The Grand Old Duke of York (Tune: The Farmer in the Dell)
The grand old Duke of York (*salute*)
He had ten thousand men. (*hold up ten fingers*)
He marched them up to the top of the hill, (*point up*)
And he marched them down again. (*point down*)
And when they're up, they're up. (*stand tall*)
And when they're down, they're down. (*squat*)
But when they're only halfway up, (*stand with knees bent*)
They're neither up nor down. (*open arms and shrug*)

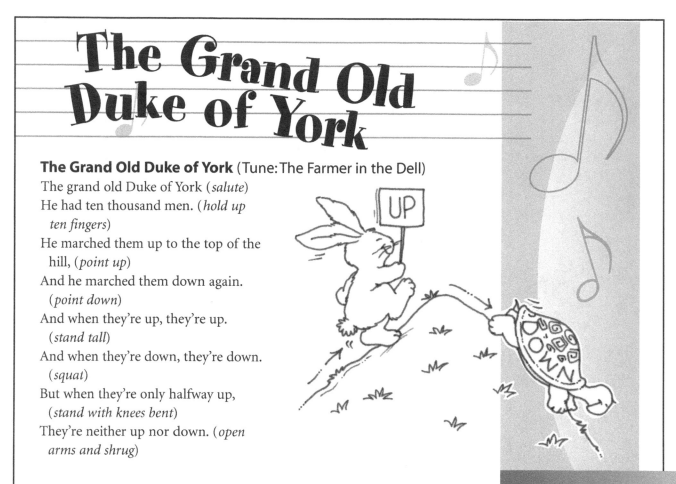

Related Songs, Chants, and Rhymes

SEE ALSO

"The Ants Go Marching," page 22
"Hickory, Dickory, Dock," page 70
"Sing a Song of Opposites," page 174

Sometimes
Sometimes I am tall, (*stand tall*)
Sometimes I am small. (*crouch low*)
Sometimes I am very, very, tall. (*stand on tiptoes*)
Sometimes I am very, very small. (*crouch and lower head*)
Sometimes tall, (*stand tall*)
Sometimes small, (*crouch down*)
Sometimes neither tall or small. (*stand normally*)

Stretching Chant
(suit actions to words)
Stretch to the windows,
Stretch to the door,
Stretch up to the ceiling
And bend down to the floor.

Yankee Doodle by Richard Shuckburgh (Tune: Traditional)
Yankee Doodle went to town
A-riding on a pony,
Stuck a feather in his hat
And called it macaroni.

Yankee Doodle, keep it up,
Yankee Doodle dandy,
Mind the music and the step
And with the girls be handy.

Father and I went down to camp
Along with Captain Gooding,
And there we saw the men and boys
As thick as hasty pudding.

Yankee Doodle, keep it up,
Yankee Doodle dandy,
Mind the music and the step
And with the girls be handy.

Follow-Up Questions

- *Can you name something in the room that is up high? Can you name something that is down low?*
- *Which way is up? Which way is down?*

Language Enrichment

- Say and do the "Stretching Chant" (see page 61) with the children. Discuss the word *stretch* before doing the actions that go with the chant. Encourage the children to stretch like a cat, like they are just waking up, and like they are trying to reach something that is slightly out of reach. Do the chant with the movements. Do the chant again, changing the word *stretch* to *point.* Substitute other verbs (*look, nod,* and so on).
- Discuss marching. Ask a volunteer to demonstrate marching. If you have a picture of a marching band available, show it to the children. Ask them questions about bands and parades. *Has anyone ever seen a band? What were the people in the band doing? Were any of the people marching?*
- Teach the children the American Sign Language signs for *up* and *down* (see appendix page 239).

STORY TIME SUGGESTIONS

The Grand Old Duke of York by Henry Sowden

The Up and Down Book by Mary Blair

Extension Activities

Cognitive Development/Science

Up and Down

Invite toddlers to drop four or five raisins in a glass of clear, carbonated soda. The raisins will drop to the bottom of the glass and then they will begin to rise as several bubbles form around them. When the raisins reach the surface, the bubbles will pop and the raisins will drop to the bottom again. Encourage the toddlers to say the words *up* and *down* as the raisins rise and fall.

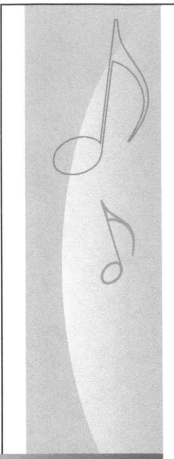

Cognitive Development/Discovery

Down the Plank

Make an inclined plank and encourage the children to roll toy cars up the plank and then down the plank. Ask questions while they play. *In which direction does the car travel more quickly?*

Cognitive and Social-Emotional Development/Games

Up and Down Hide and Seek

Hide a stuffed animal somewhere up high in the room and challenge the children to find it. After they find it, hide it again. This time hide it somewhere down low. For younger children, be sure the hidden object is clearly visible.

Physical and Cognitive Development/Fine Motor

Up and Down

Put masking tape on one end of a piece of yarn to make a "needle," and tie the other end to a door knob or other location that is similar in height. Give the children empty toilet paper tubes to string onto the yarn. Talk with them about pushing the tubes up on the yarn. Ask them why they think the tubes fall back down so easily.

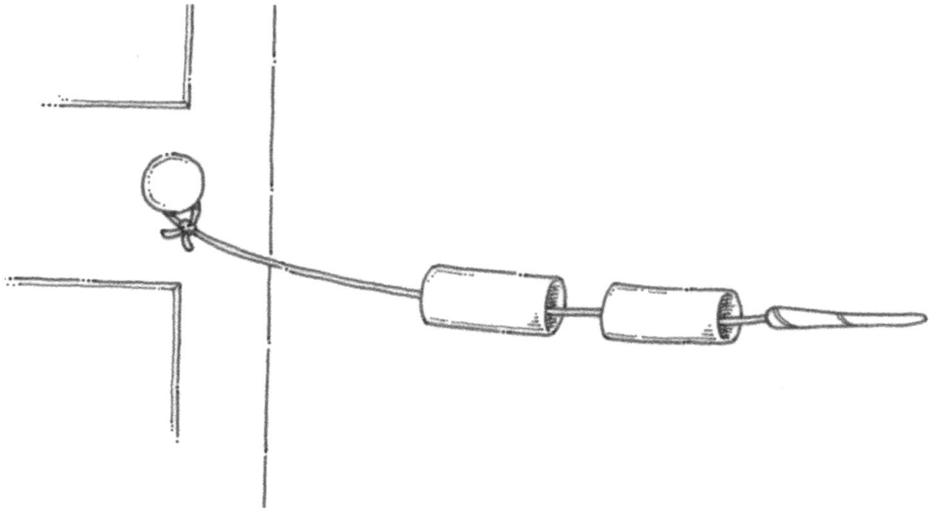

Outdoor Play or Music and Movement

- Play marching music and encourage the children to march in their own special ways.
- Give each child a beanbag. Give them directions for placing the beanbag up or down (*up* over the head, *down* on the knee, *down* on the foot, and so on).
- Sing along with "The Grand Old Duke of York" (*Where Is Thumbkin?* CD, Kimbo Educational), "The Grand Old Duke of York" (*School Days* CD, Schiller Educational Resources, LLC), or "Yankee Doodle" (*Yankee Doodle Mickey* CD, Disney).

REFLECTIONS ON THE DAY

- *Where did the Grand Old Duke march his men?*
- *In which direction did your car move more quickly: up or down?*

Head, Shoulders, Knees, and Toes

Head, Shoulders, Knees, and Toes (Tune: Traditional)
(*touch body parts as they are mentioned in the song*)
Head, shoulders, knees, and toes,
Knees and toes.
Head, shoulders, knees, and toes,
Knees and toes.
Eyes and ears and mouth and nose.
Head, shoulders, knees, and toes,
Knees and toes!

Related Songs, Chants, and Rhymes

Head, Shoulders, Baby
Head, shoulders, baby 1, 2, 3.
Head, shoulders, baby 1, 2, 3.
Head, shoulders, head, shoulders,
Head, shoulders, baby 1, 2, 3.

Shoulders, hip, baby, 1, 2, 3.
Shoulders, hip, baby, 1, 2, 3.
Shoulders, hip, shoulders, hip,
Shoulders, hip, baby, 1, 2, 3.

Hip, knees…
Knees, ankle...
Ankle, toes…
Toes, ankle…
Ankle, knees…
Knees, hips…
Hip, shoulders...
Shoulders, head...

Say and Touch
Say "red" and touch your head.
Say "sky" and touch your eye.
Say "tear" and touch your hair.
Say "near" and touch your ear.

SEE ALSO

"Open, Shut Them," page 145
"This Little Piggy," page 202
"Walk, Walk, Walk Your Feet," page 203

Say "south" and touch your mouth.
Say "hose" and touch your nose.
Say "in" and touch your chin.
Say "nest" and touch your chest.
Say "harm" and touch your arm.
Say "yummy" and touch your tummy.
Say "see" and touch your knee.
Say "meat" and touch your feet.

Follow-Up Questions

- *How many heads do you have? How many shoulders? Knees?*
- *Which body parts mentioned in the song do you have two of?*

Language Enrichment

- Discuss body parts. Talk about the names of different body parts and their functions. Count body parts.
- Chant "Head, Shoulders, Baby." Chant it a second time and substitute the Spanish form, *uno, dos, tres* for *1, 2, 3.* Tell the children they are counting in Spanish. If you know another language, have the children count in that language.
- Ask the children if they could sing the song using other body parts. For example:
  Hands, elbows, legs, and feet (legs and feet).
  Hands, elbows, legs, and feet (legs and feet).
  And chest and arms and hair and teeth.
  Hands, elbows, legs, and feet (legs and feet).
- Teach the children the American Sign Language signs for *head, shoulder, knee,* and *toe* (see appendix page 239).

Extension Activities

Cognitive and Physical Development/Discovery

Tactile Crawl
Create a tactile pathway using carpet squares, sheets of bubble wrap, and squares of felt, burlap, and so on. Ask the children to crawl over the pathway. Encourage older children to describe the feel of the items on their knees as they pass over them. Use descriptive words as younger children crawl over the pathway.

STORY TIME SUGGESTIONS

From Head to Toe by Eric Carle
Head, Shoulders, Knees and Toes by Annie Kubler

Cognitive and Physical Development/Fine Motor

Build a Face

Cut out faces, eyes, noses, ears, and mouths from felt. Provide a flannel board and invite the children to use the felt to make faces. Talk with them as they work. *What color eyes are you putting on your face? How many ears do you need?*

Physical Development/Gross Motor

Head and Shoulders

Place a strip of masking tape on the floor and give each child a beanbag. Have the children walk the line with a beanbag on their heads and then on their shoulders. Interact with them as they play. *Can you balance the beanbag on your knee? On your toes?* Discuss other body parts as the children continue to play.

Social-Emotional Development/Dramatic Play

Head Gear

Provide hats, scarves, and helmets of all kinds for the children to explore. Talk with them as they try on the head gear. *Why would someone wear this helmet? Which hat do you like best? Which hat will keep your head warm?*

REFLECTIONS ON THE DAY

- *Show me your shoulders. Can you shake your shoulders?*
- *How many toes do you have? What things can you do with your toes?*

Outdoor Play or Music and Movement

- Show the children how to shake their shoulders and hips. Say the "Head, Shoulders, Baby" chant. Ask the children to shake their hips and shoulders when they are mentioned in the chant.
- Sing along with "Head, Shoulders, Knees, and Toes" (*Me, My Family and Friends* CD, Schiller Educational Resources, LLC) or "Head, Shoulders, Knees, and Toes" (*Where Is Thumbkin?* CD, Kimbo Educational).

Hey, Diddle Diddle

Hey, Diddle Diddle (Mother Goose)
Hey, diddle diddle,
The cat and the fiddle,
The cow jumped over the moon.
The little dog laughed to see such a sight,
And the dish ran away with the spoon.

Related Songs, Chants, and Rhymes

Fiddle-I-Fee (Tune: Traditional)
I had a cat, and the cat pleased me.
Fed my cat under yonder tree.
Cat went fiddle-i-fee.

I had a hen, and the hen pleased me.
Fed my hen under yonder tree.
Hen went chimmey chuck, chimmey chuck,
Cat went fiddle-i-fee.

I had a dog, and the dog pleased me.
Fed my dog under yonder tree.
Dog went bow-wow, bow-wow,
Hen went chimmey chuck, chimmey chuck,
Cat went fiddle-i-fee.

I Never Saw a Purple Cow by Gelette Burgess
I never saw a purple cow.
I never hope to see one.
But I can tell you anyhow
I'd rather see than be one!

SEE ALSO

"Bingo," page 231
"Little Boy Blue," page 95
"Nursery Rhyme Rap," page 15
"Old King Cole," page 129

Follow-Up Questions

- *Do you think a cat could play a fiddle? Show the children a picture of a fiddle, if available. Explain that a fiddle is a string instrument, and someone must pluck the strings to make music.*
- *What made the dog laugh?*

Language Enrichment

- Ask the children open-ended questions about the rhyme. *What do you think the word* "diddle" *means?* Accept all answers. *Where do you think the dish and the spoon went?*
- Whisper the rhyme but say the rhyming words loud.
- Most children have never seen a fiddle. If one is available, share it with the children. Encourage them to talk about the parts of the fiddle and the wonderful sounds it makes.
- Children love to play with words that are alliterative and rhyming. Play an echo game with the children. Say the following rhyme and have the children echo you:

Hey, diddle diddle
Hey, diddle diddle (*children echo*)
Where is my fiddle?
Where is my fiddle? (*children echo*)
Diddle, diddle
Diddle, diddle (*children echo*)
Diddle, fiddle
Diddle, fiddle (*children echo*)
Diddle, diddle fiddle
Diddle, diddle, fiddle. (*children echo*)

STORY TIME SUGGESTIONS

Goodnight Moon by Margaret Wise Brown
Hey, Diddle, Diddle by Jeanette Winter

Extension Activities

Cognitive Development/Math

Silverware Match

Give the children spoons and plates. Encourage them to match the items using one-to-one correspondence. Talk about setting the table for a meal at home. *Will there be a plate, a spoon, a fork, and a knife for each person at the table?* Repeat the line in the rhyme, "The dish ran away with the spoon." Ask them if a dish can run. *Where are its legs?*

Physical Development/Fine Motor

Moon Sequence

Cut out several "moons" in a variety of sizes from poster board. Help the children arrange the moons from the smallest to the largest. Challenge them to stack the moons from the largest to the smallest. Cut out a set of moons in different phases (full, ¾, ½, ¼) and challenge older children to arrange them in order. Ask the children if they like the new moon, half moon, or full moon best.

Physical Development/Gross Motor

Moon Jumping

Place a paper plate on the floor to represent a moon. Encourage the children to jump over the "moon." Let younger children step over the moon. Talk about the height of the moon. *Can anyone really jump over something that high? Who jumped over the moon in the rhyme?*

Social-Emotional Development/Dramatic Play

Make Me Laugh

Give the children several stuffed dogs and cats. Encourage them to do some silly things to make the dogs and cats laugh. *What would it sound like if a dog or cat laughed? Would it sound like a human laugh?* If you have access to a Tickle Me Elmo™ or other laughing toy, use it as part of the audience. It will add fun to the game.

Outdoor Play or Music and Movement

- Sing along with "Hey, Diddle Diddle" (*Nursery Rhyme Time* CD, Kimbo Educational) or "Hey, Diddle Diddle" (*We Sing Nursery Rhymes and Lullabies* CD, Price, Stern, Sloan).
- Play fiddle music and invite the children to dance.

REFLECTIONS ON THE DAY

- *Which animal in the rhyme do you like best—the cow, the cat, or the dog? Why?*
- *What did you do to make the dog and cat laugh?*

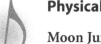

Hickory, Dickory, Dock

Hickory, Dickory, Dock (Mother Goose)
Hickory, dickory, dock (*stand, swing arm like pendulum*)
The mouse ran up the clock. (*bend over; run hand up body*)
The clock struck one, (*clap hands over head once*)
The mouse ran down. (*run hand down to feet*)
Hickory, dickory, dock. (*stand, swing arm like pendulum*)

Related Songs, Chants, and Rhymes

Cuckoo Clock
"Tick tock, tick tock," goes the happy clock.
"Cuckoo, cuckoo," sings the bird.
Cuckoo, cuckoo, tick tock, tick tock,
Hear the sounds of the cuckoo clock?

Slowly, Slowly
Slowly, slowly, very slowly (*walk fingers up arm slowly*)
Creeps the garden snail.
Slowly, slowly, very slowly
Up the wooden rail.

Quickly, quickly, very quickly (*run fingers up arm*)
Runs the little mouse.
Quickly, quickly, very quickly
'Round about the house.

Follow-Up Questions

- *Why did the mouse run down the clock? Some children may not have seen a clock that strikes the time. If a small striking clock is available, you may want to bring it to show the children.*
- *Could a bear run up a clock? How? Why not?*

SEE ALSO
"Are You Sleeping?," page 26
"The Grand Old Duke of York," page 61
"Nursery Rhyme Rap," page 15
"The Old Gray Cat," page 208

Language Enrichment

- Bring in several different types of clocks to share with the children. If real clocks are not available, gather pictures of clocks. Encourage the children to talk about the clocks. *What noise do they make? Where are the numbers on the clock? Where is the numeral 1?*
- Say the words "hickory," "dickory," and "dock" a few times. Encourage the children to play with the words. Perhaps they can clap the syllables with you or march around the room to the cadence of the words. Children love alliteration and rhyme.

- Identify famous mice (Maisy, Chuck E. Cheese, Mickey, or Minnie). Talk about what mice eat.
- Talk about *up* and *down*. Have the children demonstrate up and down by standing up and sitting down and by raising their hands up and then putting them down.

Extension Activities

Cognitive Development/Games

Find the Mouse

Hide a stuffed mouse or one you cut from paper and encourage the children to find it. Give them clues as they look for the mouse.

Physical Development/Art

Mice Fingerprints

Mix non-toxic fingerpaint and encourage the children to explore the paint. Show them how to make fingerprints. Turn their fingerprints into mice by adding a tail, ears, and eyes. Talk with the children as they paint. *How many ears do you need to make? How many tails?*

STORY TIME SUGGESTION

The Completed Hickory Dickory Dock by Jim Aylesworth

Physical Development/Fine Motor

Mouse Magnet

Cut out a small mouse (about 2") from gray construction paper, laminate it, and glue a small piece of magnetic strip on the back of the mouse. Draw a clock on a sheet of drawing paper. Show the children how to use a magnet on the underside of the clock to move the mouse on the top of the clock.

REFLECTIONS ON THE DAY

- *What do mice like to eat?*
- *What made the mouse run down the clock?*

Social-Emotional Development/Snack

Make It Cheese, Please

Serve crackers and a variety of cheeses. Ask the children which cheese they like best. *Which cheese do you think a mouse might like best?*

Outdoor Play or Music and Movement

- Sing along with "Hickory Dickory Dock" (*Wee Sing Nursery Rhymes and Lullabies* CD, Price, Stern, Sloan) or "Hickory Dickory Dock" (*Nursery Rhyme Time* CD, Kimbo Educational).
- Play "Old Gray Cat" (see page 208).

Humpty Dumpty

Humpty Dumpty (Mother Goose)
(Tune: Traditional)

Humpty Dumpty sat on a wall.
Humpty Dumpty had a great fall.
All the king's horses and all the
king's men
Couldn't put Humpty Dumpty
together again.

Related Songs, Chants, and Rhymes

Humpty Dumpty (Version 2)
(Tune: Traditional)

Humpty Dumpty sat on a hill.
Humpty Dumpty had a great spill.
All the king's horses and all the king's men
Couldn't put Humpty Dumpty together again.

Humpty Dumpty (Version 3) by Pam Schiller (Tune: Traditional)

Humpty Dumpty sat on a hill.
Humpty Dumpty had a great spill.
That genius Jack Horner pulled out his glue
And Humpty Dumpty's as good as new!

Humpty Dumpty's New Ears by Pam Schiller

Humpty Dumpty sat on a wall.
Humpty Dumpty had a great fall.
Al the king's horses and all the king's men
Couldn't put Humpty Dumpty together again.

Humpty Dumpty started to cry.
Humpty said, "Oh, please won't you try?"
His friend, Jack Horner, knew what to do.
He fixed Humpty Dumpty with his glue.

When Humpty Dumpty saw himself new,
He no longer felt all sad and blue,

SEE ALSO

"The Grand Old Duke of York," page 61
"Jack and Jill," page 84
"Nursery Rhyme Rap," page 15
"Yankee Doodle," page 61

He looked in the mirror and said with glee,
"Let's glue some ears to the side of me."
A pair of ears will look real nice,
Like they do on elephants and mice.
One on the left, and one on the right,
Humpty with ears—what a sight!

Jack made two ears and then with his glue
He carefully attached ear one then ear two.
Humpty looked in the mirror and said with glee,
"I'm a good-looking egg, don't you agree?"

Follow-Up Questions

- *Why do you think Humpty Dumpty fell?*
- *If he fell on a mattress, do you think he would have broken?*

Language Enrichment

- Explain to the children who the *king's horses* and *king's men* are. (The king's horses belong to the king and the king's men are his soldiers.) Ask the children how they would put Humpty Dumpty together.
- Encourage the children to play with the words "Humpty Dumpty." Note that *Humpty* and *Dumpty* are rhyming words, but don't expect the children to make a connection. Children might enjoy clapping the syllables in "Humpty Dumpty" or marching to the cadence of the syllables.
- Read the first version of "Humpty Dumpty" once, then read "Humpty Dumpty (Version 2)" (see page 73). Say the words *wall* and *fall* together and then the words *hill* and *spill* together. Now read one of the versions, saying only the first rhyming word (*wall* or *hill*), and let the children fill in the appropriate word (*fall* or *spill*) in the next line.

STORY TIME SUGGESTIONS

Humpty Dumpty by Daniel Kirk
Humpty Dumpty Dumpty by Thomas Moore and Pam Schiller

Extension Activities

Cognitive Development/Construction

Humpty Dumpty Puppets
Cut out ovals (egg shapes) for each child. Invite the children to decorate their "eggs" with non-toxic fingerpaint or markers and wiggle eyes. Cut out 1" x 12" strips of brown construction paper and fold them accordion-style. Help the children glue the strips to their eggs to make legs. Show them how to make their puppets dance and sing. Ask them to describe how they made their puppets. **Safety Note:** Supervise closely to ensure that children do not put wiggle eyes in their mouths.

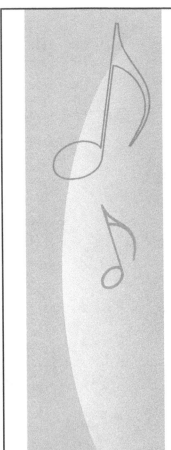

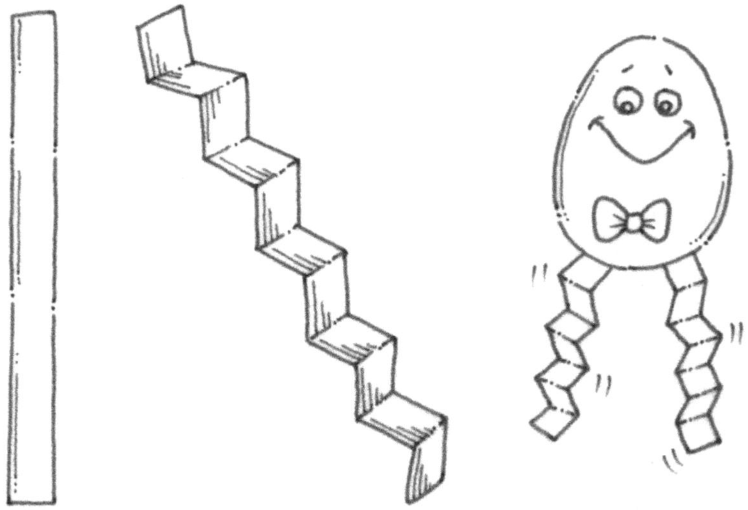

Cognitive Development/Listening

Egg Shakers

Fill plastic eggs with things that make an interesting sound (jingle bells, gravel, washers, and so on). Glue eggs together for safety. Encourage the children to shake the eggs and describe the sounds they hear. *Which eggs make a loud (or soft) sound? Which sound do you like best? Do any of the eggs make a similar sound?* Challenge older children to guess what is inside the egg. If they have trouble guessing, give them clues.

Cognitive and Social-Emotional Development/Games

Egg Hunt

Hide colored eggs and let the children find them. Provide pails for the children to carry their eggs in. Talk with children about the eggs. *How do they feel? What color are the eggs? Which color do they like best? Can you roll the eggs?*

STORY TIME SUGGESTIONS

Humpty Dumpty by Daniel Kirk

Humpty Dumpty Dumpty by Thomas Moore and Pam Schiller

Physical Development/Gross Motor

Egg Rolls

Place two strips of masking tape on the floor to create a start and a finish line. Give children large plastic eggs and encourage them to roll the eggs from the start line to the finish line by crawling on the floor and pushing the eggs with their heads or their chins. Talk with the children about their experiences. *Are the eggs easy to roll or difficult to roll? Did you use your chin or your head?*

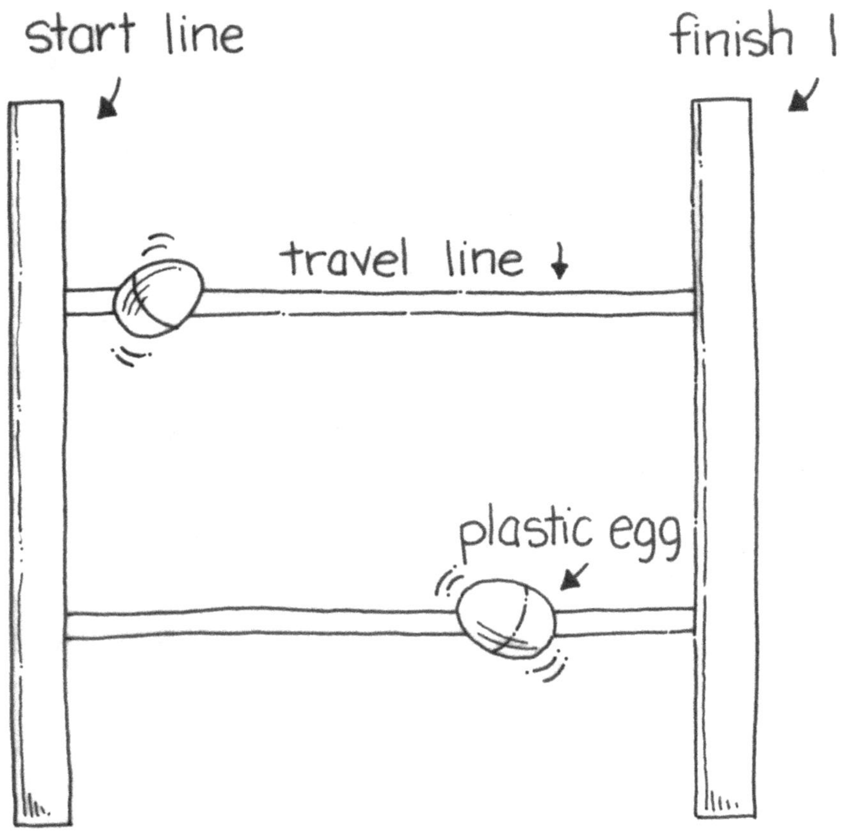

REFLECTIONS ON THE DAY

- *Do you think it was okay for the king's horses and king's men to leave Humpty Dumpty broken? Why? Why not?*
- *Explain how you rolled the egg on the floor.*

Outdoor Play or Music and Movement

- Dance to "Humpty Dumpty Dumpty" (*I Am Special* CD, Thomas Moore Enterprises).
- Sing along with "Humpty Dumpty" (*Wee Sing Nursery Rhymes and Lullabies* CD, Price, Stern, Sloan) or "Humpty Dumpty" (*Nursery Rhyme Time* CD, Kimbo Educational).
- Provide a soft surface (grass or a floor mat) and teach the children to do Humpty Dumpty Rolls (forward rolls). Supervise each child and each roll.

If You're Happy and You Know It

If You're Happy and You Know It (Tune: Traditional)
If you're happy and you know it, clap your hands.
(*clap hands twice*)
If you're happy and you know it, clap your hands.
(*clap hands twice*)
If you're happy and you know it then your face will show it. (*point to smiling face*)
If you're happy and you know it, clap your hands. (*clap hands twice*)

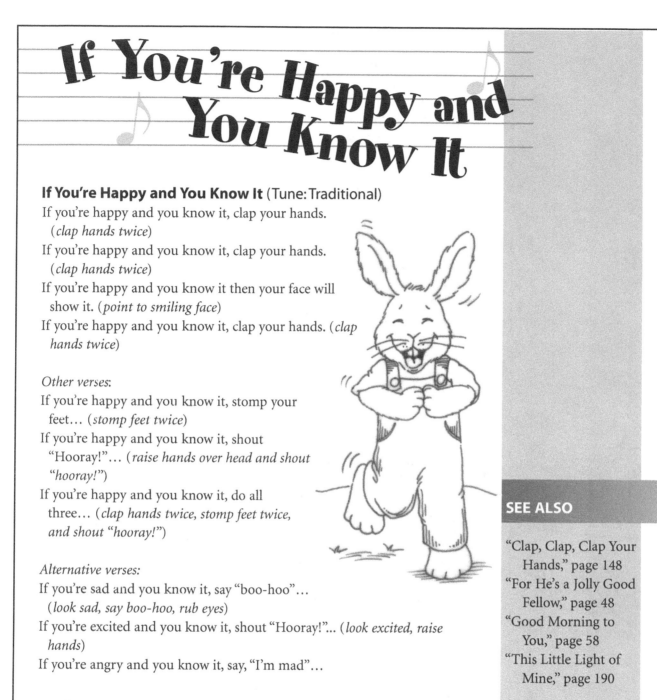

Other verses:
If you're happy and you know it, stomp your feet… (*stomp feet twice*)
If you're happy and you know it, shout "Hooray!"… (*raise hands over head and shout "hooray!"*)
If you're happy and you know it, do all three… (*clap hands twice, stomp feet twice, and shout "hooray!"*)

Alternative verses:
If you're sad and you know it, say "boo-hoo"…
(*look sad, say boo-hoo, rub eyes*)
If you're excited and you know it, shout "Hooray!"… (*look excited, raise hands*)
If you're angry and you know it, say, "I'm mad"…

SEE ALSO

"Clap, Clap, Clap Your Hands," page 148
"For He's a Jolly Good Fellow," page 48
"Good Morning to You," page 58
"This Little Light of Mine," page 190

Related Songs, Chants, and Rhymes

I Clap My Hands
I clap my hands to make a sound—
Clap, clap, clap!
I tap my toe to make a sound—
Tap, tap, tap!

I open my mouth to say a word—
Talk, talk, talk!
I pick up my foot to take a step—
Walk, walk, walk!

I Have Something in My Pocket (Tune: Traditional)
I have something in my pocket.
It belongs across my face.
I keep it very close at hand.
In a most convenient place.

I bet you could guess it,
If you guessed a long, long while
So I'll take it out and put it on,
It's a great big happy SMILE!

S-M-I-L-E (Tune: Battle Hymn of the Republic)
It isn't any trouble
Just to S-M-I-L-E,
It isn't any trouble
Just to S-M-I-L-E.
So smile when you're in trouble,
It will vanish like a bubble,
If you'll only take the trouble
Just to S-M-I-L-E.

Follow-Up Questions

- *What do you do when you are happy? What do you do when you are sad?*
- *What things make you happy?*

STORY TIME SUGGESTIONS

If You're Happy and You Know It, Clap Your Hands by David A. Carter
If You're Happy and You Know It, Clap Your Paws by Sarah Albee

Language Enrichment

- Discuss ways to show you are happy (clap hands, shout, smile, laugh, and so on).
- Show the children pictures of people who are expressing happiness. Discuss the pictures. *How do you know this person is happy? What is she doing?*
- Talk about words that demonstrate happiness and joy, such as *Hurray! Wow!* or *Yeah!*
- Teach the children the American Sign Language sign for *happy* (see appendix page 239).

Extension Activities

Cognitive Development/Language

Happy Faces

Provide a mirror and encourage the children to sit in front of it and make happy faces. After they have made happy faces for a while, encourage them to try other faces (sad, mad, or surprised). Talk with the children as they try different faces. *What things make you feel happy? What things make you sad? What things frighten you? Have you ever been surprised?*

Cognitive and Social-Emotional Development/Listening

Who's Laughing?

Tape the children laughing. Play the recording back for them to listen. Can they identify their laugh when they hear it? Talk with them about the sound of their laughter. *Does everyone sound the same when they laugh?*

Physical Development/Fine Motor

Happy Face Puzzles

Cut out large circles from poster board and draw happy faces on them. Cut the faces into simple puzzles pieces and invite the children to work the puzzles. Talk with them as they work. *How do you know which piece goes there? Can you turn the puzzle over and work it?*

Physical Development/Gross Motor

Happy Face Hop

Draw happy faces on paper plates and lay them in a path across the floor. Invite the children to jump from face to face. When the children tire of jumping, give them beanbags and challenge them to toss them so that they land on a plate. If they miss the plate, suggest they stand closer to the plate when tossing. Talk with the children as they play. *How can you make sure that the beanbags land on a plate? Is it easier to hit the plate with the beanbag when you stand closer to the plate?*

Outdoor Play or Music and Movement

- Play You Can't Make Me Laugh with the children. Start by making funny faces and doing funny antics until someone laughs. Then let one of the children be the "clown."
- Sing along with "I Love to Laugh" (*Laugh 'n Learn Silly Songs* CD, Kimbo Educational), "If You're Happy and You Know It" (*Me, My Family and Friends* CD, Schiller Educational Resources, LLC) or "If You're Happy and You Know It" (*Six White Ducks* CD, Kimbo Educational).

REFLECTIONS ON THE DAY

- *Which activity made you happiest today? Why?*
- *Which verse of the song do you like best?*

Itsy Bitsy Spider

Itsy Bitsy Spider (Tune: Traditional)
The itsy bitsy spider
Went up the water spout.
Down came the rain
And washed the spider out.
Out came the sun
And dried up all the rain.
And the itsy bitsy spider
Went up the spout again.

Related Songs, Chants, and Rhymes

Dancing Spider by Pam Schiller
Dancing spider hop, hop, hop.
Dancing spider stop, stop, stop.
Dancing spider sway, sway, sway.
Dancing spider stay, stay, stay.

My Busy Garden adapted by Pam Schiller
(Tune: She'll be Coming 'Round the Mountain)
Oh, spiders are busy spinning all around—spin, spin!
Oh, spiders are busy spinning all around—spin, spin!
See them spinning low and high, better look out, Mr. Fly,
Oh, the spiders are busy spinning all around—spin, spin!

Oh, the ants are busy digging all around—dig, dig!
Oh, the ants are busy digging all around—dig, dig!
See them scurry here and there, tossing dirt into the air,
Oh, the ants are busy digging all around—dig, dig!

Oh, the bees are busy buzzing all around—buzz, buzz!
Oh, the bees are busy buzzing all around—buzz, buzz!
See them buzzing here and there, lots of pollen in the air,
Oh, the bees are busy buzzing all around—buzz, buzz!

Oh, the beetles are busy chewing all around—chomp, chomp!
Oh, the beetles are busy chewing all around—chomp, chomp!
See them chewing leaves and flowers as they while away the hours,
Oh, the beetles are busy chewing all around—chomp, chomp!

SEE ALSO

"The Grand Old Duke of York," page 61
"Little Miss Muffet," page 101

Oh, the insects are all busy, yes, they are—busy, busy!
Oh, the insects are all busy, yes, they are—busy, busy!
My garden is a buzzin' with insects by the dozen,
Oh, the insects are all busy, yes, they are—busy, busy!

Follow-Up Questions

- *What made the spider fall down?*
- *How did the spider get dried off?*
- *Have you ever tried to do something and weren't able to do it? What did you do?*

Language Enrichment

- Define words that the children may not know, such as *water spout, washed out,* and *itsy bitsy.*
- Show the children pictures of spiders to stimulate discussion. *How do spiders move? What color are spiders? Where do we see spiders? Have you seen a spider somewhere? Where?*
- Sing the song using an itsy bitsy voice. Substitute *big gigantic* for *itsy bitsy* and sing the song with a gigantic voice.
- Substitute the word *ta* for the words in the song using the "Itsy Bitsy Spider" tune (**Note:** Using a syllable sound like *ta* or a letter sound like /t/ instead of words helps focus on one of the discrete sounds of language. For some toddlers, this is easier than saying the words. When children enter school and formal reading instruction begins, they will need to be able to hear both the discrete source of syllables and individual letters. Early experiences with these sounds wire them in the brain so they will be familiar to children later.)

Extension Activities

Cognitive Development/Discovery

Up and Down

Place a plastic spider inside an empty plastic peanut butter or similar size jar. (If you don't have a plastic spider, make one by twisting four plastic bag ties together to make eight legs and a body.) Fill the jar with mineral oil and glue the lid on. Demonstrate turning the jar upside down to make the spider go to the top of the jar. Turn the jar back upright and the spider will go back down to the bottom of the jar. Encourage the children to make the spider go up and down. Talk with them about the speed in which the spider is moving. *Does the spider move faster when it is going up or down?*

STORY TIME SUGGESTIONS

Have You Seen Bugs? by Joanne Oppenheim
Itsy Bitsy Spider by Iza Trapani
Nature Spy by Shelley Rotner

Cognitive and Social-Emotional Development/Construction

Sunshine Puppets

Place a small amount of yellow non-toxic fingerpaint on 6" paper plates and encourage the children to move the paint around to cover the plate. Tape each plate to a straw to make Sunshine Puppets. Have the children place their puppets behind their backs and sing the song. When the "sun comes out," have them hold their Sunshine Puppets in front of their faces. Talk about what the sun does in the song. *Have you ever noticed how the warm sun dries things? Have you been swimming? Do you remember the sun drying you when you got out of the pool? How does the sun feel on your skin?*

Physical and Cognitive Development/Music

Dancing Spiders

Make a spider for each child by twisting four pipe cleaners together to make a body and eight legs. You may want to use colorful pipe cleaners so the spiders don't look scary. Tie an 18" piece of elastic thread to the middle of each spider. Play classical music and show the children how to make their spiders "dance" to the music. Talk with them about how the spiders are moving. *Can you make your spider hop? Jump? Do spiders like to dance?* Count the legs on their spiders for them. *Does having so many legs make it easier to dance? Why?*

Physical Development/Gross Motor

Spider Walk

Show the children how to bend at the waist and walk on both hands and feet. Have them walk around in this position pretending to be spiders. Make a masking tape line on the floor to represent a water spout. Encourage the children to walk like spiders up and down the "water spout." Talk with them as they pretend to be spiders. *Is it easier to walk when using both hands and feet or easier when using just feet? Do you think it is more difficult to walk using eight legs or two legs? Why?*

Outdoor Play or Music and Movement

- Show the children how to wiggle their fingers between a light source and the wall to make dancing spiders.
- Dance to the instrumental version of "Itsy Bitsy Spider" (*Twinkle, Twinkle Jazzy Star* CD, Thomas Moore Enterprises).
- Sing along with "Itsy Bitsy Spider" (*Sweet Dreams* CD, O'Neill Brothers), "Itsy Bitsy Spider" (*Songs for the Whole Day* CD, Thomas Moore Enterprises), or "My Busy Garden" (*Bugs! Bugs! Bugs!* CD, Schiller Educational Resources, LLC).

REFLECTIONS ON THE DAY

- *What did you learn about spiders today?*
- *Which has more legs: a spider or a bird? A spider or a puppy?*

Jack and Jill

Jack and Jill
(Mother Goose) (Tune: Traditional)
Jack and Jill went up the hill
To fetch a pail of water.
Jack fell down
And broke his crown
And Jill came tumbling after.

Then up Jack got, and home did trot,
As fast as he could caper.
They put him to bed,
And plastered his head,
With vinegar and brown paper.

Related Songs, Chants, and Rhymes

Jack Spratt
Jack Spratt could eat no fat.
His wife could eat no lean.
And so between the two of them,
They licked the platter clean.

Who's Gonna Shoe Your Pretty Little Feet?
Who's gonna shoe
Your pretty little feet?
Who's gonna glove
Your little hand?
Who's gonna kiss
Your "booboo" away?
Who, who, who?

Papa's gonna shoe
Your pretty little feet,
Mama's gonna glove
Your little hand,
And I'm gonna kiss
Your "booboo" away,
Ooh, ooh, ooh!

SEE ALSO

"Five Little Monkeys," page 180
"The Grand Old Duke of York," page 61
"Humpty Dumpty," page 73
"Jack Frost," page 87
"Nursery Rhyme Rap," page 15
"Say, Say, My Playmate," page 124
"Wake Up, Jack-in-the-Box," page 88

Follow-Up Questions

- *What were Jack and Jill going up the hill to get?*
- *What do you think might have made Jack fall? Why did Jill tumble?*
- *Was the pail full of water when they fell?*

Language Enrichment

- Introduce new vocabulary, such as *hill, fetch, pail, crown, tumble, trot, caper,* and *vinegar.* Explain that "*plastered his head*" means to bandage it.
- Ask the children to clap the words as you say the rhyme. Clapping words is a great readiness task for clapping syllables, which will be a skill needed when the children are a little older.
- Make connections with any children who may have the same name as the characters in the rhyme. Write the names *Jack* and *Jill* on chart paper or, if working with individual children, on a piece of drawing paper. Point out that the written words are Jack's and Jill's names. With older children or children who show an interest, point out that both names begin with the same letter of the alphabet.
- Recite the rhyme in a whisper, but say the rhyming words out loud.

Extension Activities

Cognitive Development/Blocks

Up and Down the Hill

Create a small "hill" by spreading a sheet over towels or wadded paper. Provide small cars and balls to roll up and down the hill. Talk with the children about the hill and the items they are rolling. *Which way is up? Which way is down? Which way do the items roll easier? How is a hill different from a mountain?*

Cognitive Development/Discovery

Vinegar and Soda

Provide small paper plates, a small bowl of vinegar, a small bowl of baking soda, an eyedropper, and a small spoon. Younger toddlers will enjoy exploring the materials—touching the baking soda, playing with the eyedroppers, and smelling the vinegar. Show the older children how to use the spoon to place a small amount of baking soda on their plate and how to use the eyedropper to put some vinegar on top of the soda to create a fizz. Talk with the children as they explore combining vinegar and soda. *What makes the fizz? Does more vinegar make more fizz?* Have the children smell the vinegar. Remind them that vinegar was used to bandage Jack's head. The vinegar acts like alcohol—it cleanses the wound.

STORY TIME SUGGESTIONS

Jack and Jill by Heather Collins

My Big Book of Jack and Jill by Vincent Douglas

Safety Warning: Supervise closely so that children do not get the mixture in their eyes because it will burn. Also discourage putting the mixture in their mouths—it won't hurt them, but it won't taste good.

Physical Development/Gross Motor

Pail Play

Spread blocks on the floor and encourage the children to pick them up and place them into pails. Encourage them to switch the hand they use for picking up the blocks. Ask questions as they play. *Is it easier to pick things up with the first hand you used or the second hand you used? Do you think carrying blocks easier than carrying water? What will you do if your pail gets full and you still have more blocks to pick up?*

Social-Emotional and Cognitive Development/Water

Fill a Pail of Water

Fill the water table with water or provide a small tub of water for the children to explore. Provide pails or make pails by attaching a pipe cleaner handle to a paper or plastic cup. Encourage the children to fill their pails with water. Talk with them as they play. *Is the pail heavier when you have it filled with water? Is it hard to keep the water from spilling?* If you do this activity outdoors, challenge the children to try walking with their pail of water.

Outdoor Play or Music and Movement

- Locate a soft surface such as grass or a tumbling mat. Show the children some tumbling tricks, including rolling forward, rolling like a log, and rocking.
- Invite the children to act out "Five Little Monkeys" (see page 180). Discuss the bump on the head Jack received and the bump on the head the monkeys received. *Who do you think had the biggest bump on their head?*
- Sing along with "Jack and Jill" (*Nursery Rhyme Time* CD, Kimbo Educational) or "Jack and Jill" (*Wee Sing Nursery Rhymes and Lullabies* CD, Price, Stern, and Sloan).

REFLECTIONS ON THE DAY

- *Do you think it is more difficult to carry water or blocks in a pail? Why?*
- *How is a hill different from a mountain?*

Jack Be Nimble

Jack Be Nimble (Mother Goose) (Tune: Traditional)
Jack be nimble,
Jack be quick;
Jack jump over
The candlestick.

Additional verses:

Jack be nimble,
Jack be late;
Jack jump over
The dinner plate.

Jack be nimble,
Jack be soon;
Jack jump over
The silver spoon.

Jack be nimble,
Jack be up;
Jack jump over
The sippy cup.

(*Make up your own verses.*)

SEE ALSO

"Hey, Diddle Diddle," page 67
"Jack and Jill," page 84
"Jack Spratt," page 84

Related Songs, Chants, and Rhymes

Jack Frost
Jack Frost bites your nose.
He chills your cheeks and freezes your toes.
He comes every year when winter is here
And stays until spring is near.

Jack-in-the-Box
Jack-in-the-box (*tuck thumb into fist*)
Oh, so still.
Won't you come out? (*raise hand slightly*)
Yes, I will. (*pop thumb out of fist*)

Jack, Jack

Jack, Jack, down you go, (*crouch down low*)
Down in your box, down so low.
Jack, Jack, there goes the top. (*pop up*)
Quickly now, up you pop.

Wake Up, Jack-in-the-Box

(*suit actions to words*)
Jack-in-the-box, jack-in-the-box,
Wake up, wake up, somebody knocks.
One time, two times, three times, four.
Jack pops out of his little round door.

Follow-Up Questions

- *How could Jack get on the other side of the candlestick if he didn't jump over it?*
- *Have you ever jumped over anything? What was it?*

Language Enrichment

- Try some of the additional verses that change the item that Jack jumps over. Invite the children to act out the rhyme. Provide the appropriate props. Say the rhyme as the children act it out. Encourage the children to fill in the name of the item jumped over.
- Change the word *jumped* to *danced.* Ask the children how changing the word changes the rhyme. Try other verbs such as *hopped, skipped,* or *leaped.*
- Clap the words of the rhyme with the children.
- Talk with the children about fire safety and specifically candle safety.

STORY TIME SUGGESTION

Jack Be Nimble and Other Favorites (Action Nursery Rhymes) with CD by Soundprints

Extension Activities

Cognitive Development/Science

Matching Smells

Provide six small, scented votive candles (two of each scent). Invite the children to smell the candles and match the ones that smell the same. Talk with them as they smell the candles and see if they can describe the scents. Remind the children that only adults should light candles.

Cognitive and Physical Development/Construction

Candlesticks

Cut 1" x 9" strips of a variety of colors of construction paper to represent candles. Cut out flames from orange or yellow construction paper. Encourage the children to glue the candles on their paper and add a flame to "light" them.

Physical Development/ Fine Motor

Pretend Birthday Cakes

Provide playdough and birthday candles. Show the children how to shape a cake with the playdough and then add birthday candles to create a birthday cake. Talk with the children about candle safety.

Physical Development/Gross Motor

Jumping Jills and Jacks

Give the children a candlestick, paper plate, sippy cup, and spoon to jump over. *Are any of the items any more difficult than others to jump over?* Talk with the children about the items.

Outdoor Play or Music and Movement

- Show the children how to do Jumping Jacks.
- Sing along with "Nursery Rhyme Rap" (*School Days* CD, Schiller Educational Resources, LLC) or "Jack Be Nimble" (*Wee Sing Nursery Rhymes and Lullabies* CD, Price, Stern, Sloan).

REFLECTIONS ON THE DAY

- *What did you learn about candles today?*
- *What items did you jump over?*

Johnny Works With One Hammer

Johnny Works With One Hammer (Tune: Traditional)
Johnny works with one hammer,
One hammer, one hammer. (*make hammering motion with right hand*)
Johnny works with one hammer
Then he works with two.

Johnny works with two hammers… (*motion with left and right hands*)
Johnny works with three hammers… (*motion with both hands and right foot*)
Johnny works with four hammers… (*motion with both hands and both feet*)
Johnny works with five hammers… (*motion with both hands and feet and with head*)
Then he goes to bed.

SEE ALSO

"Looby Loo," page 111

Related Songs, Chants, and Rhymes

Katie Draws With One Crayon
(Tune: Johnny Works with One Hammer)
Katie draws with one crayon, (*make drawing motion with right hand*)
One crayon, one crayon,
Katie draws with one crayon
Then she draws with two.

Katie draws with two crayons… (*add left hand*)
Katie draws with three crayons… (*add right foot*)
Katie draws with four crayons… (*add left foot*)
Katie words with five crayons… (*add head*)
Then she goes to bed.

Whoops Johnny! or **Whoops Katie!**
Johnny, Johnny, Johnny, Johnny. (*tap the top of each finger for each "Johnny," starting with pinky*)
Whoops, Johnny! (*slide down forefinger and up thumb, touch thumb*)
Whoops, Johnny! (*slide back down thumb and up forefinger and touch forefinger*)
Johnny, Johnny, Johnny, Johnny. (*touch one finger for each "Johnny," back to pinky*)

Follow-Up Questions

- *How do you think Johnny holds a hammer with his foot?*
- *How do you think Johnny can hold a hammer with his head?*
- *How heavy would five hammers be?*

Language Enrichment

- Encourage children to talk about what they know about hammers. Extend the conversation to tools in general.
- Sing "Katie Draws With One Crayon" (see previous page). Ask the children to think about other tools they use, including toothbrushes, combs, spoons, paintbrushes, and so on. Sing the song using one of the tools that the children suggest. Make sure to change the words to fit the action ("Katie brushes with one toothbrush").
- If available, show the children a hammer. Talk about its parts and how it is used.

Extension Activities

Cognitive Development/Discovery

Hammer Weight

Place five plastic hammers in a bucket. Have the children pick up the bucket to feel the weight of the hammers. Gather five each of several other items, such as five blocks, five books, and five spoons. Fill a second bucket with five of another item. Have the children lift the bucket of hammers and then the bucket of the other five items to determine which bucket is heavier. Talk with children as they experiment. *Is it easy to tell which bucket is heavier?* **Safety Note:** Supervise closely to ensure that items are used as intended.

Cognitive Development/Math

Counting 1 to 5

Give the children magnetic or felt numerals 1 to 5. Provide items to count, such as hammer cutouts, snap beads, small blocks, and so on. Encourage the children to count the correct number of items for each numeral. Talk with children as they work. If they are not ready to count five items, use one or two items and numerals and count the items for the children.

Cognitive and Physical Development/Art

Five Crayons

Challenge the children to draw with more than one crayon at a time. Start with two crayons, and add more. They can hold the

STORY TIME SUGGESTIONS

This Is the House that Jack Built by Pam Adams

This Is the House that Jack Built by Simms Taback

crayons in one hand or in two hands or, if ready, they can try to hold a crayon with their toes. *How can you hold five crayons? Is it difficult to draw with two hands at one time? Which hand is it easier to draw with?*

Physical and Cognitive Development/Gross Motor

Five Balls

Give the children five small- to medium-size balls and challenge them to think of a way they can hold all five at one time. Talk with them about their solutions. *Did you find a way to hold all five balls? How did you do it?*

Outdoor Play or Music and Movement

- Sing along with "Johnny Works With One Hammer" (*Me, My Family and Friends* CD, Schiller Educational Resources, LLC).
- Say the "Che Che Koolay" rhyme (see page 163) and do the actions with the children. Not all the children will be able to do the whole chant, but encourage them to try.

REFLECTIONS ON THE DAY

- *Were you able to hold all five balls? Do you think it is possible for someone to work with five hammers at one time?*
- *Did you find something that was heavier than the hammers in the bucket?*

Little Bo-Peep

Little Bo-Peep (Mother Goose) (Tune: Traditional)
Little Bo-Peep has lost her sheep,
And can't tell where to find them;
Leave them alone, and they'll come home,
Wagging their tails behind them.

Little Bo-Peep fell fast asleep,
And dreamt she heard them bleating;
But when she awoke, she found it a joke,
For they were still a-fleeting.

Then up she took her little crook,
Determined for to find them;
She found them indeed, but it made her heart bleed,
For they left all their tails behind them.

Related Songs, Chants, and Rhymes

Baa, Baa, Sweet Sheep
Baa, baa, sweet sheep, have you any wool?
Yes, please! Yes, please! Three bags full.
One for my mother,
One for my dad,
And one for the little boy
Who looks so sad.
Baa, baa, sweet sheep, have you any wool?
Yes, please! Yes, please! Three bags full.

SEE ALSO

"Little Boy Blue," page 95
"Mary Had a Little Lamb," page 114
"Nursery Rhyme Rap," page 15
"Old MacDonald Had a Farm," page 132

Follow-Up Questions

- *Have you ever lost something and couldn't find it? What was it?*
- *What is Little Bo-Peep's job?*

Language Enrichment

- Introduce words that may be new vocabulary for the children, such as *bleat, fleeting,* and *crook.*
- Recite the first verse of the rhyme a couple of times. Recite it again and hesitate before saying the rhyming word that rhymes with the ending word in the previous sentence. Are the children able to fill it in?

- Gather wool items, such as socks, mittens, and sweaters. Show the items to the children and explain that they are made from wool. Explain that wool comes from sheep. Have them describe how the material feels.

Extension Activities

Cognitive Development/Art

Wool Prints

Cut out small squares of carpet and encourage the children to dip them into a tray of tempera non-toxic paint to make prints. Talk about the things that are made from the wool.

Cognitive Development/Games

Sheep Hunt

Hide a plastic sheep and encourage the children to find it by listening to your clues. Begin with easy clues and increase the difficulty as the children become familiar with the game.

Social-Emotional Development/Dramatic Play

Wool Wear

Fill the dramatic play center with clothing made from wool and encourage the children to explore the clothing. Talk with them about the items they choose to wear. *How does the material feel to your hands? How does it feel on your body? What is this material called?*

Social-Emotional Development/ Gross Motor

Wagging Their Tails

Sew 20" strips of elastic into circles to make waistbands. Attach 6" pieces of thick white yarn to represent tails. Invite the children to place the bands around their waists and try to "wag their tails." *How can you make the tail wag?*

Outdoor Play or Music and Movement

- Play Little Bo-Peep Hide and Seek. Choose one child to be Little Bo-Peep and the other children are the sheep. The "sheep" hide and Little Bo-Peep looks for them while calling, "Here sheep." When the sheep are found, they must go to a spot in the room that is designated as home.
- Sing along with "Little Bo-Peep" (*School Days* CD, Schiller Educational Resources, LLC).

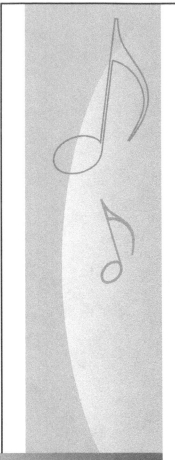

STORY TIME SUGGESTIONS

Little Bo-Peep by Tracey Campbell Pearson

Sheep in a Jeep by Nancy E. Shaw

REFLECTIONS ON THE DAY

- *Can you name something that is made from wool? Where does the wool come from?*
- *Do you think that Little Bo-Peep's sheep came back home?*

Little Boy Blue

Little Boy Blue (Mother Goose) (Tune: Traditional)
Little Boy Blue, come blow your horn,
The sheep's in the meadow, the cow's in the corn.
But where is the boy who looks after the sheep?
He's under a haystack, fast asleep.
Will you wake him? No, not I.
For if I do, he's sure to cry.

Related Songs, Chants, and Rhymes

Lavender's Blue (Tune: Traditional)
Lavender's blue, dilly dilly,
Lavender's green.
When you are king, dilly dilly,
I shall be queen.

Who told you so, dilly dilly,
who told you so?
'Twas my own heart, dilly dilly,
That told me so.

Call up your friends, dilly dilly,
Set them to work.
Some to the plough, dilly dilly,
Some to the fork.

Some to the hay, dilly dilly,
Some to thresh corn,
Whilst you and I, dilly dilly,
Keep ourselves warm.

Lavender's blue, dilly dilly,
Lavender's green.
When you are king, dilly dilly,
I shall be queen.

Who told you so, dilly dilly,
Who told you so?

SEE ALSO

"Are You Sleeping?," page 26
"Baa, Baa, Sweet Sheep," page 93
"Little Bo-Peep," page 93
"Nursery Rhyme Rap," page 15
"Old MacDonald Had a Farm," page 132
"Wynken, Blynken and Nod," page 193

'Twas my own heart, dilly dilly,
That told me so.

Lazy Mary (Tune: Here We Go 'Round the Mulberry Bush)
Lazy Mary, will you get up?
Will you get up? Will you get up?
Lazy Mary, will you get up?
So early in the morning?

No, no, Mother, I won't get up.
I won't get up.
I won't get up
No, no, Mother, I won't get up
So early in the morning.

Follow-Up Questions

- *What is Little Boy Blue doing?*
- *Why do you think Little Boy Blue fell asleep?*
- *Why do you think the boy is called Little Boy Blue?*

Language Enrichment

- Introduce words that may be new vocabulary for the children (*horn*, *meadow*, and *haystack*).
- Substitute the syllable *ba* for the words in the song. (**Note:** Using a syllable sound like *ba* or a letter sound like /b/ instead of words helps focus on one of the discrete sounds of language. For some toddlers, this is easier than saying the words. When children enter school and formal reading instruction begins, they will need to be able to hear both the discrete source of syllables and individual letters. Early experiences with these sounds wire them in the brain so they will be familiar to children later.)
- If available, share pictures of cows with the children. Use the pictures to stimulate conversation about the animal.
- After singing or saying the nursery rhyme a couple of times, stop before saying the rhyming words in the second lines (*horn* and *asleep*) and let the children fill them in.
- Whisper the rhyme until you get to the rhyming words. Say the rhyming words out loud.

STORY TIME SUGGESTIONS

Little Boy Blue and Other Rhymes by Iona Opie and Rosemary Wells
Moo, Baa, La La La! by Sandra Boynton

Extension Activities

Cognitive Development/Listening

Toot That Horn!

Give the children empty toilet paper tubes to use for horns. Encourage them to blow their horns. Help them figure out how to make their horns hit a high note and how to hit a low note by adjusting their voices. Play an echo game with the horns. You make a sound and have the children copy your sound. Make high sounds, low sounds, repetitive sounds, and so on.

Cognitive and Social-Emotional Development/Dramatic Play

Under the Haystack

Cover a table with a sheet and pretend it is a haystack. Invite the children to crawl under the "haystack" and take a nap. Provide soft music, pillows, blankets, and books to create a naptime environment. Be sure to clarify that Little Boy Blue was so tired he fell asleep without any of these comforts.

Physical Development/Art

The Color Blue

Give the children blue non-toxic fingerpaint and encourage them to paint directly on top of the table. After they have enjoyed the paint for a while, add a little red to the blue paint. What happens? In another spot, add yellow. What happens? *What would the Little Boy's name be if either of the new colors were part of his name?*

Social-Emotional and Cognitive Development/Blocks

On the Farm

Provide toy farm animals and props and encourage the children to create a farm. Sit on the floor and play with them. Model how to create a farm. Provide farm books, if available. Ask the children questions. *Where are the cows and sheep? Where is the hay?*

Outdoor Play or Music and Movement

- Sing along with "Little Boy Blue" (*Wee Sing Nursery Rhymes and Lullabies* CD, Price, Stern, and Sloan) or "Lavender's Blue" (*Me, My Friends and Family* CD, Schiller Educational Resources, LLC).
- Play a modified version of the game Freeze. Play some music and encourage the children to dance freely until they hear you blow your horn. When they hear the horn, they have to freeze. When they hear the horn a second time, they can dance again.

REFLECTIONS ON THE DAY

- *What was Little Boy Blue's job?*
- *Did you fall asleep under the "haystack" today?*

Little Hunk of Tin

Little Hunk of Tin
(Tune: I'm a Little Acorn Brown)
I'm a little hunk of tin.
Nobody knows what shape I'm in.
Got four wheels and a tank of gas.
I can go, but not too fast.

Chorus:
Honk, honk (*pull ear*)
Rattle, rattle. (*shake head*)
Crash, crash. (*push chin*)
Beep, beep. (*push nose*)
(*repeat chorus two times*)

I'm a little ice cream truck.
I wibble, wobble like a duck.
Got four wheels and lots of cream,
I make children shout and scream.

(Chorus)

I'm a little yellow bus,
Newly painted, not a spot of rust,
Brand new wheels and kids inside
Hold on tight for a happy ride.

(Chorus)

SEE ALSO

"The Bus Song," page 225
"The Freight Train," page 225
"Little Red Wagon," page 104
"Motor Boat Chant," page 167
"My Bike," page 105
"Oh, It's Wheels, Wheels, Wheels," page 105
"Row, Row, Row Your Boat," page 167
"The Wheels on the Bus," page 225

Related Songs, Chants, and Rhymes

The Car Song (Tune: When Johnny Comes Marching Home)
We like to travel in our car,
Hurrah, hurrah.
A car can take us near or far,
Hurrah, hurrah.
We buckle up before we go,
Whether we're going fast or slow,
So we'll all be safer while riding in our car!

Windshield Wiper (Tune: Row, Row, Row Your Boat)
I'm a windshield wiper. (*bend arm at elbow with fingers pointing up*)
This is how I go. (*move arm to left and right, pivoting at elbow*)
Back and forth, back and forth, (*continue back and forth motion*)
In the rain and snow. (*continue back and forth motion*)

I'm a windshield wiper,
Back and forth I go,
Swish, swash, swish, swash,
Your windshields I will wash.

Follow-Up Questions

- *Which verse did you like best: the one about the car, the bus, or the ice cream truck?*
- *Have you ever been on a bus?*

Language Enrichment

- Discuss the *onomatopoeic* words in the song (*honk, rattle, crash,* and *beep*). Explain to the children that words that sound like the sound they are describing are called *onomatopoeic* words. *Which things honk? Which things beep? Can you think of something that makes a crashing sound when it falls? Can you think of something that rattles?* This seems like a big word and complex concept, but children love the word and can grasp the concept.
- Ask the children if they have ever seen an ice cream truck. Encourage them to discuss their experiences. If they have not seen an ice cream truck, describe the experience for them. If possible, have an ice cream truck visit the school.
- Discuss an aspect of car safety, such as buckling up, staying away from the driver's seat, looking both ways when crossing the street, and so on.
- Teach the children the American Sign Language signs for *car, ice-cream truck,* and *bus* (see appendix page 239).

Extension Activities

Cognitive Development/Blocks

Honk! Honk!
Fill the block center with cars and trucks. Encourage the children to operate the vehicles and make the appropriate accompanying noises. Help them get more creative with their motor and honking sounds.

STORY TIME SUGGESTION

The Wheels on the Bus by Paul Zelinsky

Cognitive Development/Listening

Noise Makers

Provide items that rattle, beep, jingle, and honk. Encourage the children to explore the noise makers. Talk with them as they make noise. *How does that sound? Which item makes the loudest noise? Which noise do you like best?*

Cognitive and Social-Emotional Development/Snack

Tin Can Ice Cream

Mix 4 cups of milk, 4 tablespoons of sugar, and 1 teaspoon of vanilla in a 1 lb. coffee can. Close the lid and place the 1 lb. can inside a 5 lb. can. Fill the remaining space with ice and rock salt and put the lid on. Give the can to the children and encourage them to roll it back and forth across the floor for 15-20 minutes. One can serves eight children. Talk about the ingredients in the ice cream. Discuss the sound of the can rolling on the floor.

Physical Development/Motor

Crash!

Stack five small metal cans on a cookie sheet. Provide beanbags. Encourage the children to stack the cans in a pyramid and knock them down with a beanbag. Talk about the sound of the cans as they hit the cookie sheet. *Is that a crashing sound? Can you think of another word to describe the way the cans sound when they hit the cookie sheet?*

Outdoor Play or Music and Movement

- Give the children rhythm band instruments to play as they listen to marching music. Discuss the sounds the instruments make. *Do any of the instruments make a crashing sound?*
- Sing along with "Little Hunk of Tin" (*Laugh 'n Learn Silly Songs* CD, Kimbo Educational).

REFLECTIONS ON THE DAY

- *What sounds did you make with the noisemakers? Which noisemaker is your favorite?*
- *Describe the sounds the tin cans made on the cookie sheet when you knocked them down.*

Little Miss Muffet

Little Miss Muffet (Mother Goose) (Tune: Traditional)
Little Miss Muffet sat on her tuffet,
Eating her curds and whey.
Along came a spider,
And sat down beside her,
And frightened Miss Muffet away.

New verse:
Little Miss Muffet went back to her tuffet,
Looked the thing square in the eye.
"See here, you big spider,
Miss Muffet's a fighter.
And you're the one saying, 'bye-bye.'"

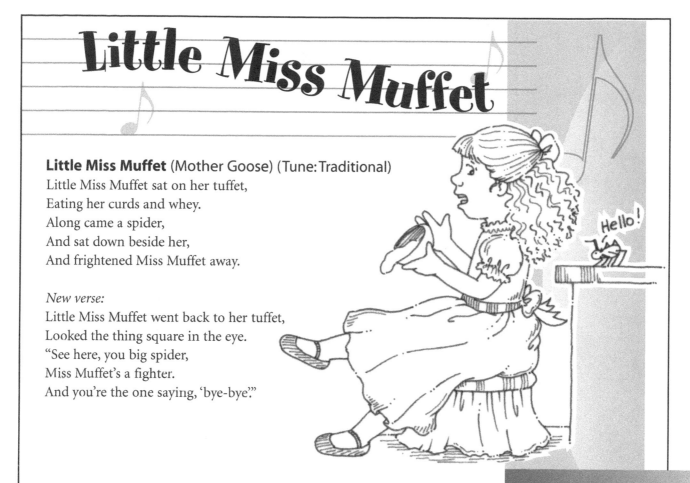

Related Songs, Chants, and Rhymes

Little Miss Spider by Pam Schiller
Little Miss Spider sat on her web
Eating her étouffée.
Along came Miss Muffet
In search of her tuffet
And frightened Miss Spider away.

(Etouffée is a spicy Cajun stew traditionally made with crawfish.)

Peas Porridge Hot
(*make up a simple partner clap*)
Peas porridge hot
Peas porridge cold,
Peas porridge in the pot
Nine days old.
Some like it hot.
Some like it cold.
Some like in the pot
Nine days old!

SEE ALSO

"Itsy Bitsy Spider," page 80
"My Busy Garden," page 80
"Nursery Rhyme Rap," page 15
"There Once Were Three Brown Bears," page 190

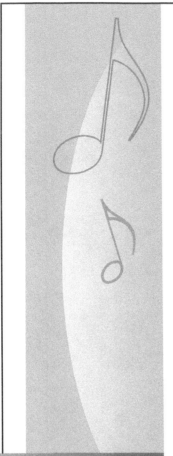

Follow-Up Questions

- *Are you afraid of spiders? Why? Why not? Should you be afraid of spiders?*
- *All the spider did was sit down beside Miss Muffet. If it really wanted to frighten her, what could it have done?*

Language Enrichment

- Introduce words that may be new vocabulary for the children, such as *tuffet*, *curds*, and *whey*. If available, provide cottage cheese for the children to sample and a footstool or floor pillow for the children to try sitting on. **Safety Note:** If any of the children are allergic or sensitive to dairy products, do not provide cottage cheese.
- After the children have heard the rhyme a few times, read it again and let the children fill in the rhyming words.
- Invite volunteers to act out the rhyme as you read it.
- Talk with children about things that frighten them. Make a list of their fears on chart paper.

Extension Activities

Cognitive Development/Art

Spider Footprints

Make a spider by twisting four pipe cleaners together at the middle and then bending the legs to look like a spider. Make a small bend at the bottom of each leg to represent a foot. Attach a clothespin to the spider's middle (back). Provide a tray of non-toxic tempera paint and sheets of drawing paper. Show the children how to dip the spider's feet in the paint and then gently press it on their paper again and again to make "spider footprints." Talk about footprints. *Would a spider really leave footprints?* Keep reminding the children to be gentle as they press the spiders on their papers.

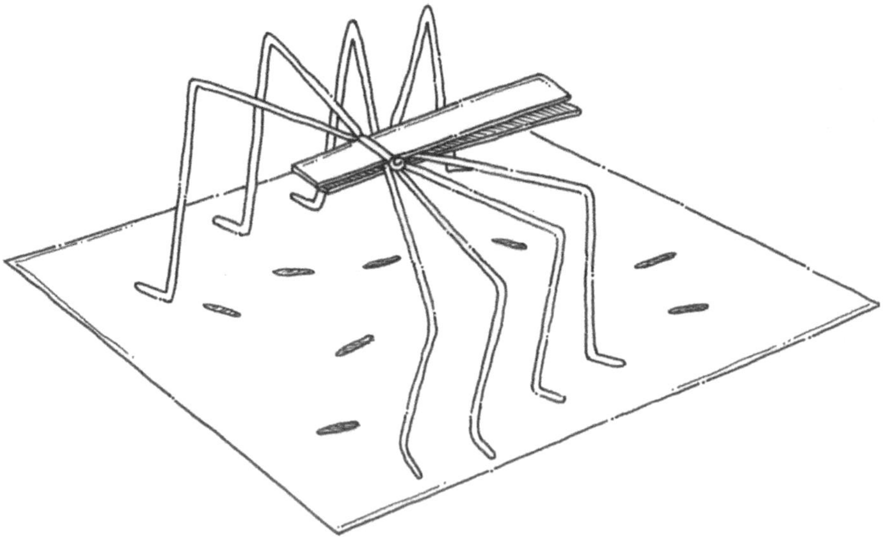

STORY TIME SUGGESTIONS

Little Miss Muffet by Tracey Campbell Pearson

Little Miss Muffet and Other Nursery Rhymes by Lucy Cousins

Cognitive and Social-Emotional Development/Gross Motor

Miss Muffet's Tuffet

Provide a variety of decorative pillows for the children to use as "tuffets." Encourage them to sit on the tuffets, and invite them to stack two tuffets together and sit. *Are the tuffets soft? How are tuffets like a chair? How are they different?*

Physical and Cognitive Development/Fine Motor

Spiders on the Wall

Provide a light source and show the children how to stand between the light source and the wall to make a shadow. Show them how to wiggle their arms and legs to make spiders. Encourage them to move slowly and quickly. Demonstrate how to bend over and walk on hands and feet to make a spider. *Can you make your spider sit still?*

Physical Development/Fine Motor

Curds and Whey

Give the children cottage cheese (curds and whey), a pot, several bowls, and large spoons. Encourage them to spoon the curds and whey from the pot and into the bowls. **Allergy warning:** Check for any food allergies before serving any food to the children.

Outdoor Play or Music and Movement

- Play Musical Tuffets with groups of four children. Place carpet squares on the floor in a circle to represent tuffets. Place one less tuffet than there are children. Play music. When the music stops, the children sit on a tuffet. The child who does not have a tuffet becomes a spider and walks on all fours (their hands and feet) as the music plays again. Spiders do not get on Miss Muffet's Tuffets. Continue until all the children have become spiders.
- Sing along with "Little Miss Muffet" (*Wee Sing Nursery Rhymes and Lullabies* CD, Price, Stern, and Sloan) or "Little Miss Muffet" (*Nursery Rhyme Time* CD, Kimbo Educational).

REFLECTIONS ON THE DAY

- *Why was Miss Muffet afraid of the spider? Did the spider do anything to Miss Muffet?*
- *Do you have a tuffet at your house?*

Little Red Wagon

Little Red Wagon adapted by Pam Schiller (Tune: Skip to My Lou)
Bumpin' up and down in my little red wagon,
Bumpin' up and down in my little red wagon,
Bumpin' up and down in my little red wagon,
Up and down, we're having fun.

Swayin' side to side in my little red wagon,
Swayin' side to side in my little red wagon,
Swayin' side to side in my little red wagon,
Side to side, we're having fun.

Rockin' back and forth in my little red wagon,
Rockin' back and forth in my little red wagon,
Rockin' back and forth in my little red wagon,
Back and forth, we're having fun.

Pickin' up treasures in my little red wagon,
Pickin' up treasures in my little red wagon,
Pickin' up treasures in my little red wagon,
Pickin' up treasures one by one.

Hey ho in my little red wagon,
Hey ho in my little red wagon,
Hey ho in my little red wagon,
Ridin' around and having fun!

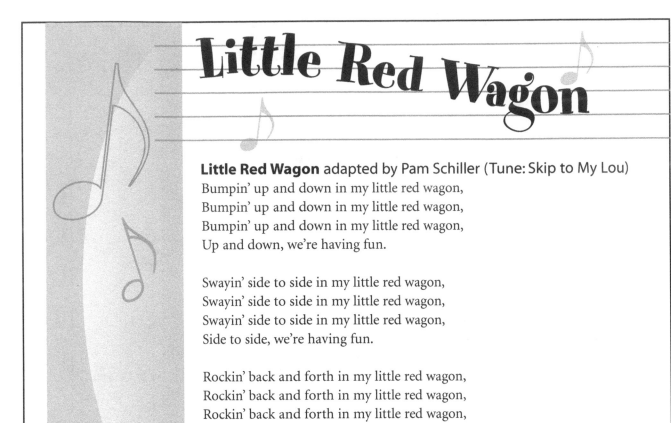

SEE ALSO

"The Car Song," page 98
"Little Hunk of Tin," page 98
"Wheels on the Bus," page 225

Related Songs, Chants, and Rhymes

Little Red Wagon (another version)
Bumpin' up and down in my little red wagon,
Bumpin' up and down in my little red wagon,
Bumpin' up and down in my little red wagon,
Havin' so much fun.

Here come my friends in their little red wagons,
Here come my friends in their little red wagons,
Here come my friends in their little red wagons,
Havin' so much fun.

Pull me around in my little red wagon,
Pull me around in my little red wagon,
Pull me around in my little red wagon,
Havin' so much fun.

Turn the corner in my little red wagon,
Turn the corner in my little red wagon,
Turn the corner in my little red wagon,
Havin' so much fun.

Bumpin' up and down in my little red wagon,
Bumpin' up and down in my little red wagon,
Bumpin' up and down in my little red wagon,
Havin' so much fun.
We're having so much fun!

My Bike

One wheel, two wheels (*make circles with thumb and index finger for wheels*)
On the ground,
My feet make the pedals (*lift feet and pretend to pedal bike*)
Go 'round and 'round.
The handlebars help me (*pretend to steer*)
Steer so straight,
Down the sidewalk (*shade eyes as if looking at something in the distance*)
And through the gate.

Oh, It's Wheels, Wheels, Wheels

(Tune: Hinky Dinky "Double D" Farm)
Oh, it's wheels, wheels, wheels
That make me want to squeal,
Want to squeal, want to squeal.
Oh, it's wheels, wheels, wheels
That give me chills and thrills,
Oh, how I love those rockin' rollin' wheels.

Oh, it's wheels, wheels, wheels
Over highway, roads, and hills
Roads and hills, roads and hills.
Oh, it's wheels, wheels, wheels
That give me chills and thrills,
Oh, how I love those rockin' rollin' wheels.

Oh, it's wheels, wheels, wheels
I love those Ferris wheels,
Ferris wheels, Ferris wheels.
Oh, it's wheels, Ferris wheels
That give me chills and thrills,
Oh, how I love those rockin' Ferris Wheels.

Follow-Up Questions

- *Do you have a wagon at home? Who takes you for a ride?*
- *How many wheels does a wagon have? How is a wagon different from a wheelbarrow? Show the children a picture of a wheelbarrow.*

Language Enrichment

- Ask a volunteer to show you how to bump up and down in a wagon. Ask another volunteer to demonstrate swaying side to side and a third volunteer to demonstrate rocking.
- Ask the children what kinds of things they might haul in a wagon. Make a list on chart paper of all the things they suggest.
- Teach the children the American Sign Language sign for *wagon* (see appendix page 239).

Extension Activities

Cognitive Development/Discovery

Wheels and Gears

Provide clocks, beaters, plastic pizza wheels, and any other items that have wheels or gears. If you have riding vehicles that can be brought indoors, include them in your collection. Talk with the children about the wheels and gears that make each object work. *Which direction do they move? Do the wheels or gears work together?*

Cognitive and Social-Emotional Development/Blocks

Cars and Trucks

Fill the block center with toy cars and trucks and any other available rolling vehicles. Talk with the children about the features of the vehicles. Count the wheels together. If you have dump trucks, provide items to pick up and dump.

Physical and Cognitive Development/Art

Wheel Designs

Prepare a tray of non-toxic tempera paint. Place a large sponge in the center of the tray to create a stamp pad. Provide butcher paper and small vehicles. Encourage the children to roll the vehicles over the sponge and onto butcher paper to create wheel designs. Talk with them as they make their designs. *How many wheels are on your car? Why are there more wheels than tracks? Can you make your design go in a circle?*

STORY TIME SUGGESTIONS

My Little Red Wagon by Rusty Fletcher

My Wagon Will Take Me Anywhere by Elizabeth Cody Kimmel

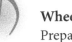

Physical Development/Gross Motor

Indoor Wagons

Collect flat shallow boxes to use for indoor wagons. Attach a 36" rope handle to one end of each box. Encourage the children to pull the indoor wagons like sleighs. Provide stuffed animals for passengers. Discuss the differences in sliding and rolling. *Which is easier?*

Outdoor Play or Music and Movement

- Create a start and finish line with masking tape. Encourage the children to choose a partner. Provide a toy car for each pair of children. Encourage them to race their vehicles.
- Let the children play with the indoor wagons outdoors. Suggest they sing "My Little Red Wagon" while they play.
- Sing along with "My Little Red Wagon" (*On the Move* CD, Schiller Educational Resources, LLC) or "My Little Red Wagon" (*Wiggles, Jiggles, and Giggles* CD, Kimbo Educational).

REFLECTIONS ON THE DAY

- *What did you learn about wheels today?*
- *If you had a little red wagon, what would you do with it?*

London Bridge Is Falling Down

London Bridge Is Falling Down (Mother Goose) (Tune: Traditional)
London Bridge is falling down,
Falling down, falling down.
London Bridge is falling down,
My fair lady.

Build it up with needles and pins,
Needles and pins, needles and pins.
Build it up with needles and pins,
My fair lady.

Pins and needles rust and bend,
Rust and bend, rust and bend.
Pins and needles rust and bend,
My fair lady.

Build it up with silver and gold…
Gold and silver I've not got…
Here's a prisoner I have got…
Take the key and lock her up…

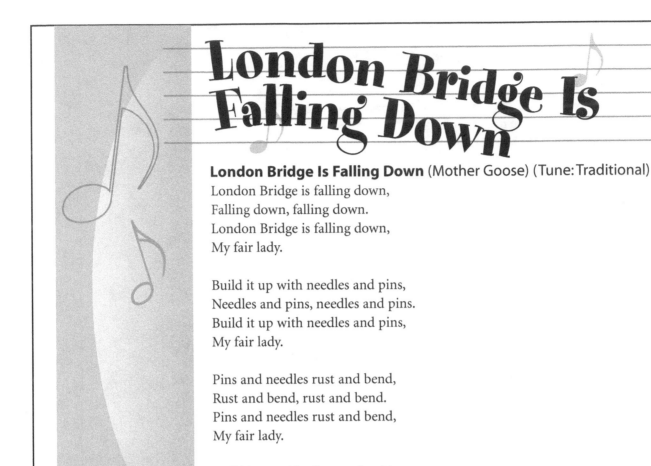

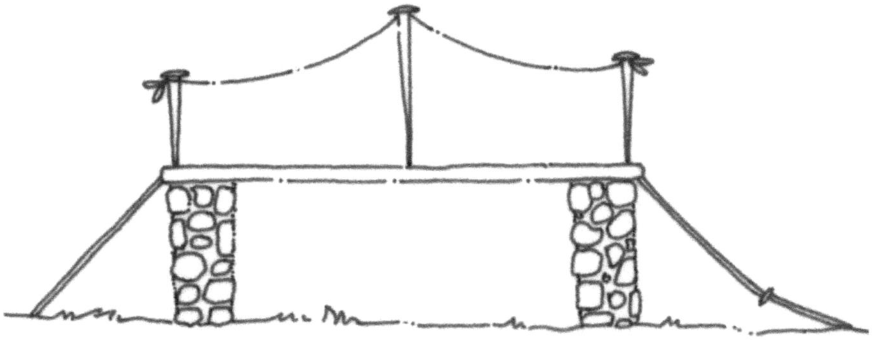

SEE ALSO

"The Grand Old Duke of York," page 61
"Jack and Jill," page 84
"Johnny Works With One Hammer," page 90
"Who's That Traipsing on My Bridge?," page 52

Related Songs, Chants, and Rhymes

Ring Around the Rosie (Tune: Traditional)
(**Directions**: *The children circle around, singing the chant. At the end of the verse, they do what the song says and all fall down.*)
Ring around the rosie
Pocket full of posies
Ashes, ashes, we all fall down.

Follow-Up Questions

- *Has anyone seen a bridge? Did the bridge go over water?*
- *Have you ever played the game London Bridge?*

Language Enrichment

- Show the children pictures of bridges. Use the pictures to stimulate conversation about bridges.
- Discuss the items that were used to build the bridge (*needles and pins* and *silver and gold*). *What travels over a bridge? Could a bridge made of sticks hold a heavy car?* You may want to show children how easily a stick can break. Add additional verses, such as *glue and gum, sticks and straws,* and *string and yarn.*
- Discuss the term *my fair lady.*

Extension Activities

Cognitive Development/Art

Silver and Gold

Have the children paint at easels using non-toxic gold and silver paint. Suggest that they paint a bridge, but let them paint anything they wish. Ask questions. *Which color paint do you like the best?*

Physical Development/Blocks

Building Bridges

Make Paper Bag Blocks by filling paper sacks ¾ full with crumpled newspaper and then folding the top over and taping with masking tape. Encourage children to build bridges with regular blocks or Paper Bag Blocks. Talk about bridges. *What holds them up? What crosses over them? What goes under them?* Provide toy cars to push over the bridge, if appropriate.

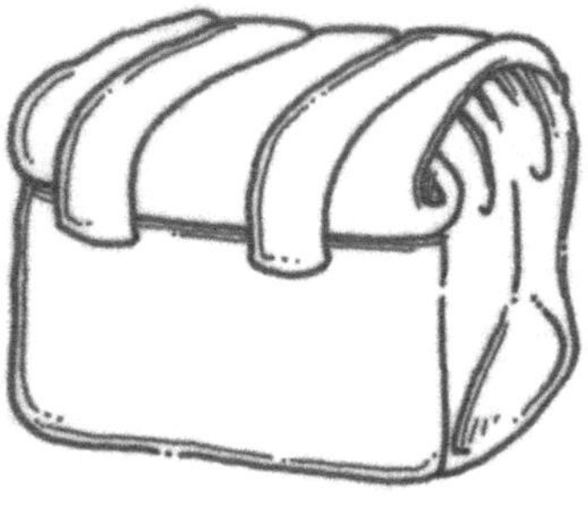

STORY TIME SUGGESTIONS

London Bridge Is Falling Down by E. Emberley
London Bridge Is Falling Down by Wendy Straw
The Three Billy Goats Gruff (Traditional)

Physical Development/Fine Motor

Locks and Keys

Provide several locks with keys. Encourage the children to match the keys to the locks. Discuss how locks work. *Do the keys work either way you turn them?* Hold two keys together. *What is different about the keys?* Match the locks and keys for younger children. They will enjoy just sticking the key in the lock.

Physical Development/Gross Motor

Walking Over the Bridge

Provide a balance beam and encourage the children to pretend it is a bridge as they walk over it. If you do not have a balance beam, use blocks to build a bridge and let the children walk over them. Hold the hands of younger children as they walk over the bridge. After the children walk over the bridge, they may want to push cars over it.

Outdoor Play or Music and Movement

- Play the game "London Bridge Is Falling Down." Form a bridge by holding hands with another adult and raising your arms. Invite the children to march around in a circle while you sing the song. When you get to the line in the song, "Take a key and lock her/him up," bring your arms down around the child beneath you. Gently rock that child and then free him and play again.
- Play the game and sing along with "London Bridge Is Falling Down" (*A Tisket, A Tasket* CD, Kimbo Educational).

REFLECTIONS ON THE DAY

- *Tell me about the bridge you built today. What did you use to build it?*
- *What do you use keys for?*

Looby Loo

Looby Loo (Tune: Traditional)
Here we go Looby-Loo
Here we go Looby-Light
Here we go Looby-Loo
All on a Saturday night.

You put your right hand in,
You put your right hand out,
You give your hand a shake, shake, shake,
And turn yourself about. Oh,

Chorus:
Here we go Looby-Loo
Here we go Looby-Light
Here we go Looby-Loo
All on a Saturday night.

You put your left hand in…
You put your right foot in…
You put your left foot in…
You put your whole self in…

SEE ALSO

"Head, Shoulders, Baby," page 64
"Head, Shoulders, Knees, and Toes," page 64

Related Songs, Chants, and Rhymes

I Can, Can You? by Pam Schiller
I can put my hands up high. Can you?
I can wink my eye. Can you?
I can stick out my tongue. Can you?
I can nod my head. Can you?
I can kiss my toe. Can you?
I can pull on my ear. Can you?
I can wrinkle my nose. Can you?
I can give myself a great big hug. Can you?
And if I give my hug to you, will you give yours to me?

Follow-Up Questions

- *How many hands do we have? How many feet?*
- *Can we add a verse about our head? How would it go?*

Language Enrichment

- Ask the children what they think *looby loo* means. There is no logical answer. Let the children make up their own definitions. *What does looby light mean?*
- Sing the song, changing the consonant /l/ sound to /t/. Try other consonant sounds.
- The song takes place on a Saturday night. *What other night of the week might we use in the song?* Try singing the song using another night. If you use a day of the week with two syllables (Monday), add a one-syllable adjective to get the same three beats as Saturday. You can also use a three-syllable adjective instead of a day of the week, for example, *wonderful, terrific,* and *beautiful.* Discuss each new word and how it changes or doesn't change the song.

Extension Activities

Cognitive and Physical Development/Art

Footprint Art

Place an 8' sheet of butcher paper on the floor. Pour non-toxic tempera paint in a shallow tray and fill a small tub with sudsy water. Place the paint tray at one end of the paper and the sudsy water and a towel at the opposite end of the paper. Invite the children to take off their shoes, step into the paint, and then walk across the paper. Help them step into the sudsy water at the end of their walk. Mark a left and right footprint for each child.

Cognitive and Physical Development/Music

Shakers

Provide jingle bells and small empty plastic juice bottles for each child. Help the children drop the bells into their bottle. Seal the lids with glue and let them shake their bottles. **Safety Note:** Supervise closely and make sure that lids are glued on securely.

Physical Development/Snack

Shake-a-Pudding

Pour 1 tablespoon of instant pudding powder and 1¼ cup of milk into a plastic baby food jar. Make one for each child. Invite the children to shake the jars until the pudding is thick. Encourage them to change hands when they get tired. Talk to them about using their right hand and their left hand.

STORY TIME SUGGESTION

The Baby Dances by Kathy Henderson

Physical Development and Social-Emotional Development/Motor

Shake, Shake, Shake

Sew jingle bells to scrunchies, or sew 1 ½" wide strips of elastic to make wristbands, leg bands, and waistbands. Sew jingle bells onto each band. Encourage the children to put the bands on their wrists and ankles and around their waist and then shake to make music. Encourage them to find a partner to shake with.

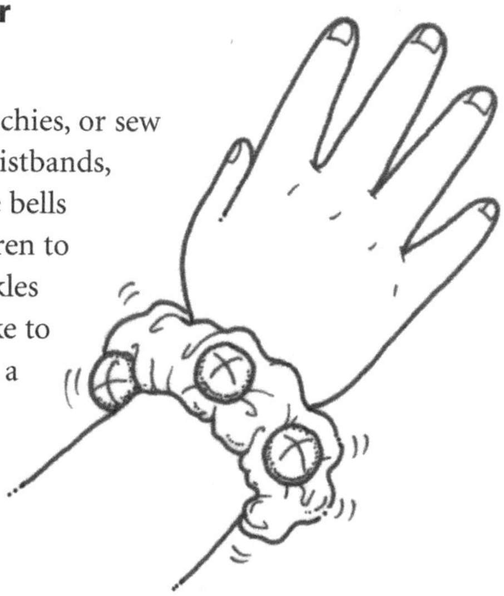

Outdoor Play or Music and Movement

- Dance to "Looby Loo" (*A Tisket, A Tasket* CD, Kimbo Educational).
- Play some marching music and invite the children to march. Chant *left, right, left, right,* as they march.

REFLECTIONS ON THE DAY

- *Which activity did you like best today?*
- *Who can show me how to shake your right hand? Left hand?*

Mary Had a Little Lamb

Mary Had a Little Lamb (Tune: Traditional)

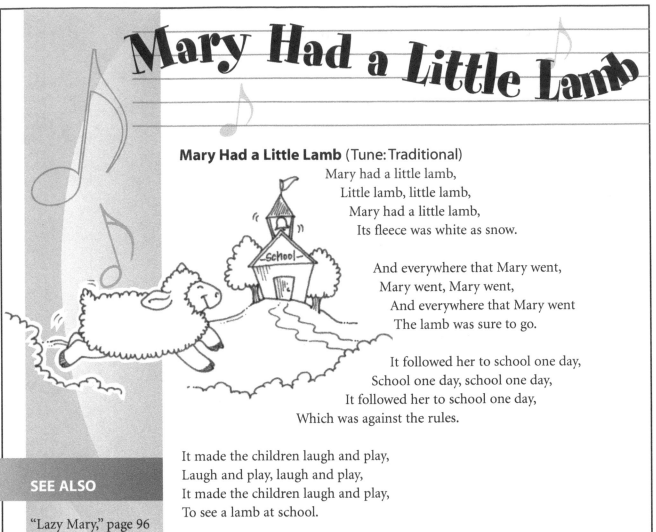

Mary had a little lamb,
Little lamb, little lamb,
Mary had a little lamb,
Its fleece was white as snow.

And everywhere that Mary went,
Mary went, Mary went,
And everywhere that Mary went
The lamb was sure to go.

It followed her to school one day,
School one day, school one day,
It followed her to school one day,
Which was against the rules.

It made the children laugh and play,
Laugh and play, laugh and play,
It made the children laugh and play,
To see a lamb at school.

"Why does the lamb love Mary so?
Love Mary so? Love Mary so?"
"Why does the lamb love Mary so?"
The eager children cry.

"Why, Mary loves the lamb, you know.
Loves the lamb, you know. Loves the lamb, you know."
"Why, Mary loves the lamb, you know."
The teacher did reply.

SEE ALSO

"Lazy Mary," page 96
"Little Bo-Peep," page 93
"Miss Mary Mack," page 120

Related Songs, Chants, and Rhymes

Mary Had a Little Goat (Tune: Mary Had a Little Lamb)
Mary had a little goat,
Little goat, little goat,
Mary had a little goat,
Its hair was white as snow.

Mary Had a William Goat
(Tune: Mary Had a Little Lamb)
(chorus)
Oh, whoop-de-doo-den-doo-den-doo,
Doo-de-doo, doo-de-doo,
Whoop-de-doo-den-doo-den-doo,
Doo-de-doo-de-doo.

Follow-Up Questions

- *Why did the lamb follow Mary to school?*
- *What do you think the lamb did that made the children laugh?*

Language Enrichment

- If available, show the children a picture of a lamb. Use the photo to stimulate conversation. *Have you ever seen a lamb? Where? Did you touch it? How did it feel? What sound does a lamb make?*
- Ask children what the words "fleece as white as snow" mean. Discuss the use of the wool.
- Talk with children about their pets. *Do you love your pet? Does your pet love you? Does your pet follow you around the house?* For children who do not have pets, encourage them to talk about what kind of pet they would like to have.
- Sing the song, substituting the chorus from "Mary Had a William Goat." Try other nonsense sounds (*ba, ta, tu, ma,* and so on) with the tune.
- Teach the children the American Sign Language sign for *lamb* (see appendix page 239).

Extension Activities

Cognitive Development/Blocks

Lamb House
Help the children build a "house" for Mary's lamb. Provide a stuffed lamb for inspiration and small cardboard boxes for accessories. Suggest creating a bed, a place to eat, and a place to play in the house. Talk with the children about other things the lamb might need in its house. Ask questions to stimulate their thinking. *Where do you think lambs sleep? What do they eat?*

STORY TIME SUGGESTIONS

Mary Had a Little Lamb by Sarah Josepha Hale
Mary Had a Little Lamb by Iza Trapani

Cognitive and Physical Development/Art

Puff Paint

Mix ¼ cup white glue, 2 tablespoons of non-toxic white tempera paint, and 2 cups of shaving cream. Put the paint directly on the table and encourage the children to fingerpaint with it directly on the table top. Talk with them as they paint. *How does the paint feel? How is it like snow? How is it different? Do you think it feels like Mary's lamb's coat?*

Physical Development/Fine Motor

Fleece as White as Snow

Make Snow Dough by mixing 1 cup of flour, ½ cup of salt, 1 cup of water, 2 tablespoons of vegetable oil, 1 tablespoon of cream of tartar, ½ cup of non-toxic white tempera paint, and clear glitter. Cook over medium heat until a ball is formed. Let cool and knead. Encourage the children to explore and play with the dough. Talk with them about snow, including its color and texture. *How is the dough like snow? How is it different?*

Social-Emotional Development/Dramatic Play

Let's Play School

Provide "school" props, such as paper, pencils, books, chalk and chalkboard, chairs and table, lunchboxes, and so on. Encourage the children to play school. Their concept of school will likely be limited to their experiences with older siblings or friends. Integrate yourself into the play experience. Provide a stuffed lamb.

REFLECTIONS ON THE DAY

- *What color was Mary's lamb?*
- *Did you prefer playing with the Snow Dough or the Puff Paint? Why?*

Outdoor Play or Music and Movement

- Play Follow the Leader, with "Mary" as the leader and the "lambs" as followers.
- Sing along with "Mary Had a Little Lamb" (*Wee Sing Nursery Rhymes and Lullabies* CD, Schiller Educational Resources, LLC) or "Mary Had a Little Lamb" (*Nursery Rhyme Time* CD, Kimbo Educational).

Mary, Mary, Quite Contrary

Mary, Mary, Quite Contrary (Mother Goose) (Tune: Traditional)
Mary, Mary, quite contrary,
How does your garden grow?
With silver bells and cockleshells,
And pretty maids all in a row.

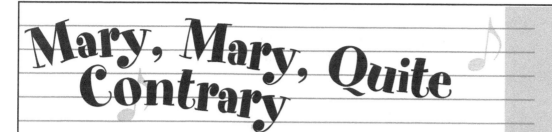

Related Songs, Chants, and Rhymes

Oats, Peas, Beans, and Barley Grow
Oats, peas, beans, and barley grow.
Oats, peas, beans, and barley grow.
Neither you nor I nor anyone knows
How oats, peas, beans, and barley grows.

The Seeds Grow (Tune: Farmer in the Dell)
The gardener plants the seeds,
The gardener plants the seeds,
Deep down inside the ground,
The gardener plants the seeds.

The clouds bring the rain,
The clouds bring the rain,
Thirsty seeds need water to drink,
So, the clouds bring the rain.

The sun warms the earth,
The sun warms the earth.
Little seeds sleep below the ground,
And the sun warms the earth.

The gardener pulls the weeds,
The gardener pulls the weeds.
Little plants need room to grow,
So, the gardener pulls the weeds.

The seeds grow into flowers,
The seeds grow into flowers
Colorful, sweet, and oh, so neat—
The garden's full of flowers.

SEE ALSO

"Lazy Mary," page 96
"Mary Had a Little Lamb," page 114
"Miss Mary Mack," page 120

There Was a Little Girl (Mother Goose)
There was a little girl, and she had a little curl
Right in the middle of her forehead.
When she was good, she was very, very good,
But when she was bad, she was horrid.

Tiny Seeds
Tiny seed planted just right, (*tuck into a ball*)
Not a breath of air, not a ray of light.
Rain falls slowly to and fro,
And now the seed begins to grow. (*begin to unfold*)
Slowly reaching for the light,
With all its energy, all its might.
The little seed's work is almost done,
To grow up tall and face the sun. (*stand up tall with arms stretched out*)

White Coral Bells (Tune: Traditional)
White coral bells upon a slender stalk,
Lilies of the valley deck my garden walk.
Oh, don't you wish that you could hear them ring?
That will happen only when the fairies sing.

Follow-Up Questions

- *Have you ever helped plant a seed? What grew from your seed?*
- *What do flowers need in order to grow?*

STORY TIME SUGGESTIONS

Jack's Garden by Henry Cole
The Tiny Seed by Eric Carle

Language Enrichment

- Introduce words that may be new vocabulary for the children, such as *contrary, silver bells,* and *cockleshells.*
- Explain the line "pretty little maids all in a row." If possible, try and obtain a photo of flowers lined up in a flower bed to help the children understand the line better.
- Whisper the rhyme, but say the rhyming words out loud.

Extension Activities

Cognitive Development/ Construction

Flower Children

Cut out the centers of 8" paper plates and give one to each child. Cut out several different colors of flower petals from construction paper. Encourage the children to glue the paper petals around the perimeter of their plate to create a flower. Cut out long stems from green crepe paper and help the children glue the "stems" to the bottom of their plates. Make sure that the stems are long enough to reach the floor when the children hold the plates in front of their faces. After several children have finished making their flowers, ask them to stand in a row with their flowers in front of their faces. Point out that this illustrates the line of the rhyme that says "pretty little maids all in a row."

Cognitive and Social-Emotional Development/Outdoors

A Flower Bed of Our Own

With the children, prepare an outdoor area for a flower bed. Let the children plant a variety of quick-sprouting seeds such as marigolds and cosmos. Make sure they monitor the seeds on a regular basis and encourage them to water as needed. When the seeds begin to sprout, place a craft stick next to each plant. Demonstrate how to make a mark on the stick to show how much the plant has grown. Help the children do this each week. If an outdoor area is unavailable, plant seeds indoors using plastic cups, potting soil, and seeds.

Physical Development/Fine Motor

Seed Sweep

Provide birdseed, a scoop, a pastry brush, and a bowl or box. Spill the seeds on the table or on a vinyl mat. Challenge children to pick up the seeds by sweeping them with the pastry brush into the scoop and then dump them into the bowl or box. Discuss the seeds as the children attempt to sweep them. *What grows from the birdseed? How do birds eat the seeds? Why do the seeds roll when they are touched?*

Social-Emotional and Physical Development/Dramatic Play

Our Florist Shop

Provide plastic or silk flowers and greenery, Styrofoam blocks, and plastic vases and pots. Encourage the children to create floral arrangements. Discuss their choices of flowers and how they arrange the flowers. *Why do these flowers not have a smell? Which flower do you like best? Why? How many flowers are you using? Are all the flowers in your arrangement the same?*

Outdoor Play or Music and Movement

- Do the action rhyme, "Tiny Seeds," with the children (see page 118–119).
- Play a waltz and encourage the children to sway like flowers in the wind or blow like petals in the wind.
- Sing along with "Mary, Mary, Quite Contrary" (*Wee Sing Nursery Rhymes and Lullabies* CD, Price, Stern, Sloan), "Miss Mary Mack" (*You Sing a Song, I'll Sing a Song* CD, Smithsonian Folkways), "Miss Mary Mack" (*Five Little Monkeys* CD, Kimbo Educational), or "White Coral Bells" (*Wee Sing Sing Along Songs* CD, Price, Stern, Sloan).

REFLECTIONS ON THE DAY

- *What did you learn about seeds today?*
- *Can you remember the names of the flowers in* "Mary, Mary, Quite Contrary?"

Miss Mary Mack

Miss Mary Mack

Miss Mary Mack, Mack, Mack,
All dressed in black, black, black,
With silver buttons, buttons, buttons,
All down her back, back, back.
She asked her mother, mother, mother,
For fifteen cents, cents, cents,
To see the elephants, elephants, elephants,
Jump the fence, fence, fence.
They jumped so high, high, high,
They touched the sky, sky, sky
And they didn't come back, back, back,
Till the fourth of July, ly, ly.

And they didn't come down, down, down
Till the fourth of July.

SEE ALSO

"Five Little Monkeys," page 180
"Teddy Bear, Teddy Bear," page 188
"Tiny Tim," page 215

Related Songs, Chants, and Rhymes

I Like Black

I like black
Not yellow, red, or blue.
I like black
I bet you like it, too.
Blackbirds, black flowers,
Tall and shiny black towers.
Tiny black baby kittens
Warm and wooly black mittens.
Blackberries, black cherries,
Black socks, black rocks.
I like black
Not yellow, red, or blue.
I like black.

Risseldy, Rosseldy (Tune: Traditional)

I married my wife in the month of June,
Risseldy, rosseldy, mow, mow, mow,
I carried her off in a silver spoon,
Rosseldy, rosseldy, hey bambassity,
Nickety, nackety, retrical quality,
Willowby, wallowby, mow, mow, mow.

Follow-Up Questions

- *Do you have any clothes that are black?*
- *Why did Miss Mary Mack ask her mother for money?*

Language Enrichment

- Ask the children about buttons. *Who helps you with your buttons?*
- Demonstrate how to clap on the rhyming words that occur in sets of three (*Mack, Mack, Mack*, and *black, black, black*).
- Sing the song in a normal voice and whisper the rhyming words, or sing the song and stop on rhyming words for the children to fill in.

STORY TIME SUGGESTIONS

Miss Mary Mack by Joanna Cole
Miss Mary Mack by Mary Ann Hoberman

Extension Activities

Cognitive and Physical Development/Art

Black Paint

Provide non-toxic black paint and encourage the children to use it to paint pictures at the easel. *What can you paint with black paint? What things come in the color black? Do you like black?*

Physical and Cognitive Development/Games

Silver Button Toss

Provide silver buttons and a small box. Encourage the children to toss the buttons in the box. Have them start the game in a position that doesn't require tossing the button very far. After a while, challenge them to toss the button from a further distance.

Physical Development/Gross Motor

Elephant Jump

Make a fence using blocks. Encourage the children to jump the "fence." *How high can you jump? Can you jump higher if you run and then jump or can you jump higher if you stand still and jump? How high would you have to jump if you were trying to reach the sky?*

Social-Emotional Development/Dramatic Play

Black Dress Up

Put black clothing in the dramatic play center. Invite the children to dress in black. Provide items that button and encourage them to practice buttoning the clothing items. Provide a mirror and encourage the children to discuss their outfits.

REFLECTIONS ON THE DAY

- *How would the song be different if Miss Mary wore a red dress?*
- *How would it be different if she had a zipper in her dress instead of buttons?*

Outdoor Play or Music and Movement

- Provide drums and encourage the children to beat on the drums as they sing the song. Try singing the song and beating the drums only on rhyming words.
- Sing along with "Miss Mary Mack" (*Songs Children Love to Sing* CD, Smithsonian Folkways/Educational Activities).

Miss Polly Had a Dolly

Miss Polly Had a Dolly
(Tune: Traditional)
Miss Polly had a dolly
Who was sick, sick, sick,
So she called for the doctor
To be quick, quick, quick;
The doctor came
With his bag and his hat,
And he knocked at the door
With a rat-a-tat-tat.

He looked at the dolly
And he shook his head,
And he said, "Miss Polly,
Put her straight to bed."
He wrote out a paper
For a pill, pill, pill,
That'll make her better,
Yes it will, will, will!

Related Songs, Chants, and Rhymes

Floppy Rag Doll
(suit actions to words)
Flop your arms, flop your feet,
Let your hand go free.
You're the floppiest rag doll
I am ever going to see.

I've a Dear Little Dolly
I've a dear little dolly
And her eyes are bright blue.
She can open and shut them
And she smiles at me, too.
In the morning, I wake her
And I take her out to play.
But what I like best is to rock her
At the close of the day.

SEE ALSO

"Five Little Monkeys," page 180
"Teddy Bear, Teddy Bear," page 188
"Tiny Tim," page 215

Say, Say, My Playmate (Tune: Traditional)

Say, say my playmate,
Come out and play with me,
And bring your dollies three.
Climb up my apple tree.
Look down my rain barrel.
Slide down my cellar door,
And we'll be jolly friends
Forever more, 1-2-3-4.

I'm sorry, playmate.
I cannot play with you.
My dollies have the flu.
Boo-hoo hoo hoo hoo hoo.
Can't climb your rain barrel.
Can't slide down your cellar door.
But we'll be jolly friends,
Forever more, 1-2-3-4.

It was a rainy day,
She couldn't come out and play.
With tearful eyes, she breathed a sigh
And I could hear her say:

Follow-Up Questions

- *Have you ever been sick? What did your family do to help you feel better?*
- *What does the doctor do for you when you are sick?*

Language Enrichment

- Discuss dolls. Show the children some of the classroom dolls. *What kind of doll do you think Miss Polly had?*
- Sing the song and have the children clap on the rhyming words that occur in groups of three *(sick, sick, sick* and *quick, quick, quick*).
- Discuss medicine safety. Explain that they should never eat anything without asking an adult first. Tell them that taking medicine without an adult's help might make them sick.
- Remind the children that in the song, the doctor knocks on the door with a *rat-tat-tat.* Encourage the children to brainstorm other sounds to represent knocking,

STORY TIME SUGGESTION

Miss Polly Had a Dolly by Liz Pichon

Extension Activities

Cognitive Development/Science

Weigh and Measure

Weigh and measure each child. Talk about the tools you are using (scale and tape measure). Point out that their weight is measured in pounds, and their height is measured in feet and inches. Talk with them about being weighed and measured at the doctor's office. *Do you remember the doctor or nurse weighing you and measuring your height?*

Physical Development/Fine Motor

Open Wide

Draw a face on a coffee can lid and, if desired, add yarn hair. Cut a small slit near the mouth. Provide chips or buttons to use as "pills" and encourage the children to feed the "baby" his or her "pills." Talk with them as they play. Use this opportunity to reinforce safety issues related to medicine. **Safety Note:** Remind the children to never take medicine unless an adult is with them.

Physical Development/Gross Motor

Pill Drop

Provide 1" pompoms to use as pretend pills. Provide a tall cylinder such as a potato chip can to use as a pill bottle. Encourage the children to drop the "pills" (pompoms) into the "bottle." Invite them to begin playing this game by holding the pompom just over the top of the bottle and then challenge them to increase the distance from which they are dropping the pill.

Social-Emotional Development/Dramatic Play

The Doctor's In

Provide props for a doctor's office, such as a play stethoscope and thermometer, bandages, and any other items you can gather. Encourage the children to pretend to take care of the dolls. Talk with them as they play. *What's wrong with this baby? What can you do to help her? How did you know she was sick?*

Outdoor Play or Music and Movement

- Encourage the children to listen to their heartbeat with a stethoscope. Encourage them to exercise to some fast tempo music and then listen to their heartbeat again. *What is different about your heartbeat after you exercise?*
- Invite the children to act out "Five Little Monkeys" (see page 180). *What did the doctor say to the monkeys? What did he say to Miss Polly about her dolly?*
- Sing along with "Miss Polly Had a Dolly" (*Children's Sing Along Songs* CD, Kidzup) or "Playmate" (*Kids Song: My Favorite Kid Songs Collection* CD, Image Entertainment).

REFLECTIONS ON THE DAY

- *What did the doctor do to help Miss Polly's dolly feel better?*
- *What do you need to remember about taking medicine?*

The More We Get Together

The More We Get Together (Tune: Traditional)
The more we get together,
Together, together.
The more we get together,
The happier we'll be.

For your friends are my friends,
And my friends are your friends.
The more we get together,
The happier we'll be.

Related Songs, Chants, and Rhymes

Make New Friends (Tune: Traditional)
Make new friends
But keep the old.
One is silver
And the other's gold.

A Rig-a-Jig-Jig
As I was walking down the street,
Down the street, down the street,
A very good friend I chanced to meet,
Hi-ho, hi-ho, hi-ho!

A rig-a-jig-jig and away we go,
Away we go, away we go,
A rig-a-jig-jig and away we go,
Hi-ho, hi-ho, hi-ho!

Will You Be My Friend Today?
(Tune: Do You Know the Muffin Man?)
Will you be my friend today?
Friend today, friend today?
Will you be my friend today?
Do you want to play?

SEE ALSO

"For He's a Jolly Good Fellow," page 48
"Hello, Good Friend," page 48
"Little Jack Horner," page 176
"Simple Simon," page 176
"Sing a Song of Sixpence," page 176
"This is Quinn," page 49

Follow-Up Questions

- *Where do you play with your friends?*
- *How do you feel when you are with your friends?*

Language Enrichment

- Discuss friendship. *What does it mean to be a friend? Who are your friends? Are mommies and daddies your friends? Can you have more than one friend?*
- Ask the children what they do with their friends. *Is it more fun to play ball with a friend or alone?*
- Invite the children to help make a list of characteristics they like to find in a friend.
- Teach the children the American Sign Language sign for *friend* (see appendix page 239).

Extension Activities

Cognitive and Social-Emotional Development/Blocks

Partner Building

Ask the children to choose a partner to work with them to build a house. Talk with them as they build. *Is it nice to have two people thinking of ideas for the house?*

Physical and Social-Emotional Development/Fine Motor

Friendship Chains

Provide 1" x 12" strips of construction paper and paste or glue. Show the children how to make a paper chain. After each child has connected a few loops, help them add their loops to a common chain. Discuss how quickly the chain grows when everyone is working together.

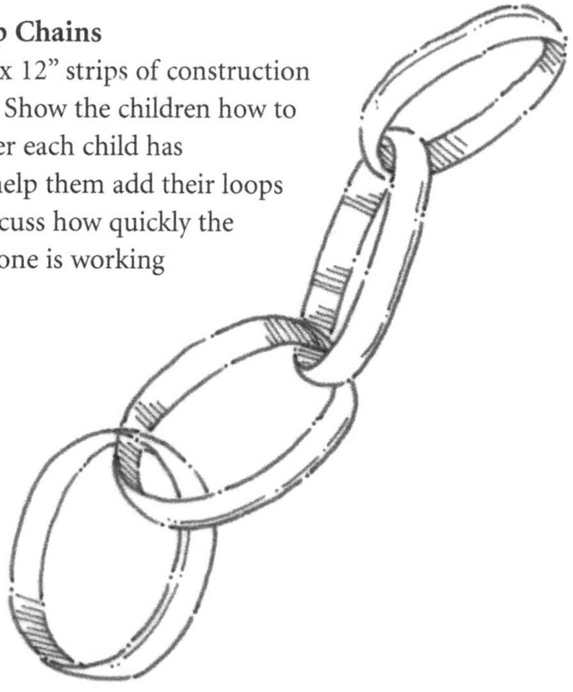

STORY TIME SUGGESTIONS

My Friend Rabbit by Eric Rohmann

Pepo and Lolo Are Friends by Ana Martin Larranaga

Physical and Social-Emotional Development/ Gross Motor

Pretzel Pass

Have children choose a partner. Give each child a straw. Show the children how to use their straws to remove a pretzel from a friend's straw. Talk with the children about working together to get a job done.

Social-Emotional Development/Art

Class Mural

Hang a piece of butcher paper on the wall. Provide crayons and encourage the children to make a group picture. *How does it feel to work with a friend? Does the work go faster?*

Outdoor Play or Music and Movement

- Play Pair, Think, and Share with older children. Divide the children into pairs. Show the children a letter "X" and encourage each pair to think of a way they can make the letter with their bodies. Try a "T, and if children do well, you might try showing them a "C" or an "O."
- Sing along with "The More We Get Together" (*Me, My Family and Friends* CD, Schiller Educational Resources, LLC) or "The More We Get Together" (*Singable Songs for the Very Young* CD, Raffi, Kimbo Educational).

REFLECTIONS ON THE DAY

- *Which activity did you enjoy most today?*
- *Where is your favorite place to be with your friends?*

Old King Cole

Old King Cole (Mother Goose) (Tune: Traditional)
Old King Cole was a merry old soul,
And a merry old soul was he.
He called for his pipe,
And he called for his bowl,
And he called for his fiddlers three.
Evr'y fiddler had a fiddle,
And a very fine fiddle had he.
Tweedle dee, tweedle dee,
Tweedle dee, tweedle dee,
Tweedle dee, tweedle dee,
Went the fiddlers three,
Oh, there's none so rare
As can compare,
With King Cole and his fiddlers three.

Related Songs, Chants, and Rhymes

The Queen of Hearts
The Queen of Hearts,
She made some tarts,
All on a summer's day.
The Knave of Hearts,
He stole those tarts,
And took them clean away.

The Queen of Hearts adapted by Pam Schiller
The Queen of Hearts,
She made some tarts,
All on a summer's day.
The King of Hearts,
He ate those tarts
And left an empty tray.

Family Music
Mother plays the tamborine, (*pretend to play instruments*)
Father plays the drum.
Little Tony plays the fiddle,
Tweedle-dee, tweedle-dee, tweedle-dum.
(*substitute the names of the children in the class—Little Justin…, Little Tasha…, etc.*)

SEE ALSO

"Hey, Diddle, Diddle," page 67
"Humpty Dumpty," page 73
"Lavender's Blue," page 95
"Nursery Rhyme Rap," page 15

Follow-Up Questions

- *Was Old King Cole happy or sad? How do you know?*
- *What kind of music did the fiddlers play? How did it sound?*
- *Do you think the music the fiddlers played help King Cole be merry?* (Tell the children that merry is the way they feel at a park when they are having fun!)

Language Enrichment

- Discuss the words that may be new vocabulary for the children, such as *merry, soul, bowl, fiddlers,* and *compare.* Discuss kings. *What do they do? What do they wear? Where do they live? Do kings marry queens?*
- Encourage the children to play with the words *tweedle dee, tweedle dee.* They might enjoy chanting the words as they clap or march.
- Say the rhyme while clapping softly until you get to a rhyming word. Clap a regular loud clap on all rhyming words.
- Recite the rhyme in a voice that gets louder and louder as you go.
- Discuss other sounds the fiddlers might make with their fiddles instead of "tweedle dee."

Extension Activities

Cognitive Development/Math

Three of This and Three of That!

Make Counting Mats. Print the numeral 3 in the center of the page on three or four sheets of construction paper. Use a margarine tub lid as a template to make five or six circles on the mat. Provide a bowl of small counters, blocks, cars, rattles, and so on. Give each child a counting mat. Invite them to count three items and put them into each circle on their mat. Younger children can just put items inside the circles. Talk with them as they work. *Is three more than two? Which number comes after three? Show me three fingers.*

STORY TIME SUGGESTIONS

Animal Orchestra by Scott Gustafson

I'm King of the Mountain by Joy Crowley

Physical Development/Blocks

Castles

Provide boxes in interesting sizes and shapes. Encourage the children to build a castle. If a picture of a castle is available, show it to the children. Younger children may simply stack the boxes to make a tower. Talk with them as they build. Provide vocabulary for castle architecture (moat, tower, dungeon, and turret).

Physical Development/Gross Motor

Crown Toss

Cut out a large crown from poster board and decorate it with glitter and sequins. Place it on the floor. Create a throw line with masking tape. Challenge the children to toss a beanbag onto the "crown." Younger children may simply drop the beanbag on the crown.

Social-Emotional Development/Dramatic Play

Here Comes the King

Turn a chair into a "throne." Provide a cape and a crown. Encourage the children to pretend to be kings.

Outdoor Play or Music and Movement

- Play some fiddle music and encourage the children to dance freely, or play marching music and invite the children to march like the king's soldiers. Hold younger children in your arms and dance or march.
- Sing along with "Old King Cole" (*Mother Goose Rocks, Vol. 2* CD, Light Years).

REFLECTIONS ON THE DAY

- *Do you think it would be fun to be a king? Why?*
- *Tell me about the castle you built.*

Old MacDonald Had a Farm

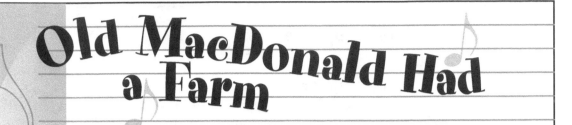

Old MacDonald Had a Farm (Tune: Traditional)
Old MacDonald had a farm, E-I-E-I-O
And on this farm she had a cow, E-I-E-I-O
With a moo, moo here,
And a moo, moo there,
Here a moo, there a moo,
Everywhere a moo, moo.
Old MacDonald had a farm, E-I-E-I-O!

Additional verses:
Pig —oink, oink
Cat —meow, meow
Dog —bow-wow
Horse —neigh, neigh

Related Songs, Chants, and Rhymes

SEE ALSO

"Bingo," page 231

Down on Grandpa's Farm (Tune: Traditional)
Down on Grandpa's farm there is a big brown cow.
Down on Grandpa's farm there is a big brown cow.
The cow it makes a sound like this: Moo! Moo!
The cow it makes a sound like this: Moo! Moo!

(Chorus)
Oh we're on our way, we're on our way,
On our way to Grandpa's farm.
Oh we're on our way, we're on our way,
On our way to Grandpa's farm.

Down on Grandpa's farm there is a little white duck.
Down on Grandpa's farm there is a little white duck.
The duck it makes a sound like this: Quack! Quack!
The duck it makes a sound like this: Quack! Quack!
(Chorus)

Additional verses:
Down on Grandpa's farm there is a big black horse…Neigh! Neigh!
Down on Grandpa's farm there are three yellow chicks...Cheep! Cheep!
Down on Grandpa's farm there are three pink pigs...Oink! Oink!

Down on Grandpa's farm there is a nice little cat...Meow! Meow!
Down on Grandpa's farm there is a little brown dog...Arf! Arf!
Down on Grandpa's farm there are two white sheep...Baa! Baa!

The Farmer in the Dell

(Directions: Choose one child to be the farmer. The rest of the children walk in a circle around the farmer. Sing the song together.)

The farmer in the dell,
The farmer in the dell.
Heigh-ho the derry-o,
The farmer in the dell.

Additional verses:
The farmer takes a wife/husband/friend... (*farmer chooses a second child to join her in the circle*)
The wife/husband/friend takes a child... (*wife chooses a third child to join in the circle, and so on*)
The child takes a dog...
The dog takes a cat...
The cat takes a rat...
The rat takes the cheese...
The cheese stands alone... (*everyone except the cheese leaves the center of the circle*)

Follow-Up Questions

- *What animals did Old MacDonald have on his farm? Did he have a giraffe?*
- *What sound does the pig make? What sound does the cow make?*

Language Enrichment

- Discuss the animals on Old MacDonald's farm. If available, show the children pictures of farm animals to stimulate conversation.
- Discuss the sounds that the animals on the farm make. Explain that these sounds are called *onomatopoeia.* This word seems large but the children will pick it up right away. Tell them that onomatopoeia refers to words that sound like the sound they are making. Good examples are found in this song and in "The Wheels on the Bus" (see page 225).
- Change "*E-I-E-I-O*" to "*A-U-A-U-O*." Try other letters. For older children, print the letters on chart paper so they can see the letters when they are singing. This activity is not intended to teach letters but is a meaningful way to build familiarity.
- Teach the children the American Sign Language signs for *cow, pig, sheep, cat, dog,* and/or *duck* (see appendix page 239).

STORY TIME SUGGESTIONS

Moo Baa La La La by Sandra Boynton
Old MacDonald Had a Farm by Pam Adams
Once Upon MacDonald's Farm by Stephen Gammell

Extension Activities

Cognitive Development/Listening

Animal Sounds

Record farm animal sounds on a cassette tape. Provide plastic farm animals or photos of farm animals. Play the tape and invite the children to find the animal that makes the sound they hear. For younger children, narrow the choice for each sound to two animals.

Cognitive and Social-Emotional Development/Blocks

Build a Farm

Provide plastic farm animals and props to build a farm. (You may want to build the farm for younger children.) Talk with the children as they build. *Where will the pigs live? How about the cows? Who lives in the barn?*

Physical and Cognitive Development/Art

Farm Animals

Provide farm animal-shaped sponges, non-toxic tempera paint, and drawing paper. Demonstrate how to use the sponges to make animal prints. Talk about the animals. *How many legs do they have? Where are their ears? Which animals have tails?*

Physical Development/Gross Motor

Animal Walks

Make a masking tape line on the floor. Show the children how to "waddle" like a duck, "saunter" like a pig or a cow, and "slink" like a cat. Encourage them to walk the line like a farm animal of their choice. Encourage younger children to walk the line holding a stuffed animal.

REFLECTIONS ON THE DAY

- *Which farm animal do you like best? What sound does it make?*
- *Who can show me how a duck walks?*

Outdoor Play or Music and Movement

- Sing "The Farmer in the Dell" (see page 133) and follow the directions to play the game.
- Sing along with "Old MacDonald Had a Farm" (*Six White Ducks* CD, Kimbo Educational), "Old MacDonald Had a Farm" (*Children's Favorite Songs, Vol. 1* CD, Disney), or "Down on Grandpa's Farm" (*The Bountiful Earth* CD, Schiller Educational Resources, LLC).

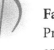

Old Mother Hubbard

Old Mother Hubbard (Mother Goose)
Old Mother Hubbard
Went to the cupboard
To get her poor dog a bone,
But when she came there
The cupboard was bare,
And so the poor dog had none.

She went to the hatter's
To buy him a hat
But when she came back
He was feeding the cat.

She went to the grocer's
To buy him some fruit,
But when she came back
He was playing the flute.

She went to the tailor's
To buy him a coat,
But when she came back
He was riding the goat.

She went to the cobbler's
To buy him some shoes,
But when she came back
He was reading the news.

Related Songs, Chants, and Rhymes

Fido (Tune: Traditional)
I have a little dog
And his name is Fido.
He is nothing but a pup.
He can stand up on his hind legs
If you hold his front legs up.

SEE ALSO

"Bingo," page 231
"The First Day of Summer," page 232
"Nursery Rhyme Rap," page 15
"This Old Man," page 205

My Dog Rags adapted by Pam Schiller (Tune: Five Little Ducks)
I have a dog and his name is Rags, (*point to self*)
He eats so much that his tummy sags, (*put hands together in front of stomach*)
His ears flip flop and his tail wig wags, (*bend each hand at wrist*)
And when he walks he zig, zig, zags! (*make an imaginary "Z" with index finger*)
Flip flop, wig wag, zig zag.
Flip flop, wig wag, zig zag.

My dog Rags he loves to play,
He rolls around in the mud all day,
I whistle for him but he won't obey,
He always runs the other way.
Flip flop, wig wag, hey, hey.
Flip flop, wig wag, hey, hey.

Whose Dog Are Thou? (Tune: Traditional)
Bow, wow, wow. (*face a partner and stomp three times*)
Whose dog are thou? (*point index finger on left and right hand at partner*)
Little Tommy Tucker's dog. (*hold hands out to side*)
Bow, wow, wow. (*face partner and stomp three times*)

Follow-Up Questions

- *Do you have a dog? What does your dog eat?*
- *How would the rhyme be different if Old Mother Hubbard had a cat instead of a dog?*

Language Enrichment

- Discuss words that may be new vocabulary for the children, including *cupboard, bare, hatter, flute, tailor,* and *cobbler.*
- Discuss dogs. Show the children pictures of dogs, if available, to stimulate discussion.
- Recite the rhyme, emphasizing the rhyming words.
- Teach the children the American Sign Language signs for *dog* and *none* (see appendix page 239).

Extension Activities

Cognitive Development/Games

Bone Puzzles
Cut out bone shapes from poster board. Cut each bone in half using a different puzzle cut. Encourage the children to work the bone puzzles. Talk with them as they work. *How do you know which pieces go together?* Older children will be able to put three-piece bones together.

STORY TIME SUGGESTIONS

Good Dog, Carl by Alexandra Day
The Pokey Little Puppy: The Hungry Puppies by Bruce Talkington

Physical Development/Fine Motor

Magnet Trail

Draw Old Mother Hubbard's house and a store on a piece of 12" x 15" poster board, connecting the two places with a line ("trail"). Glue the poster board to the top of a box. Cut out one side of the box. Draw a face on a 1 ½" circle of paper to represent Old Mother Hubbard. Attach a strip of magnetic tape to the back of the face. Show the children how to use a magnet under the box to move the face from Mother Hubbard's home to the store. If working from under the box is too difficult, show them how to move the face on the top by hold their magnet just in front of the face.

Physical Development/Gross Motor

Bone Toss

Provide a dog dish and rubber or plastic dog bones (or cut out dog bone shapes from poster board or cardboard). Make a throw line by placing a strip of masking tape on the floor. Challenge the children to toss the bones into the bowl. As the children become proficient, move the dish further from the throw line. For younger children, make a masking tape circle to represent a bowl and have them drop or toss the bone in the circle.

Social-Emotional Development/Dramatic Play

Grocery Match

Fill the dramatic play center with pairs of empty boxes and empty cans. If possible, include clean, empty dog food cans and dog biscuit boxes. Encourage the children to match the pairs of cans and boxes. Talk with them about how they know which items go together. Younger children will enjoy putting the groceries on the shelves. **Safety Note:** Make sure there are no sharp edges on the cans.

Outdoor Play or Music and Movement

- Play a modified version of Dog and Bone. Have the children sit in a circle. One child ("IT") walks around the outside of the circle, carrying a paper or plastic bone. IT drops the bone behind one of the children. That child picks up the bone and barks. The child with the bone is the new IT. Continue the game until every child has had a turn. (The children may need help choosing a child who has not had a turn.)
- Play Follow the Leader. Crawl around on the floor pretending to be a dog. Stop and smell things. Pretend to drink some water, bark, pant, and roll over.
- Sing "Whose Dog Are Thou?" or "My Dog Rags" (see page 136) and invite the children to do the movements that go with the songs.
- Sing along with "Old Mother Hubbard" (*Mother Goose Rocks, Vol. 2* CD, Light Years).

REFLECTIONS ON THE DAY

- *Would you like to have a dog for a pet? Why?*
- *What do dogs like to eat?*

One Elephant

One Elephant (Tune: Traditional)
One elephant went out to play
Out on a spider's web one day.
He had such enormous fun,
He called for another elephant to come.

Additional verses:
Two elephants went out to play...
Three elephants went out to play...
Four elephants went out to play...
Five elephants went out to play...

(**Directions**: *Children sit in a circle. Choose one child to be the "elephant." She places one arm out in front to make a trunk, and then walks around the circle while the group sings the song. When the group sings, "Called for another elephant to come," the child chooses another to become an "elephant." The second child extends one arm to make a trunk and grabs hold of the first child's waist with the other hand. The second child selects a third child and the game continues. If the children have trouble holding onto each other, have them walk in a line swinging their "trunks."*)

Related Songs, Chants, and Rhymes

Elephant
Right foot, left foot, see me go. (*put weight on right foot first, then left foot*)
I am gray and big and slow. (*sway side to side*)
I come walking down the street (*put weight on right foot first, then left foot*)
With my trunk and four big feet. (*use arm to make a trunk*)

The Elephant Goes
The elephant goes like this, like that. (*move on all fours slowly like an elephant*)
He's terribly big, (*stand up, reach arms high*)
And he's terribly fat.(*stretch arms out to the sides*)
He has no fingers, (*make fists, hiding fingers*)
He has no toes, (*wiggle toes*)
But goodness gracious,
What a nose! (*point to nose*)

SEE ALSO

"Animal Fair," page 155
"Miss Mary Mack," page 120

Follow-Up Questions

- *Have you ever seen a real elephant? Where?*
- *What does the elephant do with his trunk?*

Language Enrichment

- Discuss the word *enormous.* Most children will not be familiar with this word. Give examples of things that are enormous.
- Talk about elephants. If you have a picture of an elephant, show it to the children to stimulate conversation. *What color are elephants? How is their nose different from a dog's nose? How are their feet different from a cat's feet? What kind of ears do elephants have?*
- Ask children what they think would happen if an elephant stepped on a spider's web. Discuss the size difference in a spider web and an elephant's foot.
- Teach the children the American Sign Language signs for *elephant* and *spider* (see appendix page 239).

Extension Activities

Cognitive Development/Science

Big Ears

Provide pictures of different animals and help the children decide whether the animal has large or small ears. Be sure to include a picture of an elephant. (African elephants have larger ears than Asian elephants.)

Physical Development/Fine Motor

Gray Dough

Make gray playdough by mixing a few drops of red, yellow, blue, and green food coloring in your favorite playdough recipe. Show the children how to roll the dough into long snakes that look like an elephant's trunk. Talk with them as they work. Tell them that the playdough is the same color as an elephant's skin. Wad up a piece of aluminum foil, open it, and press it on top of a flat piece of dough (pancake shape) to create wrinkles. Point out that an elephant's skin has wrinkles.

Physical Development/Gross Motor

Spider Web Maze

Make a web maze using white yarn. Invite the children to crawl through the maze. As they crawl through the maze, discuss its likeness to a spider web. *What happens if you hit the yarn?*

STORY TIME SUGGESTION

Elephant on the Loose by Kim Watson

Social-Emotional Development/Dramatic Play

Swing Your Trunk

String three empty toilet paper tubes together. Punch two holes in the end of each tube and tie the tubes together loosely with yarn. Show the children how to hold the tube to their nose and pretend it is an elephant's trunk. Show them how to turn their head to make the truck swing. *Can you swing your trunk like an elephant?* Show them how to lift the trunk upward. *Can you make your trunk trumpet?* (Explain what this means.)

Outdoor Play or Music and Movement

- Invite the children to sing and play "One Elephant."
- Provide a light source such as a flashlight or an overhead projector. Have the children stand between the light source and a wall to create a shadow. Show them how to use their hands to make their shadow have elephant ears and their arm to make their shadow look like it has a trunk.
- Invite the children to move like elephants with "The Elephant" (*Learning Basic Skills Through Music, Vol. 1* CD, Educational Activities).
- Sing along with "One Elephant" (*Critters and Company* CD, Schiller Educational Resources, LLC) or "One Elephant (*Where Is Thumbkin?* CD, Kimbo Educational).

REFLECTIONS ON THE DAY

- *What can elephants do with their trunks?*
- *Can you think of an animal that is bigger than an elephant?*

One, Two, Buckle My Shoe

One, Two, Buckle My Shoe
One, two, buckle my shoe.
Three, four, shut the door.
Five, six, pick up sticks.
Seven, eight, lay them straight.
Nine, ten, a big fat hen.

Related Songs, Chants, and Rhymes

Counting Rhyme
One, two, three, four, five,
I caught a fish alive.
Six, seven, eight, nine, ten,
I let it go again.

Higgildy Piggildy
Higgildy Piggildy, my black hen!
She lays eggs for gentlemen.
Sometimes nine and
sometimes ten,
Higgildy Piggildy, my
black hen!

One Potato, Two Potato
(*make two fists, alternate tapping one on top of the other*)
One potato, two potato,
Three potato, four,
Five potato, six potato,
Seven potato, more.
Eight potato, nine potato,
Where is ten?
Now we must count over again.

Follow-Up Questions

- *Does anyone have shoes with buckles?*
- *Can you count? Let's count together.*

SEE ALSO

"The Ants Go Marching," page 22
"Five Little Ducks," page 183
"Five Little Monkeys," page 180
"This Old Man," page 205

Language Enrichment

- Discuss shoes. Talk about different ways to fasten shoes (*shoelaces, Velcro, buckles,* and so on).
- Invite the children to clap with the rhyme.
- After the children are familiar with the rhyme, let them fill in the second word in a rhyming word pair.
- Teach the children the American Sign Language sign for *hen* (see appendix page 239).

Extension Activities

Cognitive Development/Math

Magnetic Numerals

Give the children magnetic numerals and a magnetic board or a cookie sheet. Encourage them to play with the numbers. Talk with them as they play. Say the rhyme and point to the numerals as they are mentioned in the rhyme.

Pysical Development/Fine Motor

Straight Sticks

Give the children several sticks and ask them to lay the sticks in a row. Talk with them as they work. Say the rhyme. Explain that "lay them straight" means to lay them in a row. Invite younger children to pick up the sticks and place them in a can or box.

Social-Emotional Development/Games

Feather Blowing

Give the children feathers to play with. Place feathers on a table and show the children how to move them by blowing. Remind the children that hens are covered with feathers. Discuss how to make the feathers move further. *Can you blow the feather off the table?*

Social-Emotional and Physical Development/Dramatic Play

Shoes, Shoes, Shoes

Fill the center with shoes. Make sure to include some that buckle. Invite the children to try on the shoes. Help older children work the buckles.

STORY TIME SUGGESTION

Big Fat Hen by Keith Baker

Outdoor Play or Music and Movement

- Invite the children to march around the room while reciting "One, Two, Buckle My Shoe."
- Sing along with "One, Two Buckle My Shoe" (*Five Little Monkeys* CD, Kimbo Educational) or "Buckle My Shoe" (*Early Childhood Classics: Old Favorites With a New Twist* CD, Hap-Pal Music).

REFLECTIONS ON THE DAY

- *How do your shoes fasten?*
- *How did you move the feathers? What animal has feathers?*

Open, Shut Them

Open, Shut Them (Tune: Traditional)
Open, shut them. (*hold hands up and open and close fingers*)
Open, shut them.
Give a little clap. (*clap*)

Open, shut them. (*hold hands up and open and close fingers*)
Open, shut them.
Put them in your lap. (*place hands in lap*)

Walk them, walk them, (*walk fingers up chest to chin*)
Walk them, walk them.
Way up to your chin.
Walk them, walk them, (*walk fingers around face, but not into mouth*)
Walk them, walk them,
But don't let them walk in.

Related Songs, Chants, and Rhymes

The Finger Band (Tune: Here We Go 'Round the Mulberry Bush)
The finger band has come to town,
Come to town, come to town,
The finger band has come to town
Oh, what a lovely sound.

The finger band can play the drums,
Play the drums, play the drums,
The finger band can play the drums
Oh, what a lovely sound.

Additional verses:
The finger band can play the guitar…
The finger band can play the flute…
The finger band can play the piano…
The finger band can play the trombone…
The finger band can play the violin…

The finger band has gone away,
Gone away, gone away,
The finger band has gone away
We'll miss that lovely sound.

SEE ALSO

"Clap, Clap, Clap Your Hands," page 148
"Clap Your Hands," page 148
"Dance, Thumbkin, Dance," page 228
"Pat-a-Cake," page 148
"Sing a Song of Opposites," page 174
"Where Is Thumbkin?," page 228

Five Fingers on Each Hand

(suit actions to words)

I have five fingers on each hand,
Ten toes on my two feet.
Two ears, two eyes,
One nose, one mouth,
With which to sweetly speak.

My hands can clap, my feet can tap,
My eyes can clearly see.
My ears can hear,
My nose can sniff,
My mouth can say, "I'm me."

Five Little Fingers

One little finger standing on its own. (*hold up index finger*)
Two little fingers, now they're not alone. (*hold up middle finger*)
Three little fingers happy as can be. (*hold up ring finger*)
Four little fingers go walking down the street. (*hold up all fingers*)
Five little fingers. This one is a thumb. (*hold up four fingers and thumb*)
Wave bye-bye 'cause now we are done. (*wave bye-bye*)

Ten Little Fingers

I have ten little fingers, (*hold up ten fingers*)
And they all belong to me. (*point to self*)
I can make them do things. (*wiggle fingers*)
Do you want to see? (*tilt head*)

I can make them point. (*point*)
I can make them hold. (*hold fingertips together*)
I can make them dance (*dance fingers on arm*)
And then I make them fold. (*fold hands in lap*)

STORY TIME SUGGESTION

Hand, Hand, Finger, Thumb by Al Perkins

Follow-Up Questions

- *Where are your fingers when your hands are open? Where are your fingers when your hands are shut?*
- *Can you think of something else on your body that you can open and shut?*

Language Enrichment

- Discuss the many things our hands can do.
- Talk about things that open and shut. Show the children items that open and shut, for example, books, boxes, bottle and jars, lockets, change purses, and pots with lids. After you have shown and discussed the items, place them in a center for further exploration.
- Talk about the word *creep*. Discuss things that *creep*, such as snails, turtles,

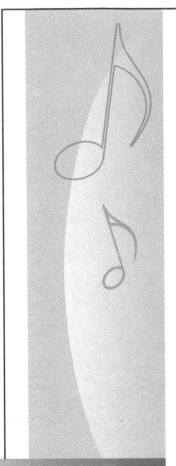

and caterpillars. Ask a volunteer to demonstrate the difference between walking and creeping. Ask another volunteer to demonstrate the difference between running and walking.

Extension Activities

Cognitive Development/Blocks

Building With and Without Fingers

Encourage the children to pick up blocks with their fingers tucked into a fist. Talk with them about how using their hands without their fingers is different from using their hands with their fingers. If mittens are available, have the children try building with mittens on.

Physical and Social-Emotional Development/Language

Creepy Crawlies

Teach the children "Caterpillar." Creep your fingers up children's arms as you recite the following rhyme:

"Who's that tickling my back?" said the wall.
"Me," said a small caterpillar, "I'm learning to crawl!"

Make a masking tape path on a tabletop. Invite children to creep their fingers like caterpillars crawling up the wall.

Physical Development/Discovery

Things That Open and Close

Provide a variety of items that open and close, such as clean water bottles (with screw-on lids and/or sports bottles), hinged boxes, margarine containers, and small boxes. Discuss the items as children play with them. Point out hinges, clasps, and so on.

Physical Development/Fine Motor

Playdough Creations

Provide playdough and encourage the children to roll it, pinch it, and pat it. Talk about the parts of the hands used for each activity. *How do you break the dough apart? Which part of your hands do you use to roll the dough? How does the dough feel? Is it smooth?*

Outdoor Play or Music and Movement

- Blow bubbles. Encourage the children to pop the bubbles using their open hands. Talk about methods they might use, including swatting, slapping, and knocking.
- Sing along with "Open, Shut Them" (*Me, My Family and Friends* CD, Schiller, Educational Resources, LLC), "Open, Shut Them" (*Preschool Action Time* CD, Kimbo Educational), or "Open, Shut Them" (*Early Childhood Classics: Old Favorites With a New Twist* CD, Hap-Pal Music).

REFLECTIONS ON THE DAY

- *Who can show me how you hold your hands when you are making a fist?*
- *Tell me something you use your hands to do.*

Pat-a-Cake

Pat-a-Cake

Pat-a-cake, pat-a-cake, baker's man. (*clap hands together*)
Bake me a cake as fast as you can.
Roll it, (*roll hands over each other*)
And pat it, (*pat hands together*)
And mark it with B, (*draw B in the air*)
And put it in the oven for baby and me. (*point to a child or tickle child's tummy*)

Related Songs, Chants, and Rhymes

Clap, Clap, Clap Your Hands

Clap, clap, clap your hands
As slowly as your can.
Clap, clap, clap, your hands
As quickly as you can.

Additional verses:
Roll, roll, roll your hands…
Shake, shake, shake your hands…
Pound, pound, pound your fist…

Clap Your Hands

(suit movements to words)
Clap your hands 1-2-3.
Clap your hands just like me.

Wiggle your fingers 1-2-3.
Wiggle your fingers just like me.

My Hands

On my head my hands I place. (*place hands on head*)
On my shoulders, (*place hands on shoulders*)
On my face, (*place hands on face*)
On my hips, (*place hands on hips*)
And at my side, (*drop hands to sides*)
Then behind me they will hide, (*hide hands behind back*)
I will hold them up so high, (*raise hands high above head*)
Quickly make my fingers fly, (*wiggle fingers*)
Hold them out in front of me, (*hands in front of body, arms extended*)
Swiftly clap them. One, two, three! (*clap, clap, clap*)

SEE ALSO

"Dance, Thumbkin, Dance," page 228
"If You're Happy and You Know It," page 77
"Open, Shut Them," page 145
"Thelma Thumb," page 229
"Where Is Thumbkin?," page 228

Follow-Up Questions

- *Do you like to eat cake?*
- *Have you ever watched someone make a cake?*

Language Enrichment

- Tell each child which letter you would mark the cake with if you were making the cake for him and wanted to use the first letter of his name. During the day, say the rhyme with the children individually and customize the words.
- Talk about making a cake. *What ingredients do you need? How do you mix the cake? How do you cook it?*

Extension Activities

Cognitive Development/Games

Cake Pan Puzzles

Find simple posters or pages from coloring books to use as puzzles. Cut the perimeter of the puzzle to fit inside a cake pan (8" round pans and 11" x 13" oblong pans work well). Laminate the picture and cut it into simple puzzle pieces. Younger children may only be able to handle two- or three-piece puzzles. Invite the children to work the puzzles inside the cake pans. Talk with them as they work. Make sure they recognize their puzzle tray as a cake pan.

Cognitive and Physical Development/Writing

Pat-a-Cake

Provide playdough, rolling pins, and magnetic letters. Demonstrate how to roll the dough and use a magnetic letter to mark it with the first letter of their names. Show each child the first letter of his name and then place it with two or three other letters and challenge him to pick it out.

Physical Development/Art

Rolling Pin Paint Designs

Provide thick, non-toxic tempera paint, paper, and a rolling pin. Help the children spoon several colors of thick tempera paint on their papers. Cover their papers with a second sheet of paper and encourage them to use the rolling pin to roll over the papers. When they are finished, separate the papers to reveal their paint designs. Talk with them about their creations. *What colors did you use? How do you like the design? How did you make this design?*

STORY TIME SUGGESTIONS

Pat-a-Cake by Joanna Cole

Pat-a-Cake by Tony Kenyon

Social-Emotional Development/Dramatic Play

Baker Shop

Provide props for pretend cake making, including bowls, spoons, empty cake boxes, egg cartons with plastic eggs, empty milk cartons, and aprons. You can use shredded paper for pretend batter. Talk about baking a cake as the children pretend to make a cake.

Outdoor Play or Music and Movement

- Show the children how to pretend to be rolling pins. Have them lie on the floor and roll like logs. Encourage older children to place their hands over their head and roll.
- Make Clappers for each child. Cut a 1" x 12" strip of paper. Tape a penny or a small washer to each end of the strip. Fold it in half and staple it over a tongue depressor. When the Clappers are wiggled back and forth they make a great clapping sound. Play some music and encourage the children to keep the beat by clapping their Clappers.

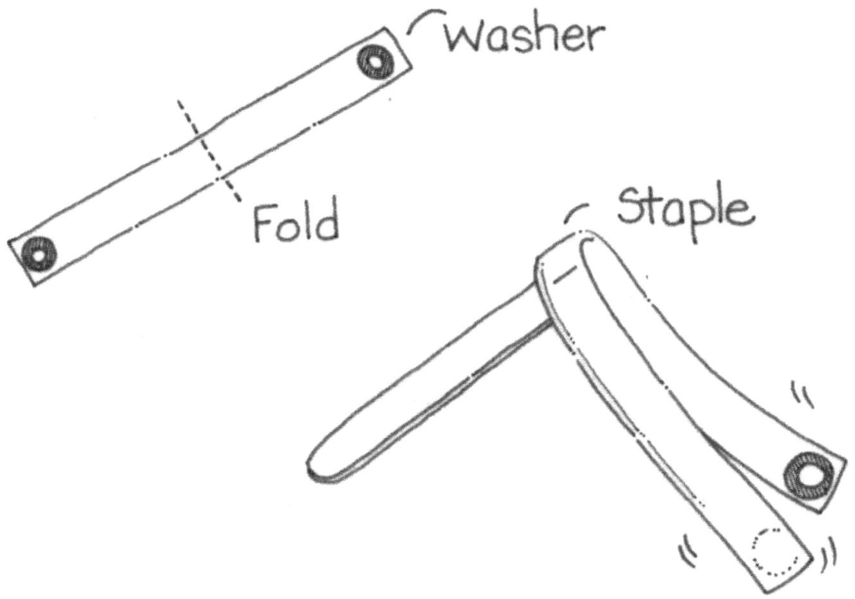

- Chant along with "Pat-a-Cake" (*Mother Goose Rocks, Vol. 1* CD, Light Years) or "Pat-a-Cake" (*Wee Sing Nursery Rhymes and Lullabies* CD, Price, Stern, Sloan).

REFLECTIONS ON THE DAY

- *Which letter would you use to mark a cake that was just for you?*
- *How do you make dough flat?*

Peanut Butter and Jelly

Peanut Butter and Jelly (Tune: Traditional)
Chorus:
Peanut, peanut butter—jelly!
Peanut, peanut butter—jelly!

First you take the peanuts and (*pretend to dig peanuts*)
You dig 'em, you dig 'em.
Dig 'em, dig 'em, dig 'em.
Then you smash 'em, you smash 'em. (*pretend to smash peanuts*)
Smash 'em, smash 'em, smash 'em.
Then you spread 'em, you spread 'em. (*pretend to spread the peanuts*)
Spread 'em, spread 'em, spread 'em.

(Chorus)

Then you take the berries and (*pretend to pick berries*)
You pick 'em, you pick 'em.
Pick 'em, pick 'em, pick 'em.
Then you smash 'em, you smash 'em. (*pretend to smash berries*)
Smash 'em, smash 'em, smash 'em.
Then you spread 'em, you spread 'em. (*pretend to spread berries*)
Spread 'em, spread 'em, spread 'em.

(Chorus)

Then you take the sandwich and (*pretend to bite a sandwich*)
You bite it, you bite it.
Bite it, bite it, bite it.
Then you chew it, you chew it. (*pretend to chew a sandwich*)
Chew it, chew it, chew it.
Then you swallow it, you swallow it. (*pretend to swallow peanut butter sandwich*)
Swallow it, swallow it, swallow it.

(Hum chorus)

SEE ALSO

"Do You Know the Muffin Man?," page 41
"Hot Cross Buns," page 41
"Oats, Peas, Beans, and Barley," page 117
"Peas, Porridge Hot," page 101
"The Raindrop Song," page 159

Related Songs, Chants, and Rhymes

Chew, Chew, Chew Your Food by Pam Schiller
(Tune: Row, Row, Row Your Boat)
Chew, chew, chew your food
A little at a time.
Chew it slow, chew it well,
Chew it to this rhyme.

Drink, Drink, Drink Your Milk by Pam Schiller
(Tune: Row, Row, Row Your Boat)
Drink, drink, drink your milk
A little at a time.
Drink it slow, drink it fast,
Drink it to this rhyme.

Go Bananas!
Ready! OK!
Bananas unite! (*put hands together over head*)
Bananas split! (*hands at side*)

Go bananas!
Go, go bananas!
Go bananas!
Go, go bananas!
(*turn in circle, moving arms up and down during these four lines*)

Bananas to the left! (*point left*)
Bananas to the right! (*point right*)

Peel your banana and, mmm, you take a bite! (*motion of peeling banana and eating it*)

Go bananas!
Go, go bananas!
Go bananas!
Go, go bananas!
Go bananas!
Go, go bananas!
Go!

I Like Peanut Butter and Jelly by Pam Schiller
(Tune: London Bridge Is Falling Down)
I like jelly on my bread, on my bread, on my bread.
I like jelly on my bread. Bread and jelly!

I like ice cream with my cake, with my cake, with my cake.
I like ice cream with my cake. Cake and ice cream!

I like ketchup with my fries, with my fries, with my fries.
I like ketchup with my fries. Fries and ketchup!

Follow-Up Questions

- *Why do we hum the part of the song after we chew the sandwich? What happens when you get too much peanut butter in your mouth?*
- *Which do you like better, peanut butter or jelly? Why?*

Language Enrichment

- Discuss the steps in preparing a peanut butter and jelly sandwich. *What do you do first? What do you use to spread the peanut butter?*
- Show the children a peanut in a shell. Remove the shell of the peanut. Explain that peanuts can be made into peanut butter. Older children may be interested in how. **Safety Note:** If any of the children have peanut allergies, do not use a real peanut.
- Talk about peanut butter and jelly sandwiches. *Do you like to eat peanut butter and jelly? What kind of jelly do you like?*

Extension Activities

Safety Note: Before doing any of the following activities, be certain that none of the children has a sensitivity or allergy to peanuts.

Cognitive and Physical Development/Math

Lid and Jar Match
Provide several empty, clean plastic peanut butter and jelly jars and lids. Take off all the lids. Encourage the children to match the jars to the lids and screw the lids back onto the jars. Use only two jars with younger children.

Physical Development/Fine Motor

Peanut Drop
If you have the tools to cut a 1" diameter hole in the top of a peanut butter jar, do so. If not, cut a 1" diameter hole in the lid of a whipped topping container. Place the lid back onto the bowl. Provide real peanuts or paper cutouts and encourage the children to drop the peanuts into the bowl or the jar.

STORY TIME SUGGESTIONS

Peanut Butter and Jelly: A Play Rhyme by Nadine Bernard Wescott
The Peanut Butter and Jelly Game by Adam Eisenson

Physical Development/Games

Peanut Search

Place peanuts in the shell in the sand table. Provide strainers and encourage the children to find the peanuts by sifting through the sand. Talk with the children as they search. *Why do you think the sand goes through the strainer but the peanut doesn't? What shape is a peanut? What is inside the shell? How many peanuts might be inside?*

Social-Emotional Development/Snack

PB & Js

Invite the children to help make peanut butter and jelly sandwiches. Explain why they are also called "PB & J" sandwiches. Discuss the steps to follow to make the sandwiches. Talk about the textures of the ingredients. Serve the sandwiches for snack or lunch.

Outdoor Play or Music and Movement

- Encourage the children to attempt to walk with a peanut on their heads. Ask them to try walking with a peanut on the backs of their hands. Modify where they carry the peanut based on their ability.
- Sing along with "Peanut Butter and Jelly" (*Fabulous Foods* CD, Schiller Educational Resources, LLC), "Peanut Butter and Jelly" (*Where Is Thumbkin?* CD, Kimbo Educational), or "Peanut Butter and Jelly" (*Fun and Games* CD, Greg and Steve Productions).
- Chant along with "Go Bananas!" (*Fabulous Foods* CD, Schiller Educational Resources, LLC).

REFLECTIONS ON THE DAY

- *What did you learn about peanuts today?*
- *How do you make a peanut butter and jelly sandwich?*

Pop! Goes the Weasel

Pop! Goes the Weasel (Tune: Traditional)
All around the cobbler's bench
The monkey chased the weasel.
The monkey thought 'twas all in fun—
Pop! Goes the weasel.

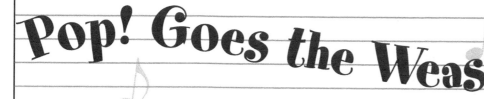

Johnny has the whooping cough,
Mary has the measles.
That's the way the money goes—
Pop! Goes the weasel.

A penny for a spool of thread
A penny for a needle.
That's the way the money goes—
Pop! Goes the weasel.

All around the mulberry bush,
The monkey chased the weasel.
That's the way the money goes—
Pop! Goes the weasel.

SEE ALSO

"Five Little Monkeys," page 180

Related Songs, Chants, and Rhymes

Animal Fair
I went to the animal fair,
The birds and the beasts were there.
The big baboon by the light of the moon
Was combing his auburn hair.
You should have seen the monk!
He sat on the elephant's trunk.
The elephant sneezed and fell on her knees.
And what became of the monk,
The monk, the monk, the monk?

Gray Squirrel (Tune: Traditional)
Gray squirrel, gray squirrel, (*stand with hands on bent knees*)
Swish your bushy tail. (*wiggle your behind*)
Gray squirrel, gray squirrel, (*stand with hands on bent knees*)
Swish your bushy tail. (*wiggle your behind*)
Wrinkle up your funny nose, (*wrinkle nose*)
Hold an acorn in your toes. (*pinch index and thumb fingers together*)
Gray squirrel, gray squirrel, (*stand with hands on bent knees*)
Swish your bushy tail. (*wiggle your behind*)

(additional verse by Richele Bartkowiak)
Gray squirrel, gray squirrel,
Swish your bushy tail.
Gray squirrel, gray squirrel,
Swish your bushy tail.
Balance on that telephone wire.
Don't look down when you get higher.
Gray squirrel, gray squirrel,
Swish your bushy tail.

Follow-Up Questions

- *Who is chasing the weasel?*
- *What is a weasel?*

STORY TIME SUGGESTIONS

Here We Go 'Round the Mulberry Bush by Annie Kubler and Pam Adams
Monkey See, Monkey Do by Marc Gave

Language Enrichment

- Discuss words that may be new vocabulary to the children, such as *weasel, cobbler, whooping cough, measles, penny, spool of thread,* and *needle.*
- Use the melody of the song but replace the words with the syllable *da* until you get to the word *pop*. Have the children say *pop*, and then continue with *da*. Do the children anticipate the place in the melody where *pop* would be?
- Discuss things that make a *pop* sound. Examples include a balloon popping, a bottle of carbonated water or soda when the lid is removed, a bubble on bubble wrap popping, a door closing, and so on.

Extension Activities

Cognitive Development/Art

Spool Prints
Provide a tray of non-toxic paint and some spools. Show the children how to press the spools into the paint and then on their paper to make spool prints. Talk about the shapes of the spool prints. *What shape is in the center of the spool print?*

Physical and Cognitive Development/Listening

Pop! Goes the Weasel

Provide several Jack-in-the Boxes for the children to explore. *What song is playing? When does the Jack pop up? How does the Jack in the Box work?* Provide a box and a small blanket or towel for children to pretend to be a Jack in the Box. Have a child squat inside the box. Play "Pop! Goes the Weasel" on a tape or CD. The child in the box emerges from the box on cue ("Pop!"). *How do you know when to pop up?* Help younger children identify the cue.

Physical Development/Fine Motor

Spool Roll

Give the children spools and a flat surface on which to roll them. Create a small ramp so that children can explore rolling the spools down a slope. Demonstrate ways to get the spools to roll. *Can you push them with a straw? Can you shove them with your fingers? Do you need to encourage the spool to roll down the slope?*

Social-Emotional Development/Dramatic Play

Shoes of Every Kind

Provide a variety of shoes (slippers, boots, dance shoes, heels, sandals, sneakers, rain boots) for the children to explore. Discuss the shoes. Provide the correct name for the shoes, for example, *galoshes*, *ballet shoes*, *high heels*, and so on. Encourage the children to try on the shoes and to walk in them. Mention that a *cobbler* is a person who makes or repairs shoes. Talk about the materials shoes are made from. You might even want to discuss the parts of the shoe, such as *sole*, *heel*, *tongue*, *laces*, and so on.

Outdoor Play or Music and Movement

- Play Chase the Weasel. Select one child to be a weasel and invite the rest of the children to pretend to be monkeys. Have the monkeys chase the weasel. When the weasel is caught, she becomes a monkey and the monkey who caught her becomes the new weasel.
- Sing along with "Pop! Goes the Weasel" (*Four Baby Bumblebees* CD, Kimbo Educational) or "Gray Squirrel" (*Where Is Thumbkin?* CD, Kimbo Educational)

REFLECTIONS ON THE DAY

- *What did you do with spools today?*
- *Which shoes did you like the best?*

Rain, Rain, Go Away

Rain, Rain, Go Away (Tune: Traditional)
Rain, rain, go away.
Come again another day.
Clouds, clouds, go away.
Little children want to play.
Thunder, thunder, go away.
Little children want to play.
Rain, rain, come back soon.
Little flowers want to bloom.

Related Songs, Chants, and Rhymes

Four Seasons Have We by Pam Schiller
Winter comes…
Quietly the snow comes drifting down,
Over the treetops to the ground,
Silently it falls all around,
Twirling and whirling to the ground.

Spring comes…
Gently the rain sprinkles the earth,
Animals and flowers give birth,
Trees and grass turn brilliant green,
The earth is a colorful scene.

Summer comes…
Brightly the sun shines from the sky
Warming the earth by and by,
Children play on sunny beaches
Grandpa picks a bushel of peaches.

Fall comes…
Playfully leaves fall to the ground,
The earth turns from green to brown,
Chilly winds send winter's warning
Every day a frosty morning.

SEE ALSO

"Cap, Mittens, Coat, and Boots," page 35
"Itsy Bitsy Spider," page 80

It Ain't Gonna Rain No More
(Tune: Peanut Sitting on a Railroad Track)
It ain't gonna rain no more, no more,
It ain't gonna rain no more.
How in the heck will we wash our neck
If it ain't gonna rain no more?

It's Raining, It's Pouring (Tune: Traditional)
It's raining, it's pouring.
The old man is snoring.
He went to bed and he bumped his head,
And he couldn't get up in the morning.

It's raining, it's pouring.
Playing inside is boring.
We want sunshine and bright blue skies,
Don't make us wait 'til morning.

Raindrop Song (Tune: Traditional)
If all the raindrops (*wiggle fingers in the air*)
Were lemon drops and gumdrops, (*tap one index finger against palm of other hand*)
Oh, what a rain that would be! (*wiggle fingers in the air*)
Standing outside, with my mouth open wide.
Ah-ah-ah-ah-ah-ah-ah-ah-ah-ah! (*stand, looking up with mouth open*)
If all the raindrops
Were lemon drops and gumdrops,
Oh, what a rain that would be!

If all the snowflakes (*repeat actions as above*)
Were candy bars and milkshakes,
Oh, what a snow that would be!
Standing outside, with my mouth open wide.
Ah-ah-ah-ah-ah-ah-ah-ah-ah-ah!
If all the snowflakes
Were candy bars and milkshakes,
Oh, what a snow that would be!

Follow-Up Questions

- *Why would you want the rain to stop?*
- *How is the rain helpful to us?*
- *If you were able to play in the rain, what would you do?*

Language Enrichment

- Talk about rainy days. *What do you wear on a rainy day? What can you do when you can't go outside? How does the rain feel on your skin?*
- Discuss the sounds that rain makes. *How does the rain sound when it hits the windows?* Invite the children to make some rain sounds (*pitter-patter, drip-drop, splish, splash*).
- Encourage the children to think of reasons the rain should go away. They might say it is messy, they want to play outside, or that there has already been enough rain. Then ask them to think of reasons the rain should come back (to water the flowers, fill a birdbath, or wash the dust away). If appropriate, print each list on chart paper.

Extension Activities

Cognitive Development/Discovery

The Sounds of Rain

Drape a shower curtain liner over a table. Provide adjustable nozzle spray bottles of water and encourage the children to spray the liner with the spray bottles. Begin with a low intensity of spray. Talk with the children as they experiment with the spray bottles. *How does the water sound when it hits the liner?* Adjust the force of the water to a higher intensity. *How does the water sound now? Does it sound different? Does it sound like rain?* Discuss soft and hard rains. *Can you hear the difference in hard and soft rains?*

Cognitive and Physical Development/Art

Rain Pictures

Provide light blue and gray non-toxic tempera paint and easel paper. Encourage the children to paint a picture of the rain. Show them how they can use their brushes to make dots of rain. Talk with them about the raindrops they are painting. *Are you painting a hard rain or a soft rain? How would you paint if the raindrops were coming down hard? What about softly?*

STORY TIME SUGGESTIONS

Listen to the Rain by Bill Martin, Jr.
Painting a Rainbow by Lois Ehlert

Physical Development/Gross Motor

Raindrop Hop

Cut out large raindrops from gray or light blue butcher paper or from a shower curtain liner. Lay the "drops" on the floor about one foot apart. Encourage the children to hop from raindrop to raindrop. If hopping this distance is easy expand the distance. Suggest that children count the hops they make. Talk with them as they play.

Social-Emotional Development/Dramatic Play

Rain Gear

Fill the center with rain gear, including a raincoat, umbrella, galoshes, rain hats, and boots. Encourage the children to try on the different types of clothing. Talk with them as they play. *Why would you wear boots when it rains? How do the boots keep your feet dry? How are boots and galoshes different? Do umbrellas all come in the same size? Is a bigger umbrella better than a small umbrella? Why?*

Outdoor Play or Music and Movement

- Give the children rainbow-colored streamers. Play classical music and invite the children to dance creatively with their streamers.
- Sing along with "Rain, Rain Go Away" (*Here Is Thumbkin* CD, Kimbo Educational), "It's Raining" (*Toddler Favorites* CD, Music for Little People), "Ain't Gonna Rain No More" (*Playing Favorites* CD, Greg and Steve Productions), or "The Raindrop Song" (*Fabulous Foods* CD, Schiller Educational Resources, LLC).

REFLECTIONS ON THE DAY

- *What is your favorite thing to do on a rainy day?*
- *What do you think animals do on a rainy day?*
- *What does the sky look like on a rainy day? How does the sky look on a sunny day?*

Ram Sam Sam

Ram Sam Sam (Tune: Traditional)
A ram sam sam (*hit one fist on top of the other*)
A ram sam sam (*hit opposite fist on top of the other*)
Guli, guli, guli, guli (*roll hands arm over arm or pull hands apart as if pulling taffy*)
A ram sam sam.
(*repeat*)

A ram sam sam (*hit fists again*)
A rafi a rafi (*lift arms*)
Guli, guli, guli, guli (*roll hands again*)
A RAM SAM SAM! (*hit fists again*)

A dancing dog (*hit one fist on top of the other*)
A dancing dog (*hit opposite fist on top of the other*)
Guli, guli, guli, guli (*roll hands arm over arm*)
A dancing dog (*hit fists again*)

A dancer (*hit fists again*)
A dancer (*lift arms*)
Guli, guli, guli, guli (*roll hands again*)
A DANCING DOG! (*hit fists again*)

Additional verses:
A rolling stone…A tumbler
An ice cream truck…A slurpee
A laughing clown…A laugher
A purple cow…A mooey
A stomping giant…A maddy
A candy kiss… A smacky

SEE ALSO

"I Never Saw a Purple Cow," page 67
"Jack Sprat," page 84

Related Songs, Chants, and Rhymes

Bim Bam Chant
Bim bam, biri, biri, bam
Biri, biri, bim-bam
Biri, biri, bam.
Bim bam, bim bam,
Bim-bam biri, biri, bam. (repeat last line)

Che Che Koolay* (Tune: Traditional)
* This is a singing game from Ghana.
Che che koolay, (*hands on head*)
Che che koolay (*echo*)
Che che kofee sa (*hands on shoulders*)
Che che kofee sa (*echo*)
Kofee salanga (*hands on waist*)
Kofee salanga (*echo*))
Kakashee langa (*hands on knees*)
Kakashee langa (*echo*)
Koommadyeday (*hands on toes*)
Koommadyeday (*echo*)

Sarasponda* (Tune: Traditional)
* This is a Dutch folk song.
Sarasponda, sarasponda, sarasponda, ret, set, set.
Sarasponda, sarasponda, sarasponda, ret, set, set.
A-do-ray-oh! A-do-ray boomday-oh!
A-do-ray boomday ret, set, set,
Asay, pahsay, oh.

Follow-Up Questions

- *Which part of the song do you like best?*
- *What are some things that dogs like to do? Do they like to dance?*

Language Enrichment

- Discuss the words of the song. Point out that many of the words are nonsense words, which are words that don't mean anything but are fun to say.
- Make up a silly rhyming name for each child, for example, *Fabrielle Gabrielle, Radison Madison, Ostin Austin,* and *Miffany Tiffany.*
- Encourage the children to chant *guli, guli, guli* as they play.

Extension Activities

Cognitive Development/Language

Name Puzzles
Print each child's name on a strip of poster board. Cut the letters apart using a simple puzzle cut (two to three pieces). Challenge the children to put their name puzzles together.

STORY TIME SUGGESTIONS

Hand Clap! Miss Mary Mack by Johanna Cole
Silly Sally by Audrey Wood

Physical Development/Fine Motor

Guli Guli Guli Goop

Make Goop. Mix 2 cups of salt and 1 ½ cup of water and cook for 4-5 minutes. Remove from heat. Add 1 cup of cornstarch and ½ cup of water. Return to heat. Stir until mixture thickens. Let cool. Encourage the children to play with the Guli Goop. Talk about its texture. *What can you make with the Guli Goop? Can you pound it with your fist?* Store the Goop in a zipper-closure plastic bag or covered container and it will last for a couple of weeks.

Physical Development/Gross Motor

Rolling Stones

Draw a six-square grid of 4" squares on butcher paper. Make each square a different color. Give the children a round stone to roll onto the grid. Encourage them to say *a tumbler, a tumbler* while the stone is rolling. Ask them to identify the color that the stone lands on. You can change the squares on the grid, if desired, to shapes, animals, or any other item that you wish children to recognize. For younger children, make a grid with fewer and larger squares.

Social-Emotional Development/Dramatic Play

Let's Pretend

Encourage the children to pretend to be some of the characters in the song, such as a dancing dog, a stomping giant, and a laughing clown. Show them how to imitate each character. Talk about the actions that make them identifiable as the character they are pretending to be. Younger children will enjoy watching their peers and may be able to do simple actions like stomping.

REFLECTIONS ON THE DAY

- *Which of the characters in the song did you pretend to be? What did you do?*
- *What did you make with the Guli Goop?*

Outdoor Play or Music and Movement

- Teach the children "Che Che Koolay" (see page 163). If you do not know the tune of the song, use the words as a chant.
- Sing along with "Ram Sam Sam" (*Laugh 'n Learn Silly Songs* CD, Kimbo Educational), "Ram Sam Sam" (*Wee Sing Sing Along Songs* CD, Price, Stern, Sloan), or "Sarasponda" (*Wee Sing Sing Along Songs* CD, Price, Stern, Sloan).

Rock-a-Bye, Baby

Rock-a-Bye, Baby (Tune: Traditional)
Rock-a-bye, baby,
In the tree top,
When the wind blows,
The cradle will rock.
When the bough breaks,
The cradle will fall,
And down will come baby,
Cradle and all.

Related Songs, Chants, and Rhymes

Be Very Quiet
Shhh! Be very quiet,
Shhh! Be very still.
Fold your busy little hands,
Close your sleepy little eyes.
Shhh! Be very quiet.

Lullaby
Sleep, my child,
Sleep, my sun,
Sleep, little piece
Of my heart.

Follow-Up Questions

- *This song is a lullaby. Lullabies are soft songs that help little children go to sleep. Does anyone sing a lullaby to you to help you sleep?*
- *Why do lullabies need to be soft and slow?*

Language Enrichment

- Encourage the children to hum the song. Explain that sometimes people hum lullabies instead of singing them.
- Help the children understand what a *bough* is (a branch of a tree). *Would a bough that was holding a baby rocker need to be thick or thin?*
- Talk with the children about their sleeping routines. *Who puts you to bed? Does anyone sing to you?*
- Stand and sing the song, swaying side to side. Stop swaying and raise your arms up on rhyming words.
- Teach the children the American Sign Language sing for *baby* (see appendix page xx).

SEE ALSO

"Are You Sleeping?," page 26
"Dream Fairy," page 26
"I've a Dear Little Dolly," page 123
"Twinkle, Twinkle, Little Star," page 219
"Wee Willie Winkie," page 27
"White Wings," page 223

Extension Activities

Cognitive Development/Science

When the Wind Blows

Place ping-pong balls on a table and encourage the children to blow through straws to make the balls fall off the table. Tie a feather to a piece of yarn and suspend it from the edge of a table. Challenge the children to rock the feather by blowing through their straws. Point out how their breath is strong enough to move things.

Cognitive and Physical Development/Art

Lullaby Pictures

Play lullaby music and invite the children to paint (with non-toxic paint) to the tempo of the music. Talk with them about the music. Help them think about the music before moving their paintbrush.

Physical Development/Gross Motor

Rock and Drop

Cut a 2" diameter hole in the bottom of a whipped topping container. Place a ping-pong ball inside the container and close the lid. Show the children how to rock the bowl to drop the ball. Sing the song and see if the children can get the ball to fall before you get to the part about the cradle falling.

Social-Emotional Development/Dramatic Play

Rock the Baby

Provide a small rocking chair. Encourage the children to rock baby dolls to sleep. Suggest that they sing "Rock-a-Bye, Baby" while they rock. Talk with them about other ways to help a baby get to sleep, for example, reading her a story or rubbing her back.

Outdoor Play or Music and Movement

- Play a lullaby. Invite the children to rock to the music. Show them different ways to rock, such as while sitting, standing, or crawling.
- Sing along with "Rock-a-Bye, Baby" (*Sweet Dreams* CD, Kimbo Educational) or "Rock-a-Bye, Baby" (*Story Time: 52 Favorite Lullabies, Nursery Rhymes, and Whimsical Songs* CD, EMI Capitol).

STORY TIME SUGGESTIONS

Rock-a-Bye Babies by Carol Nicklaus

Rock-a-Bye Baby by Jeanette Winter

REFLECTIONS ON THE DAY

- *How did you move the ping-pong ball?*
- *How did you get your baby to sleep?*

Row, Row, Row Your Boat

Row, Row, Row Your Boat (Tune: Traditional)
Row, row, row your boat
Gently down the stream.
Merrily, merrily, merrily, merrily,
Life is but a dream.

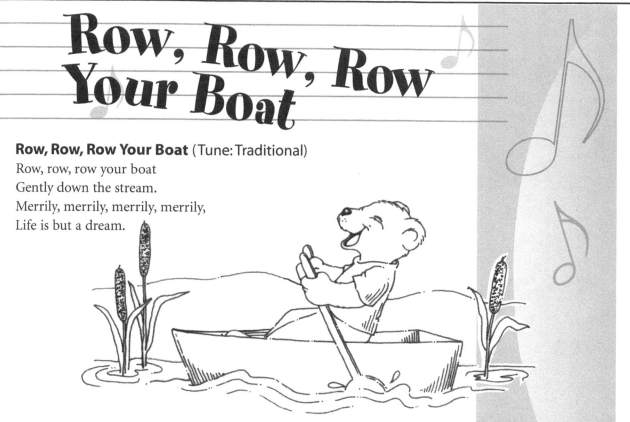

Related Songs, Chants, and Rhymes

Motor Boat Chant
Motor boat, motor boat, go so slow,
Motor boat, motor boat, go so fast,
Motor boat, motor boat, step on the gas!

Rocking Boat!
Did you ever see a rocking boat
On its back so flat?
Hands holding onto its knees,
And staying just like that.
Then a-rock and a-rock and a-rock, rock, rock,
All across the sea.
A-rock and a-rock and a-rock, rock, rock.
Rock with me.

Did you ever see a rocking boat
On its tummy flat?
Hands in front and feet in back,
And staying just like that.
Then a-rock and a-rock and a-rock, rock rock.
All across the sea.
A-rock and a-rock and a-rock, rock, rock.
Rock with me.

SEE ALSO

"The Car Song," page 98
"Little Hunk of Tin," page 98
"The Wheels on the Bus," page 225
"Oh, It's Wheels, Wheels, Wheels," page 105

Follow-Up Questions

- *Have you ever been on a boat? How did it move?*
- *Why is it necessary to row a boat?*

Language Enrichment

- Discuss words that may be new vocabulary for the children, such as *row, stream, gently,* and *merrily.*
- Demonstrate *gently.* Show how to hold a baby (use a baby doll) gently. Ask a volunteer to demonstrate how to hold someone's hands gently. Discuss things one must handle gently, such as glass, eggs, and books.
- Discuss sounds that water makes when it splashes. For example, *splish, splash, drip, drop,* and *plop.* Pour some water into a shallow tub or water table and make splashing sounds with your hands. Tell the children that boat paddles create splashing sounds.
- If available, show the children pictures of boats. Use the pictures to stimulate conversation about boats.

Extension Activities

Cognitive Development/Listening

Look and Listen

Record the song on a cassette tape and encourage the children to listen to it while they look at books about boats.

Physical Development/Gross Motor

Rocking and Rowing

Show the children how to sit on the floor and rock side to side and forward and backward like a boat when it encounters a wake or ripples. Discuss how boats move as they float on the water. Explain what a "wake" is and what "ripples" are. Show them how to sit straight and pretend to row by putting their hands together and moving them in a rowing motion, alternating the right and left sides of their body. Sing the song as you row.

Physical and Social-Emotional Development/Dramatic Play

Boat Rock

Sit on the floor. Let the children take turns sitting in your lap facing you. Rock forward, backward, and side to side like a boat floating in the water. Sing "Row, Row, Row Your Boat" as you rock.

STORY TIME SUGGESTION

Row, Row, Row Your Boat by Iza Trapani

Water Play/Social-Emotional Development

Boat Float

Provide small boats or shape aluminum foil into small boats. Encourage the children to float the boats in the water. Show them how to create a breeze by fanning the boat with a hand fan or a sheet of paper to help move the boats. Explain that rowing is another way to move the boats and that if the wind is present, rowing is easier. When there is no wind, rowing is more difficult. Discuss other things that make rowing easier, including people helping and a lighter load.

Outdoor Play or Music and Movement

- Do the "Motor Boat Chant" (see page 167) with the children. Have the children stand in a circle and hold hands. Start the rhyme walking slowly and increase your speed with each line.
- Sing along with "Row, Row, Row Your Boat" (*On the Move* CD, Schiller Educational Resources, LLC) or "Row, Row, Row Your Boat" (*Singable Nursery Rhymes* CD or *Three Little Kittens* CD, Kimbo Educational).

REFLECTIONS ON THE DAY

- *Do motor boats need to be rowed?*
- *What makes rowing a boat easier?*

Shoo Fly

Shoo Fly (Tune: Traditional)
Shoo fly, don't bother me, (walk in a circle to the left)
Shoo fly, don't bother me, (walk in a circle to the right)
Shoo fly, don't bother me, (walk in a circle to the left)
For I belong to somebody. (place hands on hips and shake head no)

Flies in the buttermilk, (*walk around shooing flies*)
Shoo fly, shoo,
Flies in the buttermilk,
Shoo fly, shoo,
Flies in the buttermilk,
Shoo fly, shoo,
Please just go away. (*place hands on hips and shake head no*)

Shoo fly, don't bother me, (*walk to the left in a circle*)
Shoo fly, don't bother me. (*walk to the right in a circle*)
Shoo fly, don't bother me, (*walk to the left in a circle*)
Come back another day. (*wave good-bye*)

Related Songs, Chants, and Rhymes

Flea, Fly, Flow Mosquito (Tune: Traditional)
Flea fly
Flea fly flow
Flea fly flow mosquito
Oh no-no, no more mosquitoes
Itchy itchy scratchy scratchy, ooh I got one down my backy!
Eet biddly oatten boatten boe boe boe ditten dotten
Wye doan choo oo.

Chase that
Big bad bug
Make it go away!
SHOO! SHOO!

Little Peter Rabbit (Tune: Battle Hymn of the Republic)
Little Peter Rabbit had a fly upon his ear
Little Peter Rabbit had a fly upon his ear
Little Peter Rabbit had a fly upon his ear
And he flicked it till it flew away!

SEE ALSO

"The Ants Go Marching," page 22
"Baby Bumblebee," page 29
"Here Is the Beehive," page 30
"Little Ants," page 22
"Little Ant's Hill," page 23
"My Busy Garden," page 80

Skip to My Lou (Tune: Traditional)

(Chorus)
Skip, skip, skip to my Lou,
Skip, skip, skip to my Lou,
Skip, skip, skip to my Lou,
Skip to my Lou, my darlin'.

Fly's in the buttermilk,
Shoo, fly, shoo,
Fly's in the buttermilk,
Shoo, fly, shoo,
Fly's in the buttermilk,
Shoo, fly, shoo,
Skip to my Lou, my darlin'.

(Chorus)

Cat's in the cream jar,
Ooh, ooh, ooh,
Cat's in the cream jar,
Ooh, ooh, ooh,
Cat's in the cream jar,
Ooh, ooh, ooh,
Skip to my Lou, my darlin'.

(Chorus)

Off to Texas,
Two by two,
Off to Texas,
Two by two,
Off to Texas,
Two by two,
Skip to my Lou, my darlin'.

(Chorus)

Follow-Up Questions

- *Have you ever been bothered by a fly? What did you do?*
- *What makes flies come around?*

Language Enrichment

- Discuss words in the song that may be new vocabulary for the children, for example, *shoo* and *buttermilk.*
- If you have a picture of a fly, use it to stimulate a discussion about flies. *How many wings does a fly have? How many legs? What is funny about a fly's eyes?*
- Ask questions about similar bugs. *What other insect do you shoo away?*

Extension Activities

Physical Development/Art

Buttermilk Drawings

Give the children a piece of paper and some chalk. Spoon a small amount of buttermilk on each child's paper. Invite them to draw by dipping the chalk in the buttermilk occasionally. Remind the children of the verse in the song about buttermilk. Talk with them about buttermilk and where it comes from. *What do you think it tastes like?* Discuss the effect the buttermilk has on their chalk.

STORY TIME SUGGESTIONS

A Fly Went By by Mike McClintock
There Was an Old Lady Who Swallowed a Fly by Simms Taback

Physical Development/Construction

Fly Fans

Invite the children to draw on a piece of drawing paper. When they have finished drawing, fold their paper into a fan. Talk with them about fanning flies away. Have them fan the air while singing, "Shoo fly, don't bother me."

Physical Development/Gross Motor

Catch a Fly

Wad up small pieces of black construction paper or tissue paper to represent flies. Give the children a large plastic or Styrofoam cup to use as a "fly catcher." Toss paper flies in the air and challenge the children to catch them. Invite younger children to pick up the flies that fall to the floor. Discuss ways that people get rid of flies, such as fly paper, sprays, swatters, and so forth.

Social-Emotional Development/Dramatic Play

Bug Eyes

Cut egg cartons apart in sets of two. Cut a small round hole in the bottom of each crate and attach a pipe cleaner to the sides to make "bug eyes." Let the children pretend to be flies. Talk with them about flies. *Where do they live? What do they do?*

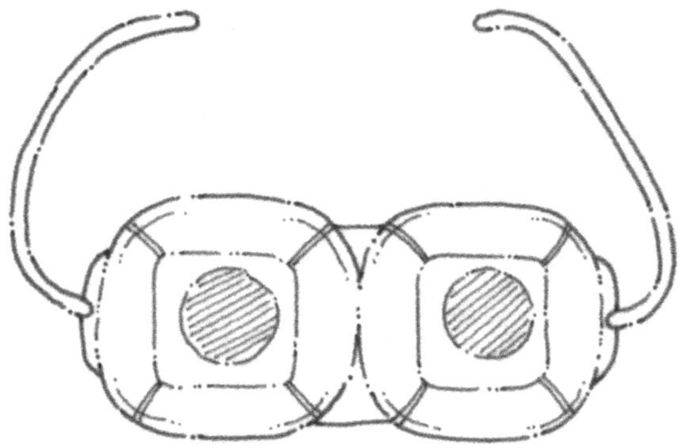

REFLECTIONS ON THE DAY

- *What did you learn about flies today?*
- *How can we get flies to leave us alone?*

Outdoor Play or Music and Movement

- Give each child two plastic plates, one to hold in each hand, to use as wings. Play classical music and invite them to fly like flies.
- Encourage the children to sing along with, "Shoo Fly, Don't Bother Me" (*Children's Sing Along Songs* CD, Kidzup), "Skip to My Lou" (*Four Baby Bumblebees* CD, Kimbo Educational), or "Flea, Fly, Flow Mosquito" (*Laugh 'n Learn Silly Songs* CD, Kimbo Educational).

Sign Along With Me

Sign Along With Me by Pam Schiller (Tune: Mary Had a Little Lamb)
(See American Sign Language signs beginning on page 239)
This is "please" and this is "thank you."
This is "please," this is "thank you."
This is "please" and this is "thank you."
Sign along with me.

This is "yes" and this is "no."
This is "yes," this is "no."
This is "yes" and this is "no."
Sign along with me.

This is "stop" and this is "go."
This is "stop," this is "go."
This is "stop" and this is "go."
Sign along with me.

This is "hi" and this is "bye."
This is "hi," this is "bye."
This is "hi" and this is "bye."
Sign along with me.

Related Songs, Chants, and Rhymes

My Body Talks by Pam Schiller
(*suit actions to words*)
When I want to say, "Hello," I wave my hand.
When I want to say, "No," I shake my head from side to side.
When I want to say, "Yes," I nod my head up and down.
When I want to say, "Good job," I stick up my thumb.
When I want to say, "I disagree," I turn my thumb down.
When I want to celebrate a success, I clap my hands.
When I want to say, "Enough" or "stop," I hold my hand out.
When I want to say, "Come here," I wave my hand toward me.
When I want to say, "Goodbye," I wave my hand or blow you a kiss.
When I want to say, "I love you," I wrap my arms around you and squeeze.

SEE ALSO

"The Finger Band," page 145
"Five Little Fingers," page 146
"Hickory, Dickory, Dock," page 70
"Motor Boat Chant," page 167
"Open, Shut Them," page 145
"There Was a Little Girl," page 118

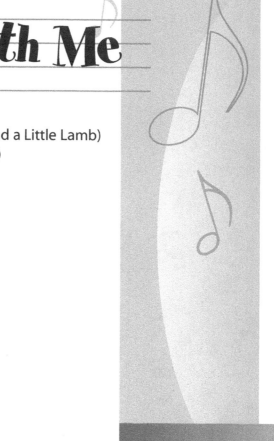

Sing a Song of Opposites by Pam Schiller
(Tune: Mary Had a Little Lamb)
This is big and this is small,
This is big, this is small.
This is big and this is small,
Sing along with me.

This is tall and this is short.
This is tall, this is short.
This is tall and this is short
Sing along with me.

This is up and this is down
This is up, this is down.
This is up and this is down.
Sing along with me.

This is in and this is out.
This is in, this is out.
This is in and this is out.
Sing along with me.

This is fast and this is slow.
This is fast, this is slow.
This is fast and this is slow.
Sing along with me.

STORY TIME SUGGESTIONS

Sing a Song of Opposites by Pam Schiller
My Hands by Aliki

Follow-Up Questions

- *Did you know you can talk with your hands? What is talking with your hands called?*
- *Who can show me how to say "thank you" with your hands?*

Language Enrichment

- Discuss opposites. Talk about each pair of opposites in the song. Provide other examples of opposites (*up/down, high/low, on/off*). *Can you think of any other opposites?*
- Review other signs the children know.
- Review the signs in the song. Suggest that children use the songs during the day.

Extension Activities

Cognitive Development/Art

Handprints

Pour non-toxic fingerpaint on top of a table and let the children fingerpaint directly on the table. While they are painting, encourage them to make handprints on a piece of paper. Discuss the many ways we use our hands. Talk about the parts of the hands, such as the palm, fingers, and so on.

Cognitive Development/Blocks

Stop and Go

Encourage the children to push toy cars by following your sign language commands to *stop* and *go.* Younger children can watch the reactions of older children as a cue and follow along.

Physical Development/Gross Motor

Hand Jive

Play some music and encourage the children to clap to the music. Encourage the children to clap hands with you. Tell them they are doing a "Hand Jive."

Social-Emotional Development/Dramatic Play

Hand Wear

Fill the center with things worn on the hands, including mittens and gloves. Include a variety of gloves, such as gardening gloves, winter gloves, and baseball gloves. Talk with the children about their hands. *What do we need our hands for? How do we take care of our hands?* Discuss hand washing and hand care.

Outdoor Play or Music and Movement

- Play "Stop and Go" using American Sign Language signs to direct children's movements. Have the children stand on a start line. Tell them to watch your hands and move toward you when you sign *go* and to stop when you sign *stop* (see appendix page 239).
- Invite the children to act out "My Body Talks" (see page 173).
- Sing along with "Sing a Song of Opposites" (School Days CD, Schiller Educational Resources LLC).
- Dance along with "Twirl These Ribbons: A Dance of Opposites" (*Leaping Literacy* CD, Kimbo Educational).

REFLECTIONS ON THE DAY

- *How do you say "thank you" in sign language?*
- *How do you say "goodbye" in sign language?*

Sing a Song of Sixpence

Sing a Song of Sixpence (Tune: Traditional)
Sing a song of sixpence,
A pocket full of rye;
Four-and-twenty blackbirds
Baked in a pie!

When the pie was opened
The birds began to sing:
Was not that a dainty dish
To set before the king?

The king was in his counting-house,
Counting out his money;
The queen was in the parlor,
Eating bread and honey.

The maid was in the garden,
Hanging out the clothes;
When down came a blackbird
And snapped off her nose.

SEE ALSO

"Do You Know the Muffin Man?," page 41
"Old King Cole," page 129
"Two Little Blackbirds," page 222

Related Songs, Chants, and Rhymes

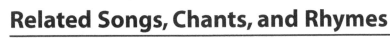

Little Jack Horner
Little Jack Horner sat in the corner.
Eating his Christmas pie.
He stuck in his thumb,
And pulled out a plum.
Then said, "What a good boy am I!"

Simple Simon
Simple Simon met a pieman,
Going to the fair;
Said Simple Simon to the pieman,
"Let me taste your ware."

Said the pieman to Simon,
"Show me first your penny."
Said Simple Simon to the pieman,

"Indeed, I have not any."
Simple Simon went a-fishing,
For to catch a whale;
But all the water he had got
Was in his mother's pail.

Simple Simon went to look,
If plums grew on a thistle;
He pricked his fingers very much,
Which made poor Simon whistle.

He went for water in a sieve,
But soon it all fell through;
And now poor Simple Simon
Bids you all adieu.

Follow-Up Questions

- *Have you ever eaten pie? What kind of pie did you eat?*
- *Do you think anyone would really put live birds in a pie?*

Language Enrichment

- Define the words in the rhyme that may be new vocabulary for the children, such as *sixpence*, *rye*, *dainty*, *counting-house*, *parlor*, and *snapped*.
- Discuss pies. Talk about the many kinds of pies. Ask children which pies they like and tell them which pie you like best.

Extension Activities

Cognitive Development/Science

Planting Rye Seeds

Provide potting soil, rye seeds, and cups. Help the children put soil in their cups and plant the seeds. Talk about the seeds—their size, shape, and what they will become. Remind the children of the line in the song about a "pocket full of rye."

Physical Development/Fine Motor

Playdough Pies

Provide rolling pins, playdough, and pie tins. Encourage the children to make playdough pies. Discuss the parts of a pie (filling, bottom crust, and top crust). Talk about possible fillings for their pies. *What would you put in your pie?* Talk about the tools used in pie making, such as rolling pins, cups, measuring spoons, and so on. If weather and setting permit, you may want to let the children make mud pies outdoors.

STORY TIME SUGGESTIONS

Old King Cole by Dianne O'Quinn Burke

Old King Cole and the Very Merry Feast by Penny Dann

Social-Emotional Development/Dramatic Play

Hanging Up the Clothes

Make an indoor clothesline with string. Provide clothing in a laundry basket and clothespins. Invite the children to hang up the clothes. Talk with them about hanging clothes out to dry. Explain that while most people use dryers to dry their clothes, sometimes they hang things on a clothesline outside. For example, people may hang clothes outside when they go camping, or if it's a nice, warm day.

Social-Emotional Development/Snack

Bread and Honey

Serve toast and honey for snack. Remind the children about the line in the rhyme: "the queen was in the parlor eating bread and honey." **Safety Note:** Check for food allergies before serving.

Outdoor Play or Music and Movement

- Provide black streamers for children to use for wings. Give each child two streamers, one to hold in each hand. Encourage the children to "fly" like birds. Play classical music and encourage the children to fly to the tempo of the music.
- Sing along with "Sing a Song of Sixpence" (*Three Little Kittens* CD, Kimbo Educational), "Sing a Song of Sixpence" (*Story Time: 52 Favorite Lullabies, Nursery Rhymes and Whimsical Songs* CD, EMI Capitol), or "Simple Simon" (*Mother Goose Rocks, Vol. 2* CD, Light Years).

REFLECTIONS ON THE DAY

- *What kind of pie did you make today?*
- *What is going to happen to the rye seed we planted? How will we take care of it?*

Six in the Bed

Six in the Bed (Tune: Traditional)
There were six in the bed (*hold up six fingers*)
And the little one said,
"Roll over! Roll over!" (*roll hand over hand*)
So they all rolled over
And one rolled out. (*hold up one finger*)

There were five in the bed... (*repeat hand motions*)
Four in the bed...
Three in the bed...
Two in the bed...

There was one in the bed
And the little one said,
"Alone at last!" (*place head on hands as if sleeping*)

SEE ALSO

"Are You Sleeping?," page 26
"It's Raining, It's Pouring," page 159
"Lazy Mary," page 96
"Rock-a-Bye, Baby," page 165
"Thelma Thumb," page 229
"There Was an Old Woman," page 193
"Wee Willie Winkie," page 27

Related Songs, Chants, and Rhymes

Deedle, Deedle, Dumpling

Deedle, deedle, dumpling, my son John,
Went to bed with his breeches on.
One shoe off and one shoe on,
Deedle, deedle, dumpling, my son John.

Five Little Monkeys

Five little monkeys jumping on the bed.
One fell off and bumped her head.
Mamma called the doctor, and the doctor said,
"No more monkeys jumping on the bed!"

Repeat the rhyme, subtracting a monkey each time. Say the rhyme using fingers or have the children act it out.

Follow-Up Questions

- *Have you ever slept in a bed with too many people? What happened? Were you crowded?*
- *Have you ever rolled out of the bed? What happened?*

STORY TIME SUGGESTIONS

Five Little Monkeys Jumping on the Bed by Eileen Christelow
Ten in the Bed by Penny Dale

Language Enrichment

- Discuss beds. Ask children what kind of bed they sleep in. *Does your bed have sides? Can more than one person fit in your bed?* Show photos of cribs, bunk beds, single beds, toddler beds, waterbeds, and so on, if available.
- Act out the rhyme. Place a sheet or a piece of bulletin board paper on the floor to represent a bed. Place five children on the "bed" and recite the rhyme. Help the children roll out of the bed, one at a time, so that they can see how rolling over creates an almost empty bed. Ask them to describe what happens when everyone rolls in the same direction.

Extension Activities

Cognitive Development/Discovery

Things That Roll

Provide a variety of items that roll, such as small balls, cars, a rolling pin, crayons, spools, and so on. Add a few items that don't roll, such as a square block, book, shoe, and sheet of paper. Encourage the children to find out which items roll and which items do not roll.

Cognitive Development/Math

Five

Make stick puppets by cutting 2" circles from tagboard and drawing facial features on each circle. Glue the circles to craft sticks. Make several puppets. Provide a sheet of construction paper to represent a bed. Print the numeral 5 in the center of the "bed." Encourage the children to place five stick puppets on the bed. Talk with the children as they work. Help them count the puppets as they place them in the bed. Younger children will enjoy placing the puppets in the bed without counting.

Physical Development/Gross Motor

Roll Over

Provide a sheet, large towel, blanket, or piece of bulletin board paper to represent a bed. Encourage the children to roll across the "bed." Supervise closely so that children don't roll into each other or injure each other as they roll. You may want to use a bed roll for this activity. It will be softer.

Social-Emotional Development/Dramatic Play

Bed Rolls

Provide several bed rolls for children to play with. Talk about where bed rolls are used—on camping trips, slumber parties, when relatives come to visit, and so on. Be sure to provide definitions for camping trips and slumber parties.

Outdoor Play or Music and Movement

- Encourage the children to re-enact "Six in the Bed" and/or "Five Little Monkeys."
- Sing along with "Ten in the Bed" (*Five Little Monkeys* CD, Kimbo Educational).

REFLECTIONS ON THE DAY

- *What items roll?*
- *Why did the children fall out of the bed?*

Six White Ducks

Six White Ducks (Tune: Traditional)
Six white ducks that I once knew,
Fat ducks, skinny ducks, they were too.
But the one little duck with the feather on her back,
She ruled the others with a quack, quack, quack!
Quack, quack, quack. Quack, quack, quack.
She ruled the others with a quack, quack, quack!

Down to the river they would go,
Wibble wobble, wibble wobble, all in a row.
But the one little duck with the feather on her back
She ruled the others with a quack, quack, quack!

Into the water they would dive,
Splish splash, splish splash, one through five.
But the sixth little duck with the feather on her back,
She ruled the others with a quack, quack, quack!
Quack, quack, quack. Quack, quack, quack.
She ruled the others with a quack, quack, quack!

SEE ALSO

"Old MacDonald Had a Farm," page 132

Related Songs, Chants, and Rhymes

Be Kind to Your Web-Footed Friends
(Tune: Stars and Stripes Forever)
Be kind to your web-footed friends,
For a duck may be somebody's mother,
Be kind to your friends in the swamp
Where the weather is always damp,
You may think that this is the end.
Well, it is!

Downy Duck (Tune: Traditional)
One day I saw a downy duck
With feathers on his back.
I said, "Good morning, downy duck."
And he said, "Quack, quack, quack."

Five Little Ducks (Tune: Traditional)
Five little ducks went out one day
Over the hills and far away,
Papa duck called with a "Quack, quack, quack."
Four little ducks came swimming back.

Repeat the song, losing one more duck with each verse until you are left with one duck. Have papa duck call and end with "Five little ducks came swimming back."

Little Ducky Duddle (Tune: Traditional)
Little ducky duddle
Went wading in a puddle,
Wading in a puddle quite small.
Said he, "It doesn't matter
How much I splash and splatter
'Cause I'm just a little ducky after all."
Quack! Quack!

Follow-Up Questions

- *Have you ever seen real ducks before? Where? What were they doing?*
- *What sounds do ducks make?*

Language Enrichment

- Discuss ducks. If possible, show the children a picture to stimulate discussion. *What color are ducks? Where do they live? What do they eat?*
- Discuss animal sounds. *What sound do ducks make? What sounds do cows make? Donkeys? Cats? Dogs?* Remind the children that animal sounds are called *onomatopoeic* sounds—words that sound like the sound they are describing.
- Discuss *fat* and *skinny*. Give examples for each size.
- Teach the children the American Sign Language sign for *duck* (see appendix page 239).

Extension Activities

Cognitive Development/Math

Fat and Skinny Sort
Provide pairs of items—one skinny and one fat. Items could include yarn, crayons, books, blocks, and so on. Encourage the children to sort the items into categories of fat and skinny. Talk with the children about their choices. *How do you know which item belongs in which category? Have you seen fatter blocks?*

STORY TIME SUGGESTIONS

Five Little Ducks by Penny Ives
Five Little Ducks by Raffi
Have You Seen My Ducklings? by Nancy Tafuri

Cognitive and Physical Development/Art

White

Provide white, non-toxic paint and encourage the children to paint a white picture. Discuss the color white. *What things are white? What part of the duck is white?*

Physical Development/Gross Motor

Feather Drop

Give the children feathers. Place a cardboard box on the floor. Have the children hold their feathers chest high and drop them into the box below. Talk with them about the course their feather travels as it drops. *Why is it difficult to get the feather to hit the box?*

Social-Emotional Development/ Water

Floating Ducks

Place rubber ducks in the water table. Show the children how to paddle the water to make the ducks "swim." For older children, place colored dots on the bottom of the ducks. Distribute the dots so that there are two ducks with each color of dot. Have the children catch two ducks in an attempt to find two with the same color.

Outdoor Play or Music and Movement

- Show the children how to waddle like a duck. Challenge older children to waddle in a row.
- Sing along with "Six White Ducks" (*Six White Ducks* CD, Kimbo Educational), "Six White Ducks (*Wee Sing 25th Anniversary Celebration* CD, Price, Stern, Sloan), or "Five Little Ducks" *(Five Little Ducks* CD, Kimbo Educational).

REFLECTIONS ON THE DAY

- *What color are the ducks in the song?*
- *Who can show me how a duck moves? What is the movement called?*

Skidamarink

Skidamarink (Tune: Traditional)
Skidamarink a dink a dink,
Skidamarink a doo,
I love you.
Skidamarink a dink a dink,
Skidamarink a doo,
I love you.

I love you in the morning
And in the afternoon,
I love you in the evening
And underneath the moon;
Oh, Skidamarink a dink a dink,
Skidamarink a doo,
I love you!

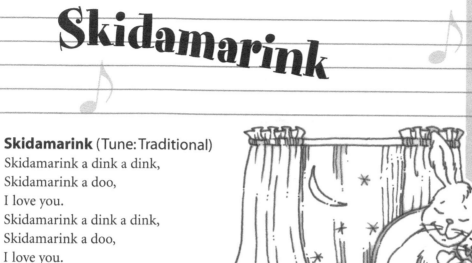

Related Songs, Chants, and Rhymes

A Bicycle Built for Two (Tune: Traditional)
Daisy, Daisy, give me your answer true.
I'm half crazy all for the love of you.
It won't be a stylish marriage.
I can't afford a carriage.
But you'll look sweet, upon the seat
Of a bicycle built for two.

Curly Locks (Mother Goose)
Curly locks, curly locks,
Will you be mine?
You shall not wash dishes,
Nor yet feed the swine,
But sit on a cushion,
And sew a fine seam,
And feast upon strawberries,
Sugar, and cream.

Five Pink Valentines by Pam Schiller
Five pink valentines from the card store, (*count off the valentines on your fingers*)
I gave one to Sam, now there are four.

SEE ALSO

"Good Morning to You," page 58
"Risseldy, Rosseldy," page 121

Four pink valentines, pretty ones to see.
I gave one to Maddie, now there are three.
Three pink valentines, pink through and through,
I gave one to Austin, now there are two.
Two pink valentines having lots of fun,
I gave one to Gabrielle, now there is one.
One pink valentine, my story is almost done,
I gave it to you, now there are none.

I Love Little Pussy

I love little pussy,
Her coat is so warm,
And if I don't hurt her
She'll do me no harm.
I'll sit by the fire
And give her some food,
And pussy will love me
Because I am good.

Follow-Up Questions

- *Who do you love?*
- *Who loves you?*

STORY TIME SUGGESTIONS

I Love You: A Rebus Poem by Jean Marzollo and Suse MacDonald

I Love You Because You're You by Liza Baker

Skidamarink! I Love You by Michael Scott

Language Enrichment

- Discuss loving someone. *How do you show someone that you love him or her? How do you know when someone "loves" you? How is "love" different from "like?"*
- Talk about the nonsense words in the song. *What does* "skidamarink" *mean? What does* "dink" *mean?* Put the words together, for example, *dinky do.* Encourage the children to play with the nonsense words. Clap the words, or march to the words.
- Teach the children how to say *I love you* in American Sign Language (see appendix page 239).

Extension Activities

Cognitive Development/Art

Heart Collages

Cut out several different sizes and colors of hearts from construction paper. Provide paper and glue. Invite the children to glue the hearts onto their paper to make a Heart Collage. Talk with them about the sizes and colors of hearts they use.

Cognitive Development/Language

Heart Puzzles

Cut out heart shapes from construction paper. Laminate them and cut them into puzzle pieces. For younger children, you may only want to cut the hearts in half using a puzzle line cut. Older children should be able to work four- to five-piece puzzles. Explain that hearts serve as a symbol for love.

Cognitive and Social-Emotional Development/Blocks

Big Hearts

Use masking tape to make two large hearts on the floor. Encourage the children to use blocks to outline the hearts. Talk with the children about the heart shapes. Remind them that hearts are used as a symbol for love.

Physical Development/Gross Motor

Tactile Heart

Cut out tactile hearts from vinyl, wallpaper samples, burlap, felt, aluminum foil, bubble wrap, and so on. Lay the hearts on the floor in a path. Encourage the children to crawl on the path and describe the texture of the hearts as they pass them. Talk with them as they reach each heart. Help them describe the feel of the heart on their hands and/or knees.

Outdoor Play or Music and Movement

- Play Musical Hearts as you would play a modified version of Musical Chairs. Cut out large hearts from vinyl or construction paper. Lay the hearts on the floor. Play music and encourage the children to dance until the music stops. When the music stops they must put their foot on a heart. Unlike Musical Chairs, it is okay for the children to share a heart. In this game no one gets put out. The fun is stopping and finding a heart to step on. Help younger children find a heart to step on.
- Sing along with "Skidamarink" (*Six White Ducks* CD, Kimbo Educational) or "Skidamarink" (*Car Songs* CD, Kimbo Educational).

REFLECTIONS ON THE DAY

- *What is the symbol for love?*
- *Who can show me how to say "I love you" using sign language? When you go home today, will you tell someone in your family you love them using the sign language sign?*

Teddy Bear, Teddy Bear

Teddy Bear, Teddy Bear
(*suit actions to words*)
Teddy bear, teddy bear,
Turn around.
Teddy bear, teddy bear,
Touch the ground.
Teddy bear, teddy bear,
Touch your shoe.
Teddy bear, teddy bear,
Say how-di-do.
Teddy bear, teddy bear,
Go up the stairs.
Teddy bear, teddy bear,
Say your prayers.
Turn out the light.
Say good night.

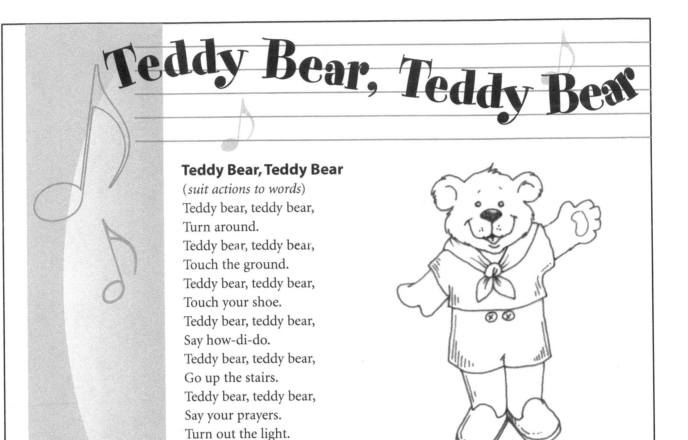

SEE ALSO

"The Bear Went Over the Mountain," page 55
"Going on a Bear Hunt," page 54
"I Met a Bear," page 55
"There Once Were Three Brown Bears," page 190
"Three Bears Rap," page 191

Related Songs, Chants, and Rhymes

Goldilocks, Goldilocks
Goldilocks, Goldilocks, turn around. (*turn around*)
Goldilocks, Goldilocks, touch the ground. (*touch the ground*)
Goldilocks, Goldilocks, knock on the door. (*pretend to knock with your hand*)
Goldilocks, Goldilocks, eat some porridge. (*pretend to eat porridge*)
Goldilocks, Goldilocks, have a seat. (*squat*)
Goldilocks, Goldilocks, go to sleep. (*put head on folded hands*)
Goldilocks, Goldilocks, run, run, run. (*run in place*)

Follow-Up Questions

- *Do you have a teddy bear? What is his/her name?*
- *Do you have a stuffed animal that you sleep with?*

Language Enrichment

- Discuss stuffed animals. Show the children several stuffed animals. Encourage them to name the animals.
- Discuss the word *how-di-do. What does it mean? What other words do we use to say* hello?
- Encourage the children to clap the words of the rhyme as they recite it.

- After saying the rhyme several times, recite it again, leaving out the second word in a rhyming word pair for the children to fill in. For example, *Teddy bear, teddy bear, turn around. Teddy bear, teddy bear, touch the _______.*
- Teach the children the American Sign Language sign for *hello* (see appendix page 239).

Extension Activities

Cognitive Development/Math

Bear Sort

Provide bear counters. Encourage the children to sort them by color. Place sheets of red, yellow, and blue construction paper on the table and have the children place the corresponding bears on top of the paper. Talk with them as they sort. *Are any of the bears the color of a teddy bear?*

Cognitive and Physical Development/Listening

Bear Acts

Record the chant on a cassette tape. Encourage the children to listen to the rhyme and use stuffed bears to do the actions as they hear them on the tape. Move the bears for younger children.

Cognitive and Social-Emotional Development/Library

Reading Buddies

Provide teddy bears and books. Encourage the children to choose a bear and then share a book with it. Older children can pretend to read a story to their bear. Help the children tell their bears a story. Encourage the children to name their bear friend.

Social-Emotional Development/Dramatic Play

Bear Fair

Fill the center with stuffed bears. Encourage the children to play with the bears. Talk with them about the many different bears. Ask them to name the colors of the bears. *Where are the bear's ears? Where is its tail?*

Outdoor Play or Music and Movement

- Encourage the children to say the rhyme and do the actions.
- Chant along with "Teddy Bear, Teddy Bear" (*Five Little Monkeys* CD, Kimbo Educational).

STORY TIME SUGGESTIONS

Teddy Bear, Teddy Bear: A Classic Action Rhyme by Michael Hague

Teddy Bears' Picnic by Jimmy Kennedy

REFLECTIONS ON THE DAY

- *Which teddy bear activity did you like best?*
- *What book did you share with your bear?*

There Once Were Three Brown Bears

There Once Were Three Brown Bears by Thomas Moore
(Tune: Twinkle, Twinkle Little Star)

There once were three brown bears,
Mother, Father, Baby Bear.
Mother's food was way too cold.
Father's food was way too hot.
Baby's food was all gone.
Someone ate it, so he cried.

There once were three brown bears,
Mother, Father, Baby Bear.
Mother's chair was way too low.
Father's chair was way too high.
Baby's chair was just so right,
But when she sat—she broke it.

There once were three brown bears,
Mother, Father, Baby Bear.
Mother's bed was way too soft.
Father's bed was way too hard.
Baby's bed was occupied.
Someone strange was sleeping there.

"Come here quickly," Baby cried.
"Someone's sleeping in my bed!"
"Who are you?" asked Baby Bear.
"Who are you?" asked Goldilocks.
"You better run," said Baby Bear.
"I will!" said Goldilocks.

SEE ALSO

"The Bear Went Over the Mountain," page 55
"Goldilocks, Goldilocks," page 188
"I Met a Bear," page 55

Related Songs, Chants, and Rhymes

Three Bears Rap

Shh, shh, shh, shh, shh, shh, shh, shh, shh, shh.
Out in the forest in a wee little cottage lived the three bears.
Shh, shh, shh, shh, shh, shh, shh, shh, shh, shh.
One was the Mama Bear, one was the Papa Bear, and one was the wee bear.
Shh, shh, shh, shh, shh, shh, shh, shh, shh, shh.
Out of the forest came a-walking, stalking, pretty little Goldilocks,
And upon the door she was a-knockin'.
Clack, clack, clack.
But no one was there, unh-unh, no one was there.
So she walked right in and had herself a bowl.
She didn't care, unh-unh, she didn't care.

Home, home, home came the three bears.

"Someone's been eating my porridge," said the Mama Bear.
"Someone's been eating my porridge," said the Papa Bear.
"Baa-baa Barebear," said the little Wee Bear.
"Someone's broken my chair."
Crash!

Just then Goldilocks woke up.
She broke up the party and she beat it out of there.

"Good-bye, good-bye, good-bye," said the Mama Bear.
"Good-bye, good-bye, good-bye," said the Papa Bear.
"Baa-baa Barebear," said the little Wee Bear.
That's the story of the three little bears—yeah!

Follow-Up Questions

- *Where were the bears when Goldilocks came to their house?*
- *How many bears are in the bear family?*

Language Enrichment

- Discuss the pairs of opposites used in the song (*hot/cold, hard/soft, low/high*).
- Encourage the children to tell you the story of "The Three Bears."
- Challenge the children to say hello in a voice that suits Mother Bear. *How would Papa Bear sound? What about Baby Bear?*
- Talk about families. *How many people are in your family?*

STORY TIME SUGGESTIONS

Goldilocks and the Three Bears (choose your favorite version)

Extension Activities

Cognitive Development/Math

Small, Medium, Large

Provide paper plates, cups, and napkins in three sizes. Encourage the children to arrange each set of items from smallest to largest.

Cognitive Development/Science

Mothers and Babies

Gather pictures of mother and baby animals. Look at the pictures with the children and talk about the animals. *What are the baby animals called?* (For example, baby bears are called "cubs.")

Cognitive and Physical Development/Art

Brown

Provide brown, non-toxic paint and paper and encourage the children to paint brown pictures. Talk with them as they paint. *What things are brown?*

Social-Emotional Development/Dramatic Play

The Three Bears

Provide props for the children to use to retell the story, such as chairs, beds (towels or blankets), bowls, spoons, plates, and so on. Encourage the children to re-enact the story or part of the story. Participate in their play. Help them develop dialogue.

Outdoor Play or Music and Movement

- Invite the children to participate in "Going on a Bear Hunt" (see page 54).
- Sing along with "There Once Were Three Brown Bears" (*School Days* CD, Schiller Educational Resources, LLC) or "Three Bears Rap" (*Where Is Thumbkin?* CD, Kimbo Educational).

REFLECTIONS ON THE DAY

- *Were the bears surprised to find Goldilocks in their house?*
- *Do you think Goldilocks ever went back to the bear's house?*

There Was an Old Woman

There Was an Old Woman adapted by Pam Schiller
There was an old woman,
Who lived in a shoe;
She had so many children,
She didn't know what to do.
She gave them some broth,
With butter and bread;
Then kissed them all sweetly,
And sent them to bed.

Related Songs, Chants, and Rhymes

There Was an Old Woman (Version 2) by Pam Schiller
There was an old woman
Who lived in a shoe;
She had so many children,
She didn't know what to do.
She got out her playdough,
Scissors and glue,
And added a playroom
To the toe of her shoe.

Wynken, Blynken and Nod
Wynken, Blynken and Nod one night
Sailed off in a wooden shoe.
Sailed on a river of crystal light
Into a sea of dew.

"Where are you going,
And what do you wish?"
The old man asked the three.
"We have come to fish
For the herring fish
That swim in the beautiful sea.
Nets of silver and gold have we!"
Said Wynken, Blynken and Nod.

SEE ALSO
"Put Your Little Foot," page 202
"Put Your Shoes On, Lucy," page 202
"Six in the Bed," page 179
"Who's Gonna Shoe Your Pretty Little Feet?," page 84

Follow-Up Questions

- *How many children do you think the old woman has?*
- *Who puts you to bed at night?*

Language Enrichment

- Discuss vocabulary that may be new to the children, such as *broth* and *soundly*.
- Recite the rhyme in a regular voice. Raise your voice on rhyming words.
- Invite the children to clap the words in the rhyme.
- Teach the children the American Sign Language sign for *children* (see appendix page 239).

Extension Activities

Cognitive Development/Dramatic Play

Too Many Children

Give the children an old, ready-to-discard large boot and some small dolls or action characters and doll furniture. Away from the children, use a craft knife to cut a door in the side or back of the boot. Encourage the children to put the characters in the shoe. *How many characters will fit in such a small place? Will any furniture fit?*

Cognitive Development/Games

Shoe Match

Provide several pairs of shoes in a basket. Encourage the children to match the shoes. Talk with them about the parts of the shoe, for example, tongue, heel, sole, toe, laces, buckles, and so on.

Physical and Social-Emotional Development/ Gross Motor

Shoe House

Obtain a large appliance box (washer or dryer box) and a second box about half the size of the first box. Use the boxes to make a boot. Use the large box as the leg and the smaller box as the toe. Decorate it like a house. Encourage the children to play in the shoe. You may want to put a few books inside.

STORY TIME SUGGESTIONS

Inside the Little Old Woman's Shoe by Charles Reasoner

Shoes, Shoes, Shoes by Ann Morris

Social-Emotional Development/Snack

Bread and Butter

Invite the children to have a slice of bread and butter. Remind them that the children in the rhyme had bread and butter with their broth for dinner.

Outdoor Play or Music and Movement

- Cut out shoe shapes from construction paper and lay them in a trail on the floor—left, right, left, right, and so on. Have the children follow the trail.
- Sing along with "Old Woman in a Shoe" (*Mother Goose Rocks, Vol. 2* CD, Light Year).

REFLECTIONS ON THE DAY

- *Could people really live inside of a shoe? Why? Why not?*
- *Who kisses you goodnight when it is time for you to go to bed?*

This Is the Way We Wash Our Hands

This Is the Way We Wash Our Hands
(Tune: Here We Go 'Round the Mulberry Bush)
(*suit actions to words*)
This is the way we wash our hands,
Wash our hands, wash our hands.
This is the way we wash our hands
Several times each day.

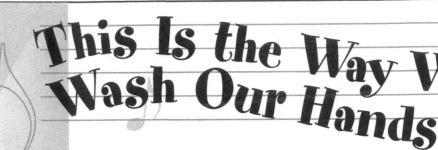

We lather the soap on our hands,
On our hands, on our hands.
We lather the soap on our hands
To get off all the dirt. (*pretend to wash hands*)

We wash between our fingers well,
Fingers well, fingers well.
We wash between our fingers well
To get off all the dirt.

We use the water to rinse our hands,
Rinse our hands, rinse our hands.
We use the water to rinse our hands
And then we go like this. (pretend to shake water from hands)

We use a towel to dry our hands,
Dry our hands, dry our hands.
We use a towel to dry our hands
Then put it in the trash.

Related Songs, Chants, and Rhymes

This Is the Way We Clean Our Teeth
(Tune: Here We Go 'Round the Mulberry Bush)
This is the way we clean our teeth,
Clean our teeth, clean our teeth.
This is the way we clean our teeth
Every night and morning.

SEE ALSO

"Open, Shut Them," page 145
"Sign Along with Me," page 173
"Slippery Soap," page 39

Take your brush, go up and down
Up and down, up and down.
Take your brush, go up and down,
Every night and morning.

Don't forget both back and front,
Back and front, back and front.
Don't forget both back and front,
Morning, noon, and night.

This Is the Way We Wash Our Face
(Tune: Here We Go 'Round the Mulberry Bush)
This is the way we wash our face,
Scrub our cheeks,
Scrub our ears,
This is the way we wash our face,
Until we're squeaky clean.

Follow-Up Questions

- *When do you wash your hands?*
- *Do you use soap when you wash your hands?*

Language Enrichment

- Talk with the children about why it is important to wash their hands. Discuss washing hands after playing outdoors, before eating, and after going to the bathroom.
- Demonstrate how to fold small towels. Discuss the difference between paper towels, which are consumable and tossed in the trash, and fabric towels that need to be hung up or folded and used again.
- Discuss the parts of the hands, such as fingers, fingernails, thumbs, knuckles, and palms.
- Teach the children the American Sign Language sign for *hands* (see appendix page 239).

Extension Activities

Cognitive Development/Science

Here Are My Hands
Provide a magnifying glass. Let the children examine their hands by looking at them through the magnifying glass. Encourage them to look at their fingernails, knuckles, and lines in their palms. Discuss all the places dirt can hide.

STORY TIME SUGGESTION

Wash Your Hands! by Tony Ross

Physical and Cognitive Development/Art

Finger Painting

Provide non-toxic fingerpaint and encourage the children to enjoy using it to paint directly on a table top. Talk about the parts of the hand as the children paint. *Where are your knuckles? Where are your fingernails? Do you use your knuckles to fingerpaint?*

Physical Development/Gross Motor

Towel Tossing

Provide wadded paper and a trash can. Encourage the children to toss the paper into the trash can. First have them toss the paper from a distance, and then have them move closer to the trash can. Talk with them about throwing away paper towels. Help them conclude that it is easier to get the paper in the trash when they are standing close to the container.

Social-Emotional Development/Water Play

Hand Washing

Provide a tub of water, soap, fingernail brushes, and towels. Encourage the children to wash their hands. Show them how to use the fingernail brush. Sing the hand washing song as you wash. Provide hand lotion when they finish.

REFLECTIONS ON THE DAY

- *What did you learn about hand washing today?*
- *Do you prefer to use paper towels or real towels to dry your hands?*

Outdoor Play or Music and Movement

- Use the tune and format of "Here We Go 'Round the Mulberry Bush" to create a new song about exercising—"This Is the Way We Build Our Muscles." Do activities with the song like marching, toe touching, jumping jacks, and so on.
- Sing along with "Brush Your Teeth" (*Health, Hygiene and Hugs* CD, Kimbo Educational) or "I'm Going to Brush My Teeth" (*Self-Help Skills* CD, Kimbo Educational).

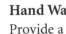

This Little Light of Mine

This Little Light of Mine (Tune: Traditional)
This little light of mine,
I'm going to let it shine.
This little light of mine,
I'm going to let it shine.
This little light of mine,
I'm going to let it shine,
Ev'ry day, ev'ry day,
Ev'ry day, ev'ry day,
Gonna let my little light shine.

Related Songs, Chants, and Rhymes

All By Myself

These are things I can do
All by myself. (*point to self*)
I can comb my hair and fasten my shoe (*point to hair and shoe*)
All by myself. (*point to self*)
I can wash my hands and wash my face (*pretend to wash*)
All by myself. (*point to self*)
I can put my toys and blocks in place (*pretend to put things away*)
All by myself. (*point to self*)

These Little Hands of Mine

These little hands of mine
Can do things, oh, so fine.
They can reach way out,
They can reach way up.
They can hold a crayon,
They can hold a cup.
They can open and close,
They can grab your nose.
These little hands of mine
Can do things, oh, so fine.
They can tell what's cold,
They can tell what's hot.
They can tell what's sticky,
They can tell what's not.
They can say, "What's that?"
They can pet the cat.
They can give a big Hi!
They can wave good-bye.

SEE ALSO

"If You're Happy and You Know It," page 77

Follow-Up Questions

- *Can you tell me something you can do well? Are you good at playing with blocks, working puzzles, or coloring?*
- *What do the words "this little light of mine" mean?*

Language Enrichment

- Talk with the children about something you do well. If you have pictures, show them. If what you do well results in a product (a painting, a knitted sweater, a baked good), show it. Help the children think of something they do well.
- Explain that when we show our talents, we are *letting our light shine.* This may be a difficult concept for younger children to understand, but older children will be able to relate to the concept.
- Discuss ways of saying *good job*, for example, thumbs up, high fives, and a pat on the back. Discuss words we use to indicate *good job*, such as *way to go, wow, super,* and *terrific.*

Extension Activities

Cognitive Development/Games

Flashlight Search

Make a construction paper star and cover it with glitter. Hide the star in a dark or semi-dark place. Give the children a flashlight and encourage them to find the hidden star.

Cognitive Development/Science

Shadow Play

Provide a light source, such as flashlight or overhead projector. Encourage the children to dance between the light source and a wall. Encourage them to "show off" the many things they can make their shadows do. Encourage them to make their shadows stand on one foot. Suggest they flap their arms like wings. Invite them to show you something special they can do.

Physical Development/Gross Motor

Step on the Light

Provide a flashlight. Select one child to be the "flashlight keeper" who is in charge of the light. Tell the "flashlight keeper" to shine the light on the floor and to slowly move it from spot to spot. If the children are young, you may need to be the "flashlight keeper." Invite the other children to try to step on the light.

STORY TIME SUGGESTIONS

All By Myself by Aliki
Look What I Can Do by Jose Aruego

Social-Emotional Development/Dramatic Play

Look What I Can Do

Provide costumes, dance shoes, a microphone (Styrofoam ball on top of an empty toilet paper tube), musical instruments, and so on. Encourage the children to perform. Talk with them about the things they can do.

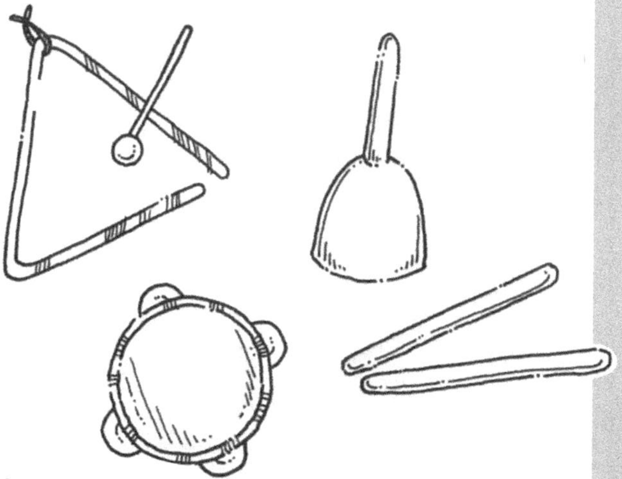

Outdoor Play or Music and Movement

- Give the children scarves or streamers and encourage them to dance creatively to classical music. Remind them to "let their light shine."
- Sing along with "I Am Special" (*I Am Special* CD, Thomas Moore Enterprises) or "This Little Light of Mine" (*Children's Sing Along Songs* CD, Kidzup).

REFLECTIONS ON THE DAY

- *What things did you have your shadow do?*
- *What is something you do well? What do people say when you do something well?*

This Little Piggy

This Little Piggy

This little piggy went to market,
(*wiggle big toe*)
This little piggy stayed home,
(*wiggle second toe*)
This little piggy had roast beef, (*wiggle middle toe*)
This little piggy had none, (*wiggle fourth toe*)
And this little piggy cried,
"Wee-wee-wee!" all the way home. (*wiggle little toe*)

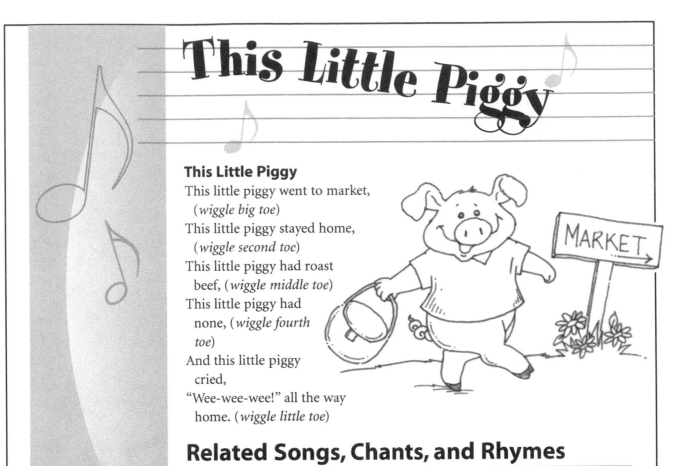

Related Songs, Chants, and Rhymes

SEE ALSO

"Head, Shoulders, Knees, and Toes," page 64
"One, Two, Buckle My Shoe," page 142
"Who's Gonna Shoe Your Pretty Little Feet?," page 84

Put Your Little Foot

Put your little foot,
Put your little foot,
Put your little foot right there.
Put your little foot,
Put your little foot,
Put your little foot right there.

Walk and walk and walk
And walk and turn,
Walk and walk and walk
And walk and turn.

Put Your Shoes On, Lucy adapted by Pam Schiller

Put your shoes on, Lucy,
Don't you know its time to go?
Put your shoes on, Lucy,
The ones with the pretty bow.

Lucy takes her shoes off
Wherever she goes,
'Cause she loves to watch the wiggle
Of her ten little toes!

Terrific Toes
I have such terrific toes
I take them with me wherever I goes.
I have such fantastic feet.
No matter what, they still smell sweet.
Toes and feet and feet and toes.
There's nothing else as fine as those.

Tiptoe by Pam Schiller
Tiptoe…tiptoe…
Quietly through the house.
Tiptoe…tiptoe…
Quietly like a mouse.
Tiptoe…tiptoe…
Whisper…
Shhh! Shhh!

Walk, Walk, Walk Your Feet (Tune: Row, Row, Row Your Boat)
Walk, walk, walk your feet,
Everywhere you go.
Walk 'em fast, walk 'em slow,
Walk them heel to toe.

Follow-Up Questions

- *Why was the little piggy crying?*
- *Which one of your toes is the little piggy? Which one of your toes is the piggy that ate roast beef?*

Language Enrichment

- Discuss feet. Ask the children to take off their shoes. Help them identify the parts of their feet. *What things can you do with your feet? Walk? Turn? Run? March? Hop? Jump?*
- Encourage the children to say the rhyme with you using their fingers instead of toes. Ask questions. *Which finger is the little piggy? Which finger didn't get any roast beef?*
- Teach the children the American Sign Language for *foot* (see appendix page 239).

STORY TIME SUGGESTIONS

The Baby Dances by Katherine Henderson
From Head to Toe by Eric Carle
This Little Piggy by Steve Haskamp
Toes, Ears and Nose by Marion Dane Bauer

Extension Activities

Cognitive Development/Gross Motor

Tactile Walk

Prepare a pathway of tactile squares. Cover 5" x 7" poster board squares with burlap, sandpaper, bubble wrap, corrugated cardboard, and so on. Place the squares on the floor. Encourage toddlers to walk along the path, stopping to explore each square with their toes. Talk with them about the feel of each square. *Is it rough? Is it smooth? Is it bumpy?*

Physical Development/Games

Toe Rings

Place a service bell on the floor. Ask the children to take off their shoes and see if they can ring the bell by tapping it gently with their "big" toe. Talk about what they have to do in order to make the bell ring. Hold the hands of the younger children—they may not have the balance it takes to stand on one foot.

Physical Development/Gross Motor

Tiptoe

Place a masking tape line on the floor. Show the children how to "tiptoe" over the line. Hold the hands of younger children. Say the "Tiptoe" poem (see page 203) as the children tiptoe over the line.

Social-Emotional and Cognitive Development/Language

Toes

Ask the children to take off their shoes and recite "This Little Piggy" with you. Help the children name their toes (big toe, middle toe, etc.). Ask questions about toes. *Why do you think we have toes? How do you use your toes? Has anyone ever stepped on your toe?*

REFLECTIONS ON THE DAY

- *What did you learn about feet today?*
- *Which part of the feet are called "piggies?"*

Outdoor Play or Music and Movement

- Place several sheets of construction paper on the floor. Play classical music and encourage the children to dance freely. Tell them that when the music stops, they must tap their big toe on a piece of the construction paper.
- Dance along with "Put Your Little Foot" (*Baby Face* CD, Kimbo Educational) or "Put Your Little Foot (*Honk, Honk, Rattle, Rattle* CD, Schiller Educational Resources, LLC).

This Old Man

This Old Man (Tune: Traditional)
This old man, he played one. (*hold up one finger*)
He played knick-knack on my thumb. (*pretend to knock on thumb*)

Chorus:
With a knick-knack paddy whack give a dog a bone. (*knock on head, clap twice, pretend to throw a bone over your shoulder*)
This old man came rolling home. (*roll hand over hand*)

This old man, he played two. (*hold up two fingers*)
He played knick-knack on my shoe. (*knock on shoe*)

(Chorus)

This old man, he played three. (*hold up three fingers*)
He played knick-knack on my knee. (*knock on knee*)

(Chorus)

This old man, he played four. (*hold up four fingers*)
He played knick-knack on the door. (*pretend to knock on door*)

(Chorus)

This old man, he played five. (*hold up five fingers*)
He played knick-knack on a hive. (*pretend to knock on a hive*)

(Chorus)

…six…sticks (continue hand motions)
…seven…heaven
…eight…gate
…nine…line
…ten…over again!

SEE ALSO

"The Ants Go Marching," page 22
"Counting Rhyme," page 142
"One, Two, Buckle My Shoe," page 142

Related Songs, Chants and Rhymes

This Old Man Is Rockin' On by Pam Schiller and Tracy Moncure
(Tune: This Old Man)
This old man, he played drums
With his fingers and his thumbs.

Chorus:
With a knick-knack paddy whack give a dog a bone.
This old man is rockin' on.

This old man, he played flute,
Made it hum and made it toot.

(Chorus)

This old man, he played strings,
Twangs and twops and zips and zings.

(Chorus)

This old man, he could dance.
He could strut and he could prance.

(Chorus)

This old man was a band,
Very best band in the land.

(Chorus)

Follow-Up Questions

- *What did the old man throw to the dog?*
- *On what body part did the old man play paddy whack when he played three?*

Language Enrichment

- Sing the song several times with the children. Sing it again, but do not say the objects on which the old man plays paddy whack so the children can fill them in.
- Encourage the children to play with the words *knick-knack paddy whack.* They can clap the words, march to the words, or just chant the words.
- Teach the children the American Sign Language sign for *dog* (see appendix page 239).

Extension Activities

Cognitive Development/Discovery

Behind the Door

Cut four flaps (small doors) in the front of an 8 ½" x 11" envelope. Make the flaps look like little doors. Put a simple 8" x 10" picture inside. (If you can find large photos of musical instruments, place them inside the envelope. If not, use easy to recognize items such as a bell, top, zebra, and so on.) Explain that each "door" is a clue to what the picture is. Have the children open one flap at a time, trying each time to determine what the picture is illustrating. *What do you see? What might the picture be?*

Physical Development/Fine Motor

Thumbprints

Provide non-toxic fingerpaint and paper. Show the children how to make thumbprints. Remind them of the first verse of the song, "This old man he played one, he played knick-knack on my thumb."

Physical Development/Games

Feed the Dog

Cut out ten dog bone shapes (approximately 2" x 3") from poster board and laminate them. Draw a dog face or find one in a coloring book. Glue the picture of the dog face on top of a shoebox. Use an exacto knife to cut an opening around the dog's mouth and through the lid of the shoebox. Invite the children to "feed the dog" bones by slipping them through the opening in his mouth and into the box.

Physical Development/Gross Motor

Knee Walk

Show the children how to walk on their knees. Talk with them as they try some "knee walking." *Do things in the room look different when you look at them from a lower height?*

Outdoor Play or Music and Movement

- Give the children rhythm band instruments. Encourage them to play the instruments while they are singing "This Old Man Is Rockin' On" (see previous page).
- Sing along with "This Old Man" (*Here Is Thumbkin* CD, Kimbo Educational) or "This Old Man Is Rockin' On" (*Laugh and Learn Silly Songs* CD, Kimbo Educational).

STORY TIME SUGGESTION

This Old Man by Pam Adams

Three Little Kittens

Three Little Kittens (Tune: Traditional)
Three little kittens lost their mittens;
And they began to cry,
"Oh, mother dear, we very much fear
Our mittens we have lost."

"What! Lost your mittens! You naughty kittens!
Then you shall have no pie."
"Mee-ow, mee-ow, mee-ow, mee-ow."
"No, you shall have no pie."

The three little kittens they found their mittens;
And they began to cry,
"Oh, Mother dear, see here, see here!
Our mittens we have found."

"What! Found your mittens! You good little kittens!
Now you shall have some pie."
"Purr, purr, purr, purr,
Purr, purr, purr."

SEE ALSO

"Fiddle-I-Fee," page 67
"Simple Simon," page 176

Related Songs, Chants, and Rhymes

Old Gray Cat
The old gray cat is sleeping, sleeping, sleeping.
The old gray cat is sleeping in the house.
(*one child, the cat, curls up, pretending to sleep*)

The little mice are creeping, creeping, creeping.
The little mice are creeping through the house.
(*other children, the mice, creep around the sleeping cat*)

The old gray cat is waking, waking, waking.
The old gray cat is waking through the house.
(*cat slowly sits up and stretches*)

The old gray cat is chasing, chasing, chasing.
The old gray cat is chasing through the house.
(*cat chases mice*)

All the mice are squealing, squealing, squealing.
All the mice are squealing through the house.
(*mice squeal; when cat catches a mouse, that mouse becomes the cat*)

Pussy Cat, Pussy Cat

Pussy cat, pussy cat,
Where have you been?
I've been to London to see the Queen.
Pussy cat, pussy cat,
What did you there?
I frightened a little mouse under the chair.

Senor Don Gato (Tune: Traditional)

Oh, Senor Don Gato was a cat
On a high red roof Don Gato sat.
He went there to read a letter,
Meow, meow, meow
Where the reading light was better,
Meow, meow, meow
'Twas a love note for Don Gato.

"I adore you," wrote the lady cat,
Who was fluffy, white and nice and fat.
There was not a sweeter kitty,
Meow, meow, meow
In the country or the city.
Meow, meow, meow
And she said she'd wed Don Gato.

Oh, Don Gato jumped so happily,
He fell off the roof and broke his knee.
Broke his ribs and all his whiskers,
Meow, meow, meow
And his little solar plexus.
Meow, meow, meow
"Ay caramba," cried Don Gato.

Then the doctors all came on the run
Just to see if something could be done.
And they held a consultation,
Meow, meow, meow
About how to save their patient,
Meow, meow, meow
How to save Senor Don Gato.

But in spite of everything they tried,
Poor Senor Don Gato up and died.
And it wasn't very merry,
Meow, meow, meow
Going to the cemetery,
Meow, meow, meow
For the ending of Don Gato.

When the funeral passed the market square,
Such a smell of fish was in the air.
Though his burial was slated,
Meow, meow, meow
He became reanimated.
Meow, meow, meow
He came back to life, Don Gato.

Follow-Up Questions

- *Have you ever lost something? What did you lose?*
- *Do you think kittens like pie? What kind?*

Language Enrichment

- Ask the children questions about the rhyme. *Do you think kittens can wear mittens? How many mittens would a kitten need?*
- Discuss the onomatopoeic sounds in the rhyme (sounds that sound like the sound they are making). *What sounds do kittens make when they are happy? What sound do they make when they are hungry?* Discuss a sound that kittens make that is not in the rhyme. *What sound do they make when they are angry or frightened?* (hiss)
- Discuss kittens and cats. *What is the difference between a kitten and a cat? How are they alike? How are they different?*
- Teach the children the American Sign Language signs for *kitten* and *cat* (see appendix page 239).

STORY TIME SUGGESTIONS

Three Little Kittens by Paul Galdone
Three Little Kittens by Lorianne Siomades
Top Cat by Lois Elhert

Extension Activities

Cognitive Development/Math

Mitten Match

Give the children a basket of mittens and encourage them to match the mittens one–to–one. Talk with them as they make matches. Use the correct language, such as matching one–to–one and making pairs. Younger children will enjoy trying on the mittens. Observe their ability to try on a matching pair.

Cognitive, Physical, and Social-Emotional Development/Games

Mitten Hunt

Hide a mitten and encourage the children to find it. Occasionally make the hiding place easy so that younger children can participate. When you hide the mitten in a more challenging spot, provide clues to help them locate the hidden mitten.

Physical Development/Fine Motor

Playdough Cherry Pies

Provide yellow and pink playdough, rolling pins, and pie tins. Show the children how to roll the yellow playdough with the rolling pin to make a "crust." Then show them how to roll the pink dough into balls to make "cherries" to fill the pie.

Physical Development/Water Play

Mitten Wash

Provide a tub of soapy water, a second tub of rinse water, and some mittens. Encourage the children to wash the mittens. Make a clothesline by stringing a line between two chairs and provide clothespins so that the children can hang the mittens up to dry. Talk with the children as they wash.

Outdoor Play or Music and Movement

- Play "The Old Gray Cat." You will need to be the cat for the first few games.
- Sing along with "Three Little Kittens" (*Singable Nursery Rhymes* CD, Kimbo Educational).

REFLECTIONS ON THE DAY

- *Where do you think the kittens lost their mittens?*
- *Where do you think the kittens found their mittens? How do you think they knew where to look?*

Three Little Monkeys

Three Little Monkeys
Three little monkeys swinging in a tree, (*hold up three fingers*)
Teasing Mr. Alligator,
Can't catch me, can't catch me. (*shake finger as if teasing*)
Along comes Mr. Alligator, quiet as can be
And SNAPS that monkey right out of the tree! (*creep fingers on floor or up arm*)
Snap! (clap)

Two little monkeys swinging in a tree, (*hold up two fingers*)
Teasing Mr. Alligator,
Can't catch me, can't catch me. (*shake finger as if teasing*)
Along comes Mr. Alligator, quiet as can be
And SNAPS that monkey right out of the tree! (*creep fingers on floor or up arm*)
Snap! (*clap*)

One little monkey swinging in a tree, (*holds up one finger*)
Teasing Mr. Alligator,
Can't catch me, can't catch me. (*shake finger as if teasing*)
Along comes Mr. Alligator, quiet as can be
And SNAPS that monkey right out of the tree! (*creep fingers on floor or up arm*)
Snap! (*clap*)

No more monkeys sitting in a tree.

SEE ALSO

"Five Little Monkeys," page 180
"Old Gray Cat," page 208
"Three Tricky Turtles," page 217

Related Songs, Chants, and Rhymes

Crocodile Song (Tune: Traditional)
She sailed away on a bright and sunny day,
On the back of a crocodile.
"You see," said she, "he's as tame as he can be;
I'll ride him down the Nile."
The croc winked his eye as she bade her mom goodbye,
Wearing a happy smile.
At the end of the ride the lady was inside
And the smile was on the crocodile!

Ten Little Monkeys by Pam Schiller (Tune: Little Red Wagon)
One little, two little, three little monkeys,
Four little, five little, six little monkeys,
Seven little, eight little, nine little monkeys,
Ten little monkeys at the zoo.

One little monkey doing some tricks.
Two little monkeys picking up sticks.
Three little monkeys standing in lines.
Four little monkeys swinging on vines.

One little, two little, three little monkeys,
Four little, five little, six little monkeys,
Seven little, eight little, nine little monkeys,
Ten little monkeys at the zoo.

Follow-Up Questions

- *What happened to the monkeys?*
- *Has anyone ever teased you?*

Language Enrichment

- Talk about teasing. *What does it mean to tease?* Tell the children that the best thing to do if someone teases them is to walk away. If the teaser doesn't get a reaction, she won't think it is any fun to tease. Demonstrate how to ignore teasing with the help of another adult.
- Talk about monkeys and alligators. Show pictures of each animal, if available. *Where do monkeys live? What do they eat? How do they move? Where do alligators live? What color are they? How do they move?*
- Teach children the American Sign Language signs for *monkey* and *alligator* (see appendix page 239).

Extension Activities

Cognitive Development/Library

Monkey See, Monkey Do
Encourage the children to copy your monkey antics. Scratch your sides, scratch your head, jump up and down, pretend to swing on a vine, and so on.

STORY TIME SUGGESTION

Five Little Monkeys: Best Loved Action Rhymes by David Melling

Physical Development/Fine Motor

Alligator Pick Up

Away from the children, spray paint spring-type clothespins using non-toxic green paint. Draw two small eyes at the top of each clothespin. Show the children how to pinch the clothespin to open it, and tell them that the open part is the alligator's mouth. Encourage the children to use the alligator clothespins to pick up 1" pompoms.

Physical Development/Gross Motor

Alligator Crawl

Show the children how to crawl on their tummies like an alligator. Identify a start and finish line on the floor with masking tape. Have the children do the alligator crawl between the two lines. Talk with them as they play. *Do alligators move quickly or slowly?*

Physical and Cognitive Development/Fine Motor

Shadow Gators

Provide a light source. Demonstrate how to make an "alligator" shadow by pressing your index, middle, ring, and little finger against your thumb. Show the children how the alligator can snap.

Outdoor Play or Music and Movement

- Play Can't Chase Me. Encourage the children (the "monkeys") to run as you or another child (the "alligator") try to catch them.
- Chant along with "Three Little Monkeys" or sing along with "The Crocodile Song" (*Where Is Thumbkin?* CD, Kimbo Educational).

REFLECTIONS ON THE DAY

- *Why were the monkeys teasing the alligator?*
- *How many monkeys were in the tree at the beginning of the rhyme? How many were left at the end of the rhyme?*

Tiny Tim

Tiny Tim (Tune: Traditional)
I had a little turtle,
His name was Tiny Tim.
I put him in the bathtub,
To see if he could swim.

He drank up all the water,
He ate up all the soap,
Tiny Tim was choking
On the bubbles in his throat.

I picked up the telephone,
I pressed in 9-1-1
I asked for the doctor
And said he better run.

In came the doctor,
In came the nurse,
In came the lady
With the alligator purse.

They pumped out all the water,
They pumped out all the soap,
They popped the airy bubbles
As they floated from his throat.

Out went the doctor,
Out went the nurse.
Out went the lady
With the alligator purse.

Related Songs, Chants, and Rhymes

Kissy Kim adapted by Pam Schiller
I had a little goldfish,
Her name was Kissy Kim.
I put her in the bathtub,
To see if she could swim.

SEE ALSO

"B-B-B-Bubbles," page 32
"Bubbles in the Air," page 32
"Miss Polly Had a Dolly," page 123
"Say, Say, My Playmate," page 124
"Three Little Monkeys," page 212

She drank up all the water,
She ate up all the soap,
Kissy Kim was choking
On the bubbles in her throat.

I picked up the telephone,
I pressed in 9-1-1.
I asked for the doctor
And said she better run.

In came the doctor,
In came the nurse,
In came the lady
With the alligator purse.

They pumped out all the water,
They pumped out all the soap,
They popped the airy bubbles
As they floated from her throat.

Out went the doctor,
Out went the nurse.
Out went the lady
With the alligator purse.

I guess I learned my lesson
I won't try that again.
Tiny Tim and Kissy Kim
In bubbles cannot swim.

There Once Was a Turtle

There was a little turtle (*make a fist*)
He lived in a box. (*draw a square in the air*)
He swam in a puddle. (*pretend to swim*)
He climbed on the rocks. (*pretend to climb*)
He snapped at a mosquito. (*use your hand to make a snapping motion*)
He snapped at a flea. (*snapping motion*)
He snapped at a minnow. (*snapping motion*)
And he snapped at me. (*snapping motion*)
He caught the mosquito. (*clap hands*)
He caught the flea. (*clap hands*)
He caught the minnow. (*clap hands*)
But he didn't catch me. (*wave index finger as if saying no-no*)

Three Tricky Turtles by Pam Schiller (Tune: Three Blind Mice)
Three pokey turtles.
Three pokey turtles.
See how they move.
See how they move.
They decided to race a fox one day,
Their friends and family began to pray.
The fox got beat by a trick I hear.
Three tricky turtles.
Three tricky turtles.

Follow-Up Questions

- *Have you ever seen a live turtle? Where? What was it doing?*
- *Do you know how to swim?*

Language Enrichment

- Discuss turtles. If you have a photo of a turtle, show it to the children to help stimulate conversation. *Where do turtles live? What do they eat? What color are they? How do they move?*
- Talk with the children about dialing 911 on the phone in an emergency. Show them the numbers on the phone and let them practice pushing the numbers. Define emergency, and give examples, such as when someone is gets hurt or if there is a fire. **Note:** Make sure children understand never to dial this number unless they feel it is an emergency.
- Talk about an alligator purse. *How is it different from other purses?* If you have something made from alligator skin, show it to the children.
- Sing "Kissy Kim" (see page 215). *What is different in the two songs? What is alike in the songs?*
- Teach the children the American Sign Language signs for *fish* and *turtle* (see appendix page 239).

Extension Activities

Cognitive Development/Math

911

Provide a couple of play or real unplugged telephones. Show the children how to dial 911 on the phones. Encourage them to have pretend conversations with the doctor or nurse who needs to come see Tiny Tim or Kissy Kim. Younger children will enjoy pushing the buttons on the phone.

STORY TIME SUGGESTION

Little Turtle and the Song of the Sea by Sheridan Cain

Physical Development/Gross Motor

Bubble Fun

Encourage the children to blow and chase bubbles. *How are these bubbles like the ones that Tiny Tim got in his throat? What would happen if any of these bubbles got in your throat?*

Social-Emotional Development/Dramatic Play

Alligator Purse

Give the children old purses to explore. Provide interesting items to go inside the purses, such as small mirrors, change purses, billfolds, and so on.

Social-Emotional Development/Water Play

Water Animals

Provide plastic fish, turtles, and any other plastic water animals available for children to play with in the water. Talk about how the animals are alike and how they are different. *Do any of the animals live only in water?*

Outdoor Play or Music and Movement

- Take the children outdoors to blow bubbles. Encourage them to chase the bubbles as you blow them.
- Sing along with "Tiny Tim" (*Laugh 'N Learn Silly Songs* CD, Kimbo Educational).

REFLECTIONS ON THE DAY

- *If you had a pet turtle, what would you name it?*
- *What phone number do you dial if you have an emergency?*

Twinkle, Twinkle, Little Star

Twinkle, Twinkle, Little Star
Twinkle, twinkle, little star,
How I wonder what you are.
Up above the world so high,
Like a diamond in the sky.
Twinkle, twinkle, little star.
How I wonder what you are.

When the blazing sun is set,
And the grass with dew is wet,
Then you show your little light,
Twinkle, twinkle, all the night.

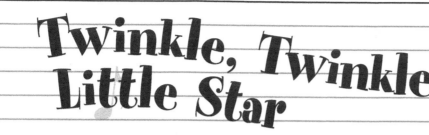

Related Songs, Chants, and Rhymes

Little Drop of Dew (Tune: traditional)
Little drop of dew
Like a gem you are
I believe that you
Must have been a star.

When the day is light
On the grass you lie.
Tell me then at night
Are you in the sky?

Star Light, Star Bright
Star light, star bright,
First star I've seen tonight.
I wish I may, I wish I might
Have this wish I wish tonight.

Follow-Up Questions

- *Do you think the stars look like diamonds?*
- *When do you see the most stars?*

SEE ALSO

"I Can, Can You?," page 111
"This Little Light of Mine," page 199

Language Enrichment

- Discuss the new vocabulary in the song, such as *wonder, world, diamond, blazing,* and *dew.*
- Sing the song, changing the word *little* to other adjectives, for example, *tiny, gigantic, jazzy, blinking,* and so on. Use your voice, when possible, to indicate the meaning of the adjective. For example, if you sing about a *gigantic star,* use a *gigantic* voice. Be sure you define each new adjective for the children.
- Discuss stars. *Where are they found? When can you see them best? Has anyone ever wished on a star?*
- Explain what it means to wish on a star. Tell the children what you would wish for if you wished upon a star. Ask them what they would wish for.
- Teach the children the American Sign Language sing for *star* (see appendix page 239).

Extension Activities

Cognitive Development/Games

Star Search

Hide cut-out stars all over the room. Give the children a basket or a sack and invite them to find the stars and place them in the sack.

Cognitive Development/Math

Star Sort

Provide star stickers or cut-out stars in several different colors of construction paper. Encourage the children to sort the stars by color.

Physical Development/Fine Motor

Star Cookies

Mix Star Dough. Mix 1 cup flour, ½ cup salt, 1 cup water, 2 tablespoons vegetable oil, 1 teaspoon cream of tartar, ⅓ cup silver glitter, and ¼ cup white, powdered, non-toxic tempera paint. Cook over medium heat, stirring until the mixture forms a ball. Let cool and then knead. Give the children Star Dough and star-shaped cookie cutters and invite them to make star shaped "cookies." Explain to the children that these are not real cookies and should not be eaten. **Safety Note**: Make sure that the children don't rub their eyes while playing with the dough. Have the children wash their hands when they are finished playing with the dough.

STORY TIME SUGGESTION

Twinkle, Twinkle Little Star by Iza Trapani

Physical Development/Sand Table

Diamond Find

Place rock salt in the sand table. Give the children a strainer and a bucket. Encourage them to strain the sand to find the "diamonds." Talk with the children about the rock salt diamonds. *Do the grains of salt look like diamonds? Why do they stay in the strainer?*

Outdoor Play or Music and Movement

- Play Star Catch. Cut out stars from Styrofoam meat trays. Toss the stars and invite the children to catch them in empty ice cream cartons or other soft buckets.
- Sing along with "Twinkle, Twinkle Little Star" (*Twinkle, Twinkle Jazzy Star* CD, Thomas Moore Enterprise), or "Little Drop of Dew" (*The Bountiful Earth* CD, Schiller Educational Resources).
- Listen to the instrumental version of "The Opera Singer" (*Singing, Moving, and Learning* CD, Thomas Moore Enterprises).

REFLECTIONS ON THE DAY

- *How did you get the rock salt diamonds out of the sand?*
- *What would you wish for if you made a wish on a star?*

Two Little Blackbirds

Two Little Blackbirds (Tune: Twinkle, Twinkle Little Star)
Two little blackbirds (*hold up index finger of each hand*)
Sitting on a hill.
One named Jack. (*hold right hand/finger forward*)
One named Jill. (*hold left hand/finger forward*)
Fly away, Jack. (*wiggle right finger and place behind your back*)
Fly away, Jill. (*wiggle left finger and place behind your back*)
Come back, Jack. (*bring right hand back*)
Come back, Jill. (*bring left hand back*)

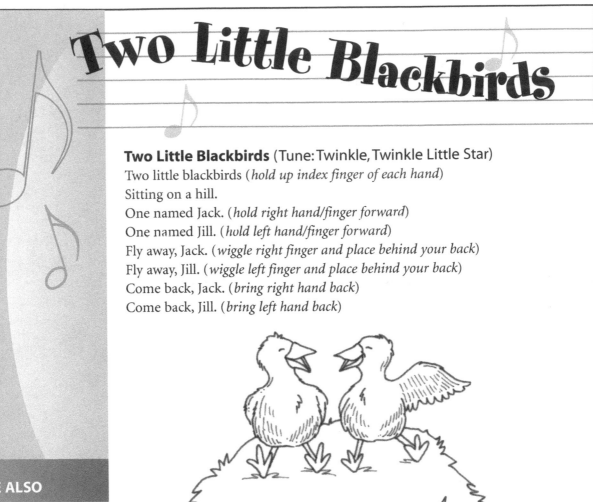

SEE ALSO

"Animal Fair," page 155
"Jack and Jill," page 84
"Sing a Song of Sixpence," page 176

Related Songs, Chants, and Rhymes

Birdie, Birdie, Where Is Your Nest? (Tune: Traditional)
Birdie, birdie, where is your nest?
Birdie, birdie, where is your nest?
Birdie, birdie, where is your nest?
In the tree that I love best.

Birdie, birdie, where do you rest?
Birdie, birdie, where do you rest?
Birdie, birdie, where do you rest?
In the nest that I love best.

Little Polly Parakeet by Pam Schiller (Tune: Little Bunny Foo Foo)
Little Polly Parakeet
Sits on Daddy's shoulder.
When he turns his face to her,
She kisses him on the cheek.

Little Polly Parakeet
Sits on Mommy's shoulder.
Whistling a happy song
Before she goes to sleep.

Little Polly Parakeet
Sits upon my shoulder.
She's soft and green and little
She's really kinda sweet.

White Wings (Tune: Traditional)
White wings, they never grow weary
They cheerfully carry me over the sea,
White wings, I long for thee dearly
I lift up my white wings and fly home to thee.

Follow-Up Questions

- *Where do you think the birds flew away to?*
- *Have you ever seen a black bird? Where was it?*

Language Enrichment

- Discuss new vocabulary words in the song, including *fly* and *hill.* Show the children a picture of a blackbird. Discuss the bird's feathers, wings, beak, and feet.
- Read the nursery rhyme "Jack and Jill" (see page 84). Point out the similarities in the names of the children and the names of the birds.
- Sing "Birdie, Birdie, Where Is Your Nest?" (see previous page) with the children. If available, share photos of birds and/or bird's nests. Use the photos to encourage conversation about birds and their nests.

Extension Activities

Cognitive Development/Art

Feather Collages

Give the children art paper, feathers, and glue or paste. Encourage them to make a collage with the feathers. Talk with them about the feathers as they work. *How do they feel? Are they light? Which color feather do you like best? Which animals have feathers? Do you think feathers keep birds warm?*

STORY TIME SUGGESTIONS

Are You My Mother? by P.D. Eastman
The Best Nest by P.D. Eastman

Physical Development/Fine Motor

Nest Building

Give the children a box of twigs, string, and dried grass. Encourage them to stack the twigs to build a nest. Talk with them about where birds get the building material for their nests. *How do birds carry the things to their nests since they do not have any hands?* **Safety Note:** Supervise closely to ensure that children do not put small twigs and grass in their mouths.

Physical Development/Gross Motor

Feather Drop

Place a shallow box or box lid on the floor. Give the children feathers and have them try to drop the feathers into the box. This is not as easy as it sounds. Challenge the children to hold the feathers chest high. Once they get the hang of this, suggest that they hold the feathers over their heads before dropping. Talk about how the feathers drop. Discuss other things that float when they are dropped, such as a leaf, piece of paper, or piece of thin cloth. Encourage younger children to drop the feathers without worrying about hitting the box.

Social Development/Dramatic Play

Nesting

Give the children a large basket to use as a nest. Encourage them to make their nest more comfortable by lining it with a blanket or other soft materials. Talk with them as they play. *Do you think birds get tired of sitting in their nest? Why? Why not? Do you think they get cold?*

REFLECTIONS ON THE DAY

- *What did you learn about birds today?*
- *Would you like to fly like a bird? Where would you fly?*

Outdoor Play or Music and Movement

- Play Fly Away Birdie! Place several sheets of brown construction paper on the floor. Ask the children to form a circle around you. Say, "Fly away, fly away, little birdies" and then count to three. As soon as you say "fly away," the children must run to a "nest" (brown paper) before you can catch them. If they get to the paper before you catch them, they are safe. If they do not, they help you catch other children.
- Give each child two paper plates to represent wings. Play classical music and invite the children to dance like birds.
- Sing along with "Birdie, Birdie, Where Is Your Nest?" (*Critters and Company* CD, Schiller Educational Resources, LLCB).

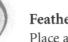

The Wheels on the Bus

The Wheels on the Bus
(Tune: Traditional)

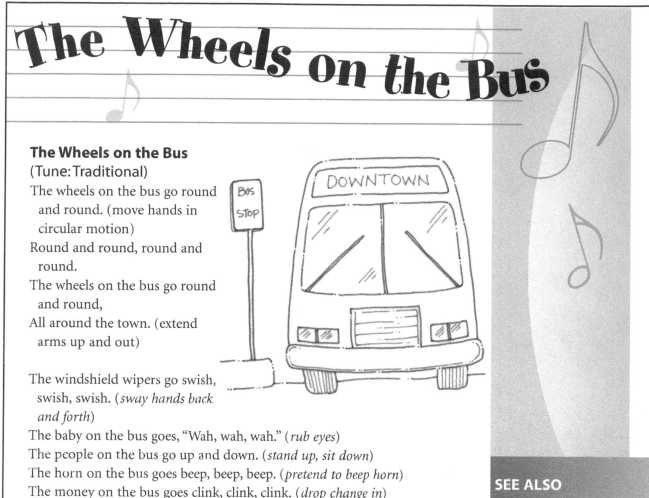

The wheels on the bus go round and round. (move hands in circular motion)
Round and round, round and round.
The wheels on the bus go round and round,
All around the town. (extend arms up and out)

The windshield wipers go swish, swish, swish. (*sway hands back and forth*)
The baby on the bus goes, "Wah, wah, wah." (*rub eyes*)
The people on the bus go up and down. (*stand up, sit down*)
The horn on the bus goes beep, beep, beep. (*pretend to beep horn*)
The money on the bus goes clink, clink, clink. (*drop change in*)
The driver on the bus says, "Move on back." (*hitchhiking movement*)

Related Songs, Chants, and Rhymes

The Bus Song (Tune: Pop Goes the Weasel)
I drive the bus around the town,
I stop at every corner.
My blinking lights and brakes go on,
Swish goes the door.
A dollar for a ride around town,
A quarter for a transfer.
Put your money in the slot.
Swish goes the door.

The Freight Train (Tune: Mary Had a Little Lamb)
Clickity, clackity, clickity clack!
The train speeds over the railroad track.
It rolls and rattles and screeches its song,
And pulls and jiggles its freight cars.

SEE ALSO

"The Car Song," page 98
"Little Hunk of Tin," page 98
"Little Red Wagon," page 104
"Motor Boat Chant" page 167
"My Bike," page 105
"Oh, It's Wheels, Wheels, Wheels," page 105
"Row, Row, Row Your Boat," page 167
"Windshield Wiper," page 99

Clickity, clackity, clickity, clack!
The engine in front is big and black.
The cars are filled with lots of things
Like milk or oil or mattress springs.

Clickity, clackity, clickity, clack!
The engineer waves, and I wave back.
I count the cars as the freight train goes,
And the whistle blows and blows...and blows!

Follow-Up Questions

- *Have you ever ridden on a bus? Tell us about your ride.*
- *Why do the people move up and down on a bus?*

Language Enrichment

- Discuss the sound words in the song, such as *swish*, *clink*, and *beep*. These words are called *onomatopoeic* words. Even though onomatopoeia seems like a large word, use it with the children. Many of them will use the word because they like the way it sounds.
- Make up some new sounds for the song. For example, the daddies could be snoring, the babies could be laughing, or the wipers could go *swipe* instead of *swish*. Sing the song with the new sounds. *What sound would kittens make in the bus?*
- Teach the children the American Sign Language sign for *bus* (see appendix page 239).

STORY TIME SUGGESTIONS

The Wheels on the Bus by Raffi
The Wheels on the Bus by Paul O. Zelinsky

Extension Activities

Cognitive Development/Art

Tire Tracks
Lay butcher paper on the floor. Use a rubber band or tape to attach a colored marker to the back of a toy car or truck. Make sure the marker touches the ground so that when the children push it, it will leave a track behind. Talk with the children about the trail they are making. *What happens if you back up?*

Cognitive Development/Discovery

Things That Roll
Provide a basket of items that roll (cars, skates, a pizza wheel, rolling pin, and so on) and items that don't roll. Help the children sort the items—those that roll and those that don't. Encourage younger children to just explore the rolling items. *What is the same about all the items that roll?*

Cognitive Development/Science

Sound Center

Provide musical items that make sounds, such as bells, drums, rhythm band instruments, horns, shakers, and so on. Encourage the children to make sounds with the items and then describe the sounds they make. *Do any of the sounds sound like the sounds mentioned in the song?*

Cognitive and Social-Emotional Development/Blocks

All Around the Town

Help the children build a town with blocks. Make paper bag houses by turning brown paper lunch bags upside down and drawing buildings on them. Add paper bag houses, trees, toy people, and plastic animals. Provide a toy bus and have the children drive the bus "all through the town." You might want to suggest that they sing, "The Wheels on the Bus" as they make their way through town.

Outdoor Play or Music and Movement

- Encourage the children to march around the room while singing "The Wheels on the Bus." When they are not doing the hand motions for "swish, swish, swish" or "clink, clink, clink," have them roll arm over arm as they do for "wheels on the bus go round and round."
- Sing along with "The Wheels on the Bus" (*Six White Ducks* CD, Kimbo Educational) or "The Wheels on the Bus" (*Early Childhood Classics: Old Favorites With a New Twist* CD, Hap-Pal Music).

REFLECTIONS ON THE DAY

- *Can you name something that rolls?*
- *Can you think of a sound other than beep that a horn on the bus might make?*

Where Is Thumbkin?

Where Is Thumbkin? (Tune: Frere Jacques)
Where is thumbkin? (*hands behind back*)
Where is thumbkin?
Here I am. Here I am. (*bring out right thumb, then left*)
How are you today, sir? (*bend right thumb*)
Very well, I thank you. (*bend left thumb*)
Run away. Run away. (*put right thumb behind back, then left thumb behind back*)

Other verses:
Where is Pointer?
Where is Middle One?
Where is Ring Finger?
Where is Pinky?
Where are all of them?

Related Songs, Chants, and Rhymes

SEE ALSO

"Open, Shut Them," page 145
"Sign Along With Me," page 173

Dance, Thumbkin, Dance
Dance, Thumbkin, dance. (*dance thumb around, moving and bending it*)
Dance, ye merrymen, everyone. (*dance all fingers*)
For Thumbkin, he can dance alone,
Thumbkin he can dance alone.

Dance, Foreman, dance. (*dance index finger around, moving and bending it*)
Dance, ye merrymen, everyone. (*dance all fingers*)
For Foreman, he can dance alone,
Foreman, he can dance alone.

Dance, Longman, dance. (*dance middle finger around, moving and bending it*)
Dance, ye merrymen, everyone. (*dance all fingers*)
For Longman, he can dance alone,
Longman, he can dance alone.

Dance, Ringman, dance. (*dance ring finger around—It won't bend alone*)
Dance, ye merrymen, everyone. (*dance all fingers*)
For Ringman, he cannot dance alone,
Ringman, he cannot dance alone.
Dance, Littleman, dance. (*dance little finger around, moving and bending*)

Dance, ye merrymen, everyone. (*dance all fingers*)
For Littleman, he can dance alone,
Littleman, he can dance alone.

Thelma Thumb

(*move thumb as directed*)
Thelma Thumb is up and Thelma Thumb is down.
Thelma Thumb is dancing all around the town.
Dance her on your shoulders, dance her on your head.
Dance her on your knees and tuck her into bed.

Name other fingers: Phillip Pointer, Terry Tall, Richie Ring, Baby Finger, and Finger Family and dance them on other body parts.

Where Is A? (Tune: Where Is Thumbkin?)

(*Use finger spelling for letters—see appendix page 244*)
Where is A? (bring right hand from behind back and make letter "A")
Where is A?
Here I am. (bring left hand from behind back and make letter "A")
Here I am.
How are you today A? (*wiggle right hand*)
Very Well I thank you. (*wiggle left hand*)
Run away. (*move right hand behind back*)
Run away. (*move left hand behind back*)

Follow-Up Questions

- *What do you say when someone asks "How are you?"*
- *Where was Thumbkin hiding?*

Language Enrichment

- Discuss hands. Give the names for each of the fingers again. If there is more than one name used for the finger, tell the children the alternate name, for example, *pinky* and *little finger*, and *ring man* and *ring finger*.
- Teach the children the American Sign Language signs for *finger*, *thumb*, and *hand* (see appendix page 239).

Extension Activities

Cognitive Development/Language

Hand Tracing

Trace around each child's hands. Draw fingernails on the fingers and encourage the children to paint the nails with non-toxic paint. Label the fingers. Talk about the parts of the fingers, such as fingernails, knuckles, and fingertips.

STORY TIME SUGGESTIONS

Hand, Hand, Finger, Thumb by Al Perkins
Hand Rhymes by Marc Tolon Brown

Physical Development/Art

Finger Painting

Provide non-toxic fingerpaint and encourage the children to use each of their fingers to make a design in the paint. As they paint, talk with them about the feel of the paint on their hands.

Physical Development/Fine Motor

Fingerprints

Make Gak. Combine 2 cups of glue, 1 ½ cups of water, and a few drops of food coloring in a bowl. In a larger bowl, dissolve 2 teaspoons of Borax in 1 cup of hot water. Slowly add glue mixture to Borax. It will thicken quickly and be difficult to mix. Mix well and drain off excess water. Let stand for a few minutes. Pour into a shallow tray. Let dry for 10 minutes. Store in zipper-closure plastic bags and it will keep for 2-3 weeks. Encourage the children to explore the Gak. Have them make fingerprints in the Gak.

Social-Emotional Development/Dramatic Play

Finger and Hand Puppets

Make Finger Puppets for each child using pipe cleaners. Roll each end of a pipe cleaner into two coils. Fold the pipe cleaner into a "U" shape. Hot glue a wiggle eye to each of the coiled ends of the pipe cleaner. Show the children how to place their middle finger into the "U" in the center to create a Finger Puppet. Show them how to move the puppet by wiggling their fingers. Ask the puppets questions and encourage the children to answer. For younger children, make Hand Puppets. Help each child make a fist. Use a washable marker to make eyes on the side of the fist, on either side of the index finger knuckle. Demonstrate how the puppet works by moving the thumb as if it is a mouth.

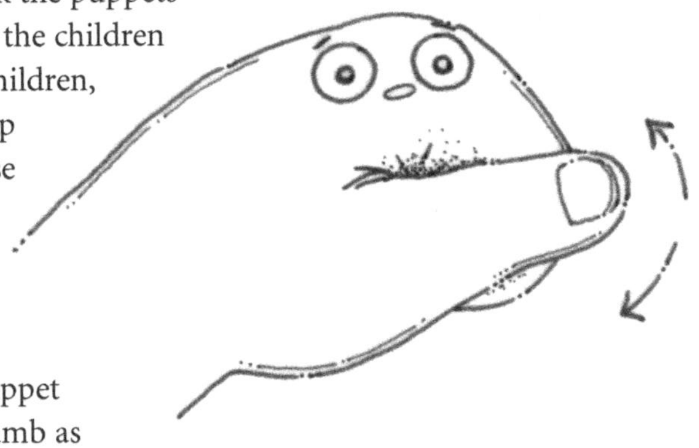

REFLECTIONS ON THE DAY

- *Can you name your fingers?*
- *Which finger do you use to point?*

Outdoor Play or Music and Movement

- Make drums for the children using empty coffee tins or empty half-gallon ice cream cartons. Show the children how to play the drums with their fingers. Play marching music and invite the children to play their drums.
- Sing along with "Where Is Thumbkin?" (*Where Is Thumbkin?* CD, Kimbo Educational).

Where, Oh, Where Has My Little Dog Gone?

Where, Oh, Where Has My Little Dog Gone? adapted by Richele Bartkowiak (Tune: Traditional)
Where, oh, where has my little dog gone?
Where, oh, where can he be?
With his ears cut short and his tail cut long,
Oh, where, oh, where can he be?

I saw him outside with his squeaky toy,
Rolling around in the sun.
He was pouncing and bouncing in a pile of leaves.
Oh, it looked like jolly good fun.

I called his name six times or more.
I listened for his happy bark.
I looked in the shed, even by the back door.
I'm worried 'cause it's getting dark.

I looked in the garden and over the fence.
I even looked under two trees.
And then when I thought it was almost too late,
I found him asleep in those leaves.

Related Songs, Chants, and Rhymes

Bingo (Tune: Traditional)
There was a farmer had a dog,
And Bingo was his name-o.
B-I-N-G-O!
B-I-N-G-O!
B-I-N-G-O!
And Bingo was his name-o!
(*Sing slowly so that the children can actually hear the letters as they are spoken. Do not drop letters with this age.*)

SEE ALSO

"Fido," page 135
"My Dog Rags," page 136
"Old Mother Hubbard," page 135

The First Day of Summer by Pam Schiller
(Tune: The Twelve Days of Christmas)
On the first day of summer,
My doggie brought to me
A branch from a sycamore tree.
On the second day of summer,
My doggie brought to me
Two chewed-up bones,
And a branch from a sycamore tree.

On the third day of summer,
My doggie brought to me
Three squeaky toys,
Two chewed-up bones,
And a branch from a sycamore tree.

On the fourth day of summer,
My doggie brought to me
Four bouncing balls,
Three squeaky toys,
Two chewed-up bones,
And a branch from a sycamore tree.

On the fifth day of summer,
My doggie brought to me
Five playful puppies,
Four bouncing balls,
Three squeaky toys,
Two chewed-up bones,
And a branch from a sycamore tree.

On the sixth day of summer,
This is what I said—
"Stop!"

STORY TIME SUGGESTIONS

How Much Is That Doggie in the Window? by Iza Trapani

Oh, Where, Oh Where Has My Little Dog Gone? by Iza Trapani

Follow-Up Questions

- *Where was the puppy?*
- *Have you ever been lost? Who found you?*

Language Enrichment

- Talk about dogs. If you have pictures show them to the children to help stimulate conversation. *What do dogs eat? Where do they sleep? How do they move?*
- Talk about losing things. *Have you ever lost something and had a hard time finding it?*
- Teach the children the American Sign Language signs for *dog* and *puppy* (see appendix page 239).

Extension Activities

Cognitive Development/Art

Dog Paws

Provide non-toxic fingerpaint. Show the children how to cover their closed hand (palm down) in paint and then press it to a sheet of paper to make a "dog paw" print. Encourage them to make several paw prints.

Cognitive Development/Listening

Puppy Sounds

Record dog sounds, for example, a growl, bark, whimper, snoring, and chewing. Make a happy face, mad face, sad face, chewing face (showing teeth), and sleeping face out of construction paper. (If possible, make puppy faces, but if this is too difficult, simple round faces will do.) Encourage the children to listen to the tape and find the face that goes with the sounds. Talk with them as they match the pictures to the sounds. *How do you know the dog is angry? How do you know she is sad? How do you know the dog is sleeping?*

Physical Development/Sand Table

Find the Dog

Bury plastic dogs in the sand table. Cover them with real or paper leaves. Challenge the children to find the dogs. Talk with them as they search. Remind them of the dog in the song.

Social-Emotional Development/Dramatic Play

Dog Ears

Cut off the feet from a pair of panty hose and tie a knot in the opening of each leg. Place the waist of the panty hose on a child's head. The legs of the panty hose look like dog ears. Give the children the panty hose dog ears to wear, and other dog props such as a dog food dish and play bones. Encourage them to pretend to be dogs. Talk about their ears. *Are your ears long or short? What kind of ears did the dog in the song have?*

Outdoor Play or Music and Movement

- Play Find the Dog. Take the children outdoors. Play hide and seek. The children pretend to be dogs and hide, and you try and find them.
- Sing along with "Oh, Where, Oh, Where Has My Little Dog Gone?" (*Critters and Company* CD, Schiller Educational Resources, LLC).

REFLECTIONS ON THE DAY

- *Did the dog in the song have long ears or short ears?*
- *What sound does a dog make when he is angry? What sound does a dog make when he gets hurt? What sound does he make when he is happy to see you?*

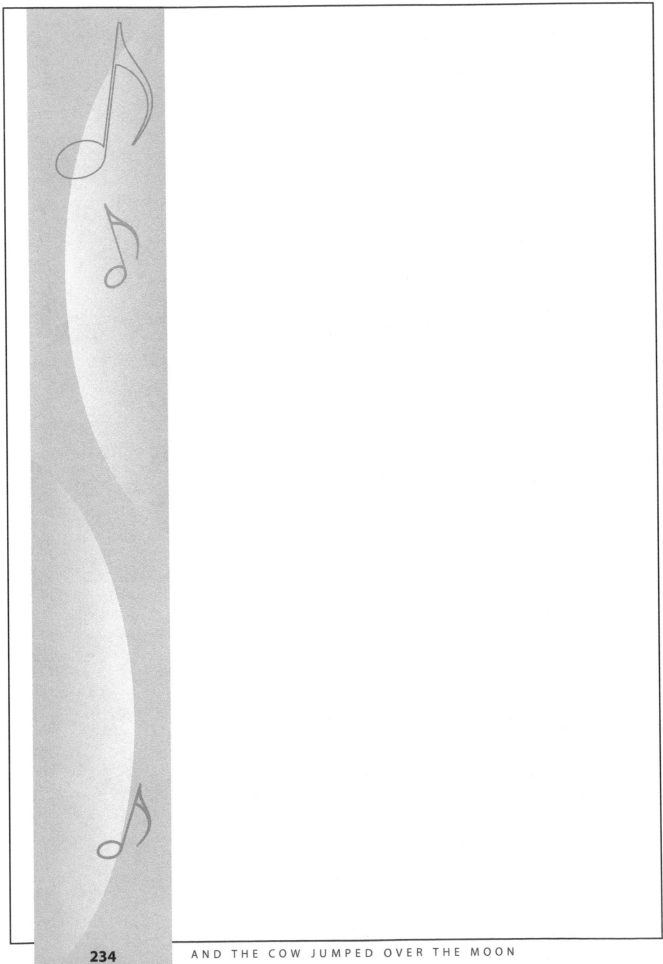

Appendix

Thematic Chart

American Sign Language

MUSIC WEBSITES

www.kididdles.com

www.geocities.com

www.judyanddavid.com

www.usscouts.org

www.drthomasmoore.com

Thematic Chart

Theme	Song	Chants and Rhymes
All About Me	Cap, Mittens, Coat, and Boots Do Your Ears Hang Low? The Finger Band Head, Shoulders, Knees, and Toes I Have Something in My Pocket If You're Happy and You Know It Open, Shut Them Put Your Little Foot S-M-I-L-E This Little Light of Mine Walk, Walk, Walk Your Feet Where Is Thumbkin?	After My Bath Clap, Clap, Clap Your Hands Dance, Thumbkin, Dance Five Fingers on Each Hand Head, Shoulders, Baby Here Are My Ears I Can Clap My Hands I Can, Can You? My Hands My Ten Little Fingers Pat-a-Cake Put Your Shoes On, Lucy Say and Touch Stretching Chant Teddy Bear, Teddy Bear Terrific Toes Thelma Thumb These Little Hands of Mine This Little Piggy
My School	The Alphabet Song Are You Listening? Be Very Quiet Good Morning to You I Like Black Katie Draws With One Crayon Make New Friends Mary Had a Little Lamb The More We Get Together Morning Greeting Nursery Rhyme Rap One, Two Buckle My Shoe Sign Along With Me Sing a Song of Opposites Which Things Go Together? Will You Be My Friend Today?	A Rig-a-Jig-Jig Alphabet Boogie The Alphabet Chant Counting Rhyme
Counting	The Ants Go Marching Five Little Ducks One, Two, Buckle My Shoe Six in the Bed Six White Ducks This Old Man Three Bear Rap	Counting Rhyme Five Little Fingers Five Little Monkeys Higgilty Piggilty One Potato, Two Potato Ten Little Fingers Put Your Shoes On, Lucy

My Family and Friends	The First Day of Summer For He's a Jolly Good Fellow Hello, Good Friend Make New Friends My Dog Rags Risseldy, Rosseldy Rock-a-Bye Baby Six in the Bed Skidamarink There Was an Old Woman This Is Quinn Will You Be My Friend Today?	
Animal Friends	Animal Fair The Bear Went Over the Mountain Bingo Birdie, Birdie, Where Is Your Nest? Crocodile Song Down on Grandpa's Farm The Farmer in the Dell Fiddle-I-Fee The First Day of Summer Little Ducky Duddle Little Peter Rabbit My Dog Rags Old Gray Mare Old MacDonald Had a Farm Old Mother Hubbard Pop! Goes the Weasel Ten Little Monkeys Three Little Kittens Two Little Blackbirds Where, Oh Where Has My Little Dog Gone? White Wings Whose Dog Are Thou?	Elephant The Elephant Goes Five Huge Dinosaurs Five Little Monkeys Going on a Bear Hunt Higgilty Piggilty I Never Saw a Purple Cow Old Gray Cat Pussy Cat, Pussy Cat There Once Was a Turtle
Farm Life	Baa, Baa, Sweet Sheep Bingo Down on Grandpa's Farm The Farmer in the Dell Five Little Ducks Little Boy Blue Little Ducky Duddle Old Gray Mare Old MacDonald Had a Farm Six White Ducks	I Never Saw a Purple Cow

Insects and Bugs	The Ants Go Marching Baby Bumblebee The Bee and the Pup Flea, Fly, Flow Mosquito Itsy Bitsy Spider Little Ant's Hill Little Ants My Busy Garden Shoo Fly	Buzzy, Buzzy Baby Bee Dancing Spider Here Is the Beehive
Transportation	A Bicycle Built for Two The Bus Song The Car Song The Freight Train Little Hunk of Tin Little Red Wagon Little Red Wagon (Another Version) Oh, It's Wheels, Wheels, Wheels Row, Row, Row Your Boat The Wheels on the Bus Windshield Wipers	My Bike Motor Boat Chant Rocking Boat
Workers	Do You Know the Muffin Man? Johnny Works With One Hammer Nursery Rhyme Rap Simple Simon	
Nursery Rhymes	Baa, Baa, Sweet Sheep Curly Locks Deedle, Deedle, Dumpling Hey, Diddle Diddle Hickory, Dickory, Dock Humpty Dumpty Jack and Jill Jack, Be Nimble Jack Spratt Little Boy Blue Little Jack Horner Little Miss Muffet Mary Had a Little Lamb Mary Had a William Goat Mary, Mary, Quite Contrary Nursery Rhyme Rap Old King Cole Old Mother Hubbard Pussy Cat, Pussy Cat Simple Simon Sing a Song of Sixpence There Was an Old Woman There Was an Old Woman (Version 2) Three Little Kittens Wee Willie Winkie	Humpty Dumpty (Version 2) Humpty Dumpty's New Ears Little Miss Spider

American Sign Language

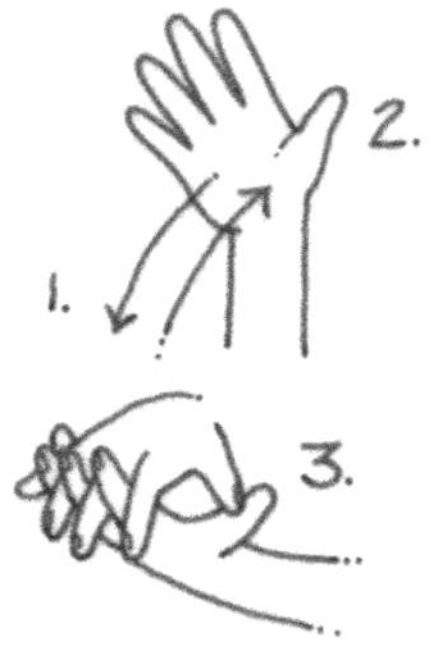

Alligator

Ant

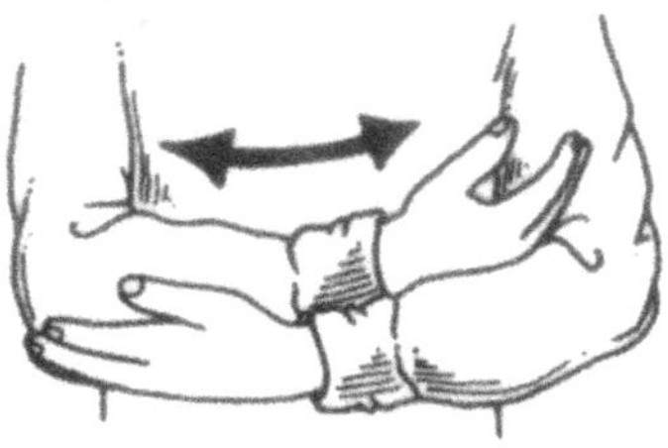

Baby

Bath

Bear

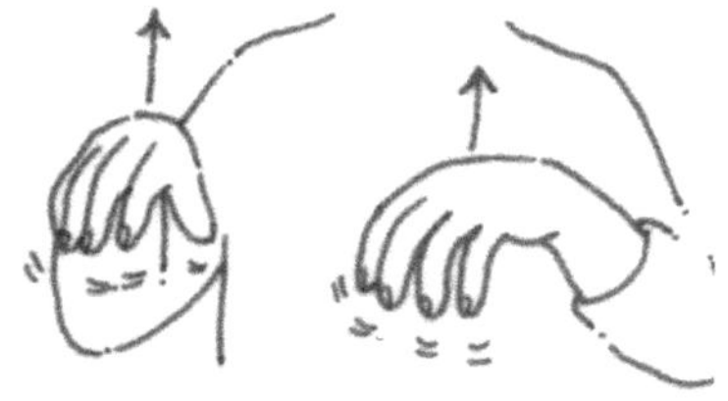

Bubbles

Bee

Bus

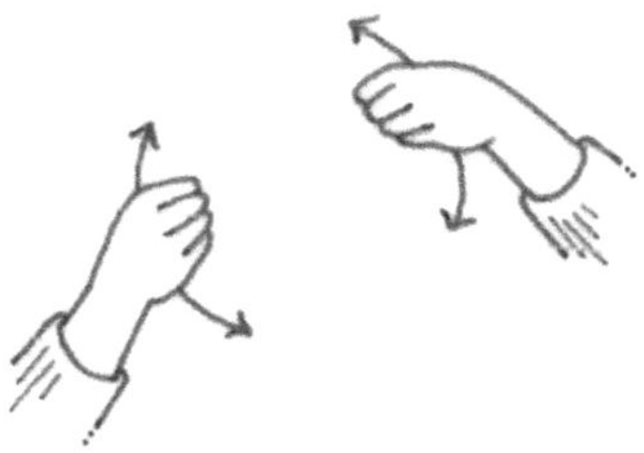

Car

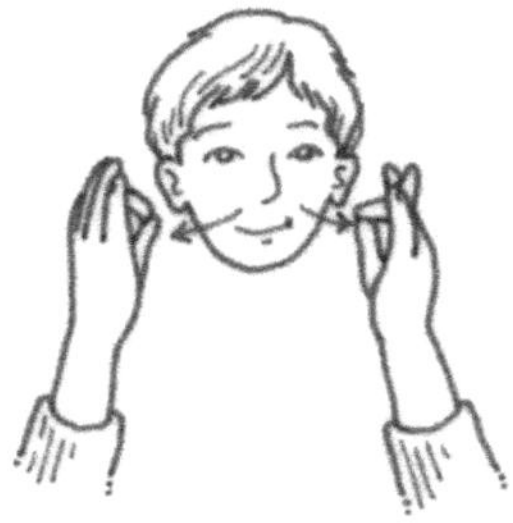

Cat

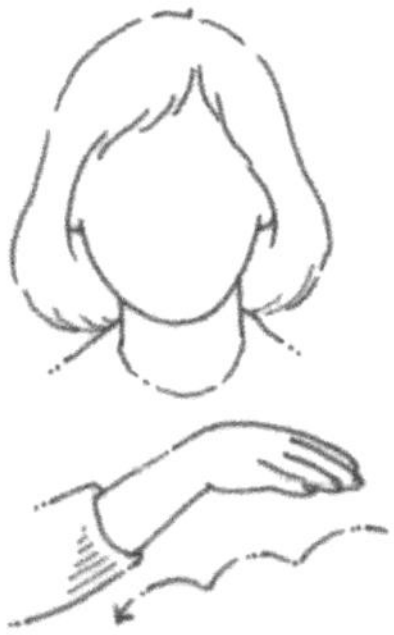

Children

Cow

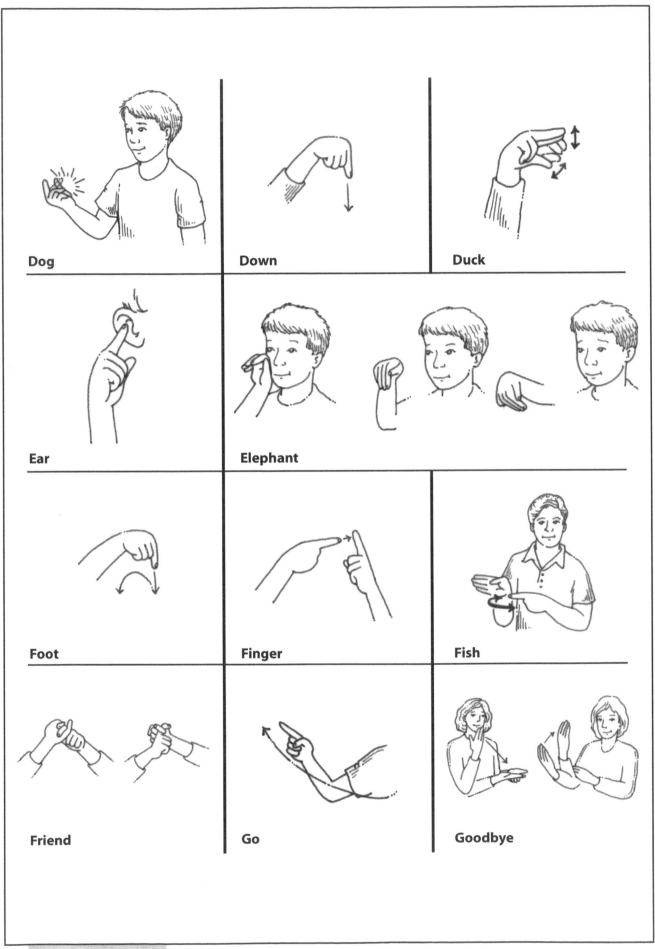

Dog

Down

Duck

Ear

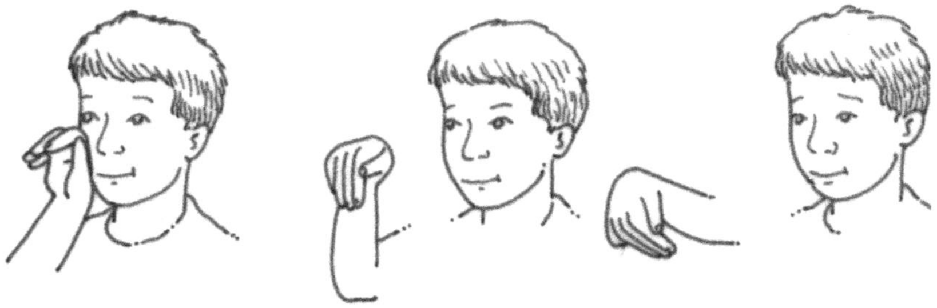

Elephant

Foot

Finger

Fish

Friend

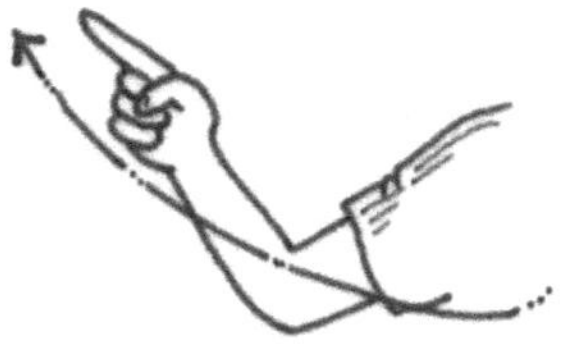

Go

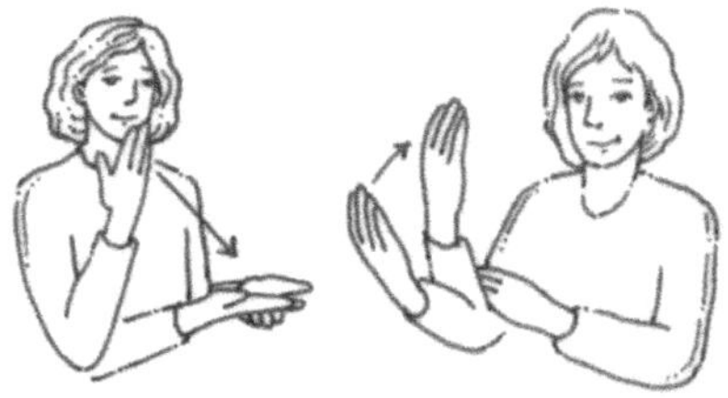

Goodbye

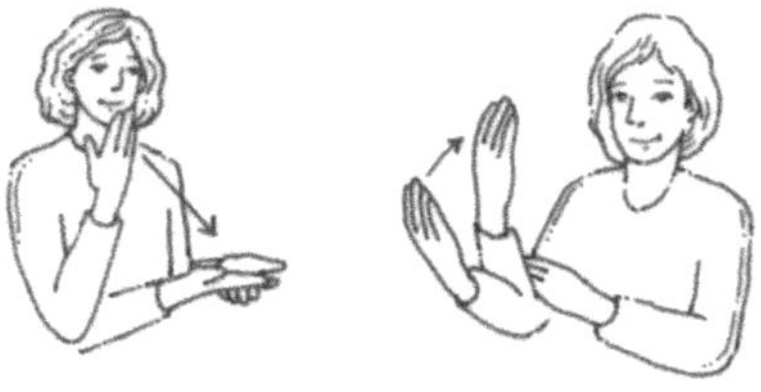

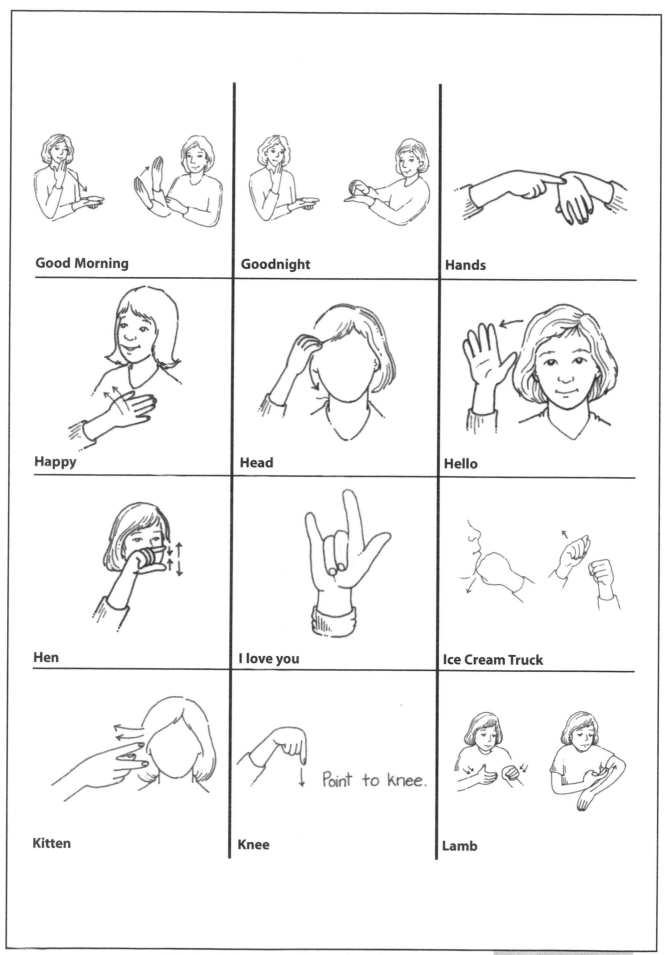

Good Morning

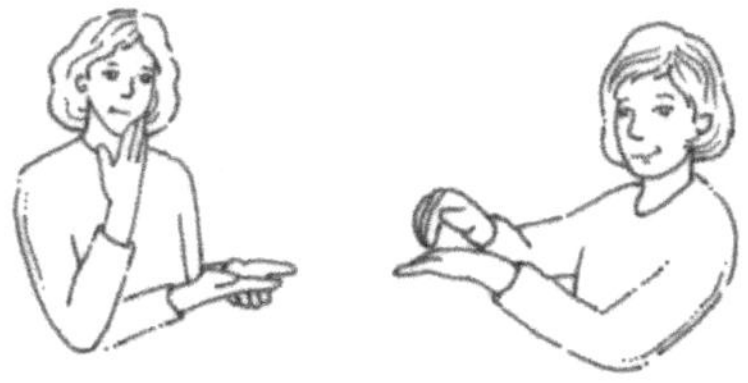

Goodnight

Hands

Happy

Head

Hello

Hen

I love you

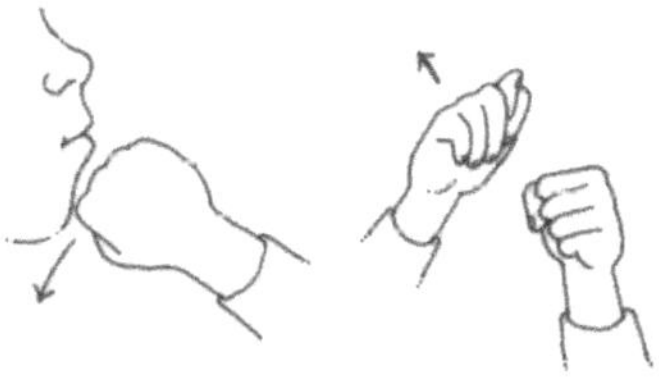

Ice Cream Truck

Kitten

Knee

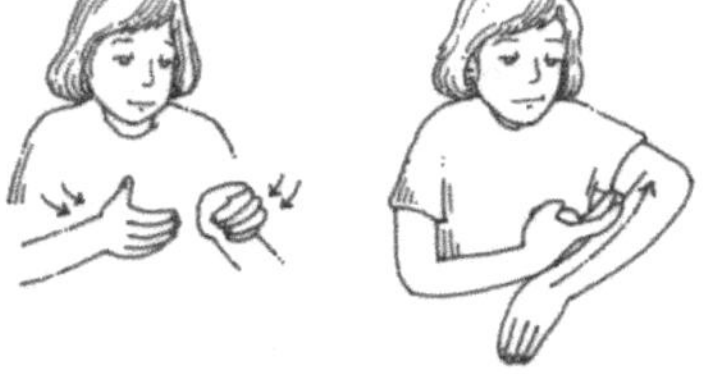

Lamb

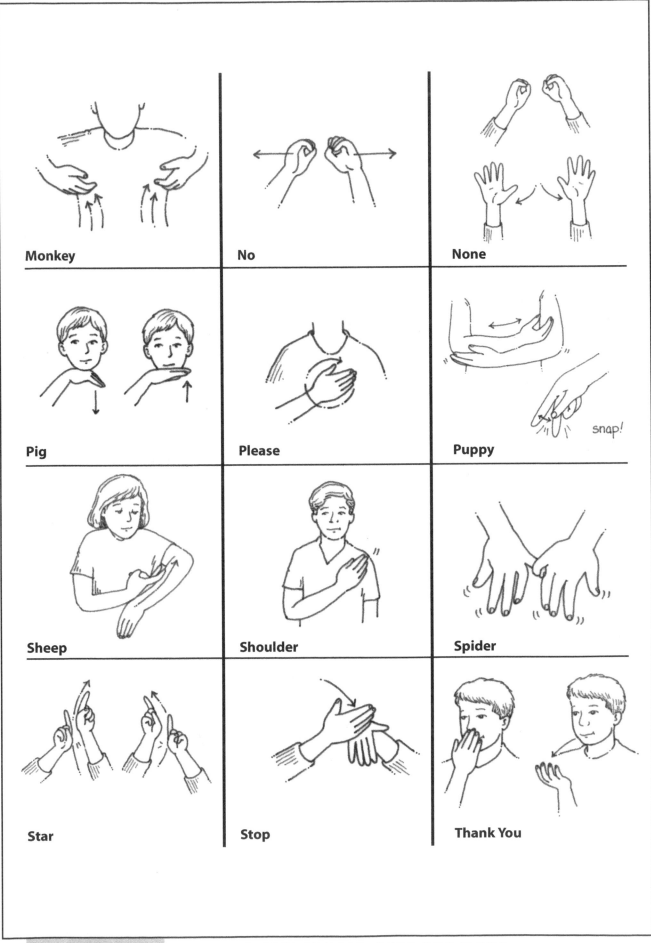

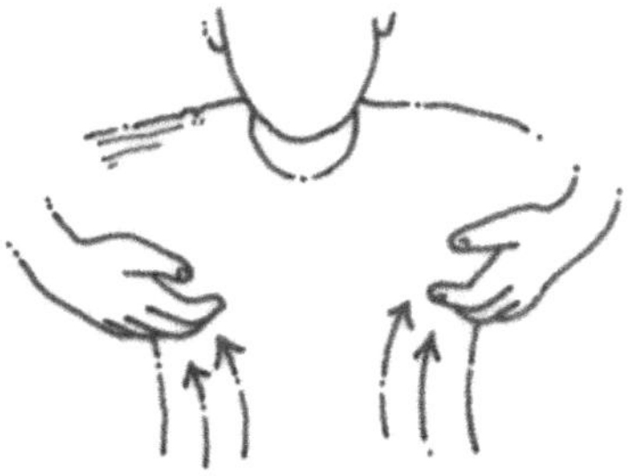

Monkey

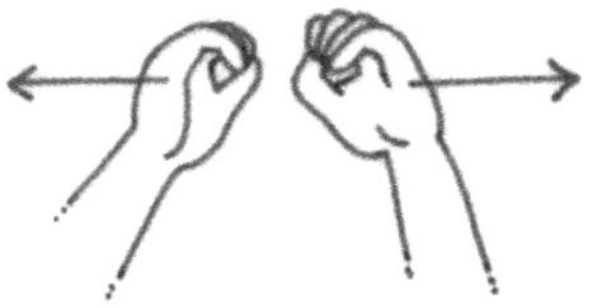

No

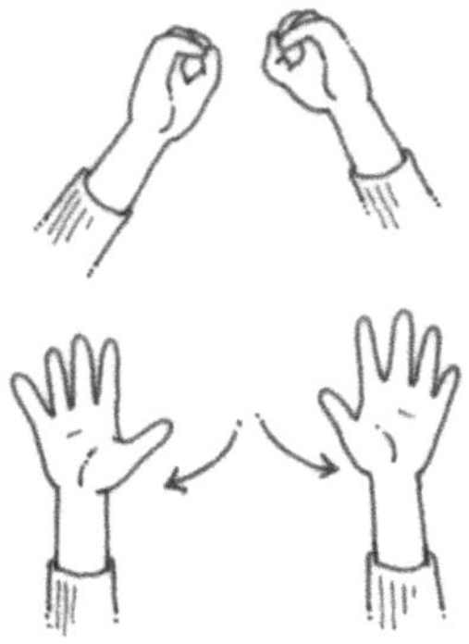

None

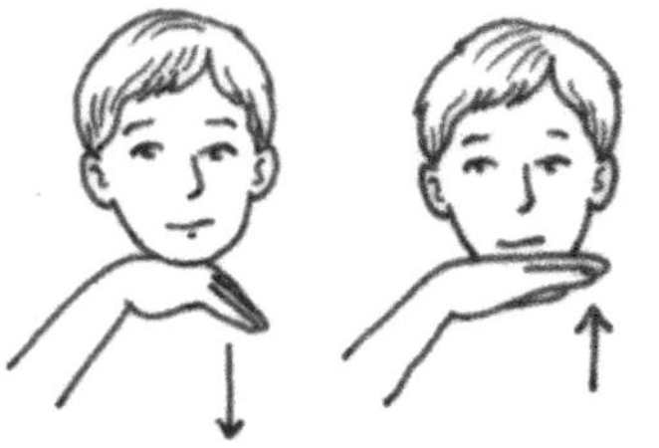

Pig

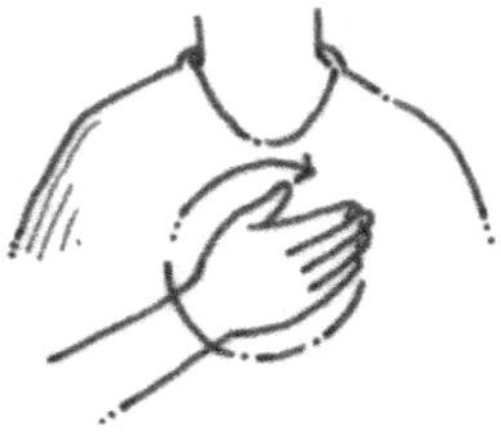

Please

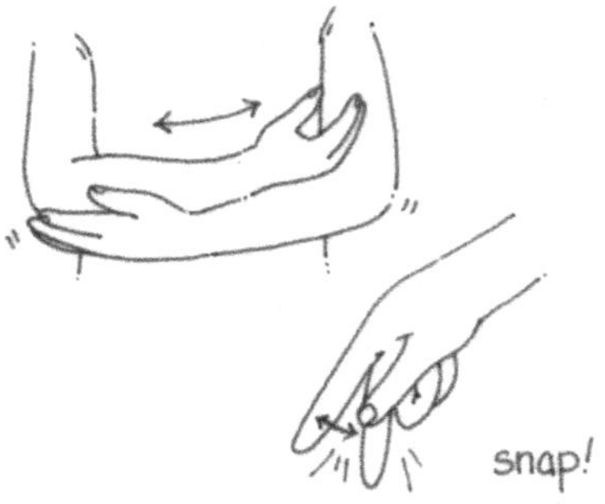

Puppy

Sheep

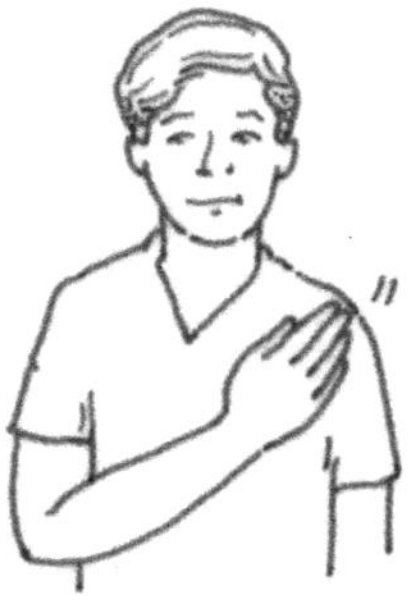

Shoulder

Spider

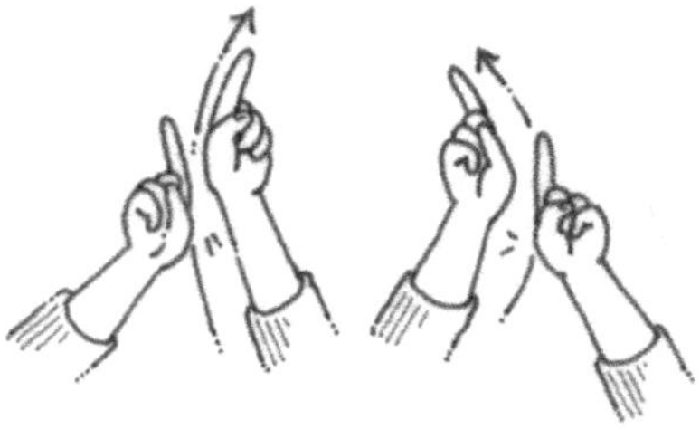

Star

Stop

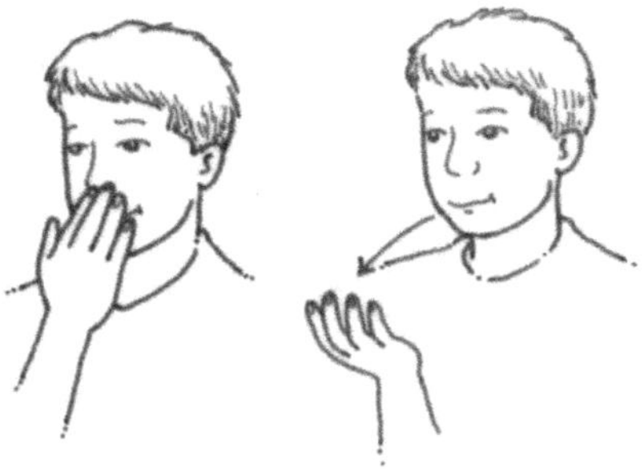

Thank You

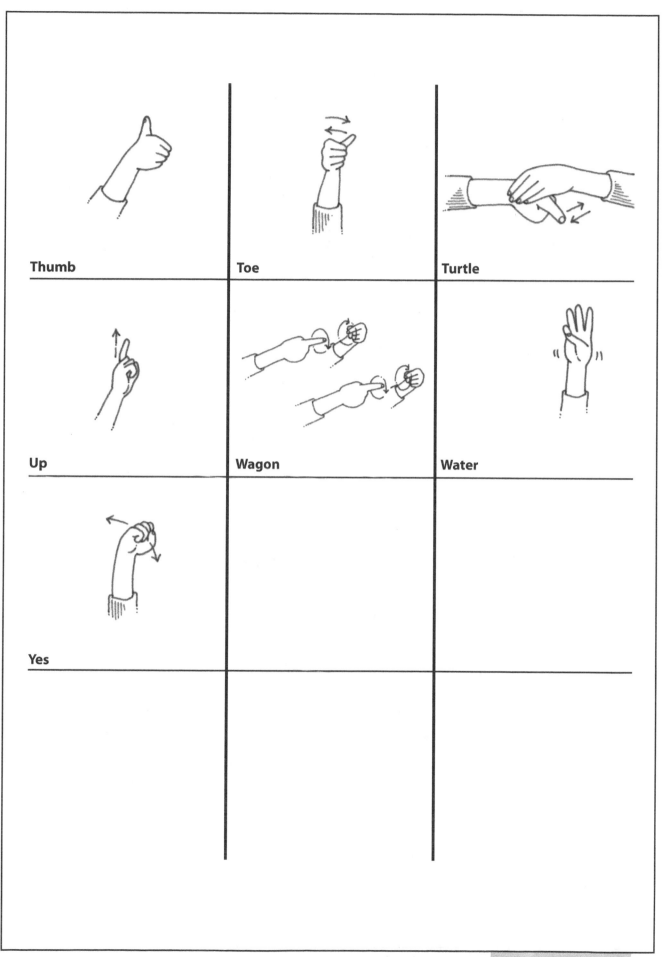

Thumb

Toe

Turtle

Up

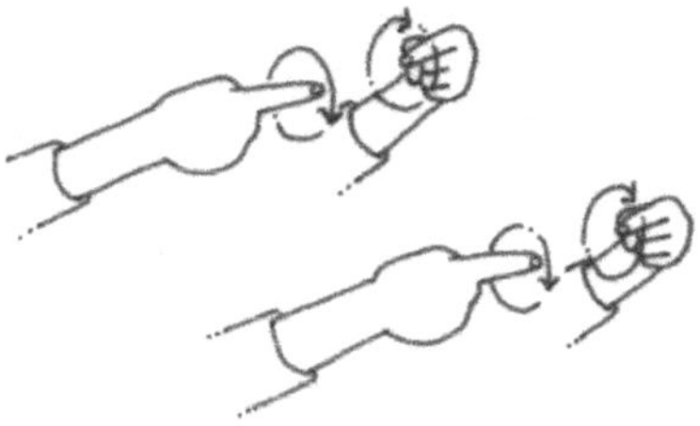

Wagon

Water

Yes

Alphabet Finger Spelling

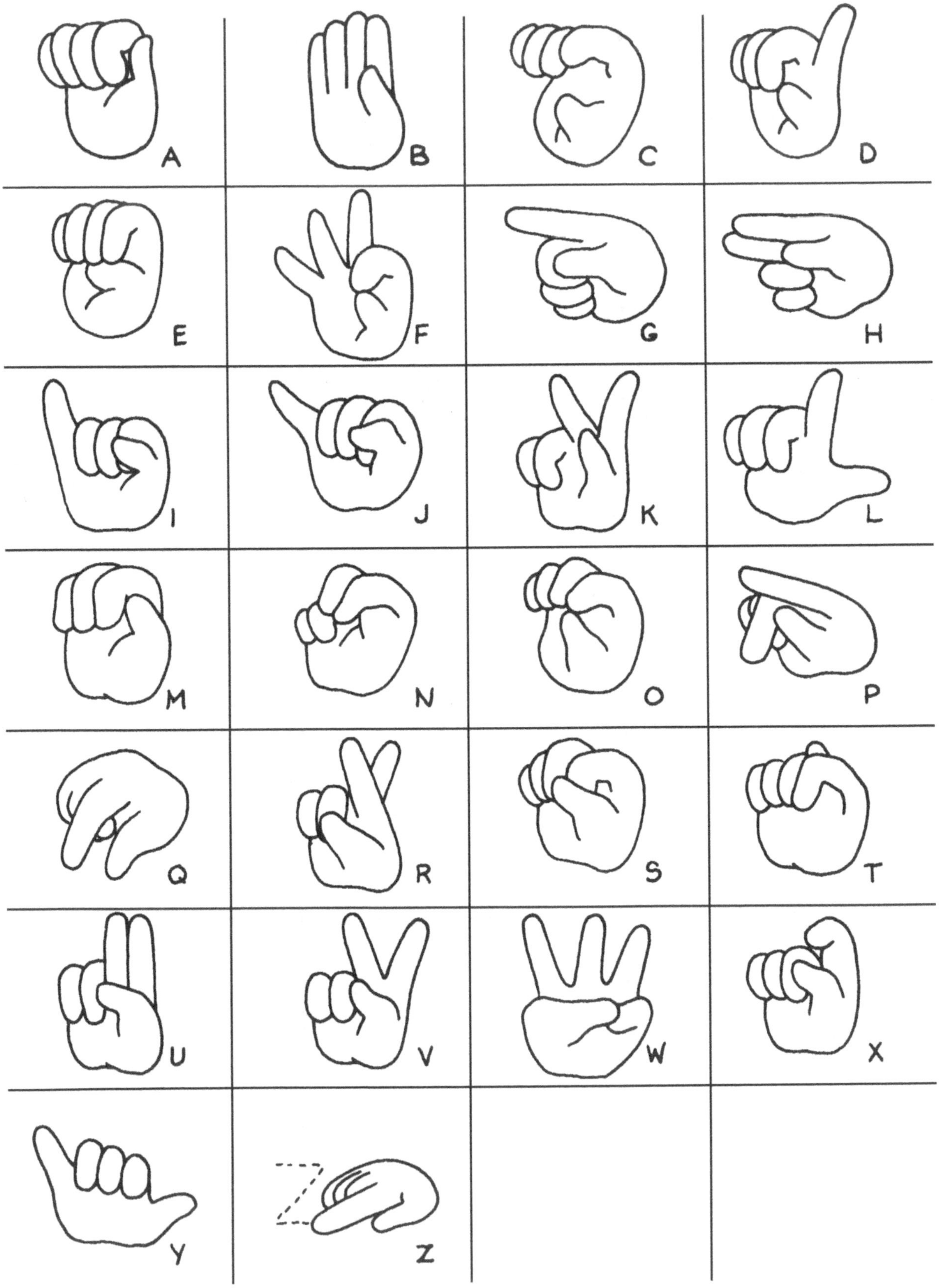

Indexes

Children's Book Index

Song Index

W

Chants and Rhymes Index

Index